Asia-Pacific Security

This book examines the recent upgrading of Australia–Japan–United States security interactions and their implications for Asia-Pacific regional security. The convergence of the strategic interests of these three states makes it imperative that such interests and the policy ramifications receive extensive investigation. This need is particularly compelling given that the 'Trilateral Strategic Dialogue' is one of several contending approaches for reshaping Asia-Pacific regional security architectures and mechanisms to confront new challenges in a post-Cold War and post-9/11 environment.

The current volume provides the first systematic and comprehensive treatment of trilateral security alliance politics as it is developing in the Asia-Pacific. It is also a study of the key evolving security trends in the region, such as how domestic politics in each country relate to regional security politics.

This book will be of much interest to all students of Asia-Pacific security, US foreign policy, Asian politics and International Relations in general.

William T. Tow is Professor of International Security in the Australian National University's Department of International Relations.

Mark J. Thomson is Director of the Budget and Management Program at the Australian Strategic Policy Institute.

Yoshinobu Yamamoto is a Professor of the University of Tokyo and Director of the Research Institute for Peace and Security (RIPS).

Satu P. Limaye is Director of the East–West Center, Washington. He was previously a research staff member at the Institute of Defense Analysis (IDA) and Director of Research and Publications at the Asia Pacific Center for Security Studies.

Asian Security Studies

Series Editors: Sumit Ganguly
Indiana University, Bloomington
Andrew Scobell
US Army War College

Few regions of the world are fraught with as many security questions as Asia. Within this region it is possible to study great power rivalries, irredentist conflicts, nuclear and ballistic missile proliferation, secessionist movements, ethnoreligious conflicts and inter-state wars. This new book series will publish the best possible scholarship on the security issues affecting the region, and will include detailed empirical studies, theoretically oriented case studies and policy-relevant analyses as well as more general works.

China and International Institutions

Alternate paths to global power
Marc Lanteigne

China's Rising Sea Power

The PLA navy's submarine challenge
Peter Howarth

If China Attacks Taiwan

Military strategy, politics and economics
Edited by Steve Tsang

Chinese Civil-Military Relations

The transformation of the People's Liberation Army
Edited by Nan Li

The Chinese Army Today

Tradition and transformation for the 21st century
Dennis J. Blasko

Taiwan's Security

History and prospects
Bernard D. Cole

Asia-Pacific Security

US, Australia and Japan and the
New Security Triangle

Edited by
William T. Tow, Mark J. Thomson,
Yoshinobu Yamamoto and
Satu P. Limaye

Routledge
Taylor & Francis Group

LONDON AND NEW YORK

ASPI
AUSTRALIAN
STRATEGIC
POLICY
INSTITUTE

First published 2007
by Routledge
2 Park Square, Milton Park, Abingdon, Oxon OX14 4RN

Simultaneously published in the USA and Canada
by Routledge
711 Third Avenue, New York, NY 10017, USA

Routledge is an imprint of the Taylor & Francis Group, an informa business

Typeset in Baskerville by
Book Now Ltd, London

British Library Cataloguing in Publication Data
A catalogue record for this book is available from the British Library

Library of Congress Cataloging in Publication Data
Asia-Pacific security: US, Australia and Japan and the new security
triangle/edited by William Tow [et al.].
    p. cm.
Includes bibliographical references and index.
1. National security–Pacific Area. 2. National security–United States.
3. National security–Japan. 4. National security–Australia. 5. Pacific Area–Defenses.
6. United States–Military policy. 7. Japan–Military policy. 8. Australia–Military
policy. I. Tow, William T.

UA830.A7688 2007
355′.03305–dc22   2006101512

ISBN10: 0–415–41710–4 (hbk)
ISBN10: 0–415–49088–X (pbk)
ISBN10: 0–203–08909–X (ebk)

ISBN13: 978–0–415–41710–5 (hbk)
ISBN13: 978–0–415–49088–7 (pbk)
ISBN13: 978–0–203–08909–5 (ebk)

Contents

Illustrations

Figure

Tables

Contributors

Desmond Ball is a Professor at the Strategic and Defence Studies Centre (SDSC) at the Australian National University. His research interests include Australian defence, nuclear strategy and Asia-Pacific security. Professor Ball has published extensively on defence and security matters and has previously been Head of SDSC and co-chairman of the Steering Committee of the Council for Security Cooperation in the Asia-Pacific.

Richard A. Bitzinger is a Senior Fellow with the S. Rajaratnam School of the International Studies in Singapore, where his work focuses on military and defence issues relating to the Asia-Pacific region, including the challenges of defence transformation in the Asia-Pacific, regional military modernization activities, and local defence industries, arms production, and weapons proliferation.

Satu P. Limaye is Director of the East–West Center, Washington. He was previously a research staff member at the Institute of Defense Analysis (IDA) and Director of Research and Publications at the Asia Pacific Center for Security Studies. Dr Limaye works on US relations with Asia and Asia-Pacific international relations.

Charles E. Morrison is President of the East–West Center. His interests include Asia-Pacific international relations, especially regional institutions. He is currently the international chair of the Pacific Economic Cooperation Council.

Yoshihide Soeya is Professor of International Relations at the Faculty of Law, Keio University. His research interests are politics and security in East Asia and Japanese diplomacy therein. Professor Soeya's most recent book, *Japan's Middle-Power Diplomacy* (2005, in Japanese), is being translated into Korean and English.

Brendan Taylor is a Lecturer in the Graduate Studies in Strategy and Defence (GSSD) Program at the Australian National University, where he coordinates courses on 'Asia-Pacific security' and 'US approaches to East Asian security'. Dr Taylor's research interests include Northeast Asian security, American foreign policy, economic statecraft and alliance politics.

Mark J. Thomson is a Program Director at the Australian Strategic Policy Institute. Dr Thomson's research interests include defence economics, North Asian security, Australian strategic policy and the interplay between economics, trade and international security.

William T. Tow is Professor of International Relations at the Australian National University. Previously Professor of International Relations both at the University of Queensland and at Griffith University and an Assistant Professor of International Relations at USC, Professor Tow's research interests include alliance politics, US security policy in the Asia-Pacific, security politics in the Asia-Pacific and Australian security policies.

Taizo Watanabe is a member of the Board of the Research Institute for Peace and Security, Tokyo. He is especially interested in the security environment of the Southeast Asian region. Mr Watanabe is also actively involved in the grassroots exchange of people between the United States and Japan as Chairman of the John Manjiro Whitfield Commemorative Center for International Exchange.

Michael Wesley is Professor of International Relations and Director of the Griffith Asia Institute at Griffith University. Previously Assistant Director-General for Transnational Issues in the Australian government's Office of National Assessments, his most recent book is *The Howard Paradox: Australian Diplomacy in Asia, 1996–2007*.

Hugh White is the Professor of Strategic Studies and the Head of the Strategic and Defence Studies Centre (SDSC) at the Australian National University, and a Visiting Fellow at the Lowy Institute for International Policy. He was the first Director of the Australian Strategic Policy Institute, and earlier served as a senior ministerial and prime ministerial advisor and as a senior official in the Australian Department of Defence.

Thomas S. Wilkins is a full-time lecturer in International Security at the University of Salford, UK. He is currently a Kiriyama Research Fellow at the Center for the Pacific Rim, University of San Francisco. Dr Wilkins specializes in the study of alliances, coalition warfare and the security architecture of the Asia-Pacific.

Susan Windybank is Director of Foreign Policy Research at the Centre for Independent Studies (CIS) in Sydney. She joined CIS in 2000 as Editor of *Policy*, the Centre's quarterly magazine, and all other CIS publications before being appointed Director in late 2004. Ms Windybank has researched and published widely including on the South Pacific, Australian security policy and the Australia–United States alliance.

Yoshinobu Yamamoto is a Professor of International Politics at Aoyama Gakuin University and a vice president of the Research Institute for Peace and Security, Tokyo. He is a graduate of the University of Tokyo and received a PhD degree from the University of Michigan. Professor Yamamoto specializes in international political theories and security affairs.

Executive summary

Satu P. Limaye

- As an initiative formalized at the ministerial level only as recently as March 2006, the United States–Japan–Australia Trilateral Strategic Dialogue's (TSD) purpose and implications are still evolving. Even the TSD's sustainability is unclear.
- The TSD owes its origins to the new international and regional security environment, the intensification and expansion of United States–Japan and United States–Australia bilateral alliances, a concomitant enhancement of Japan–Australia relations, similar values as well as political and economic systems, and a coincidence of extraordinarily close personal relationships between President Bush, and Prime Minister Koizumi, Prime Minister Howard and senior officials in the three countries. The impetus for the TSD has come from Japan and Australia.
- Japan primarily views the TSD as a mechanism to facilitate its security and foreign policy 'normalization' without creating perturbations in the region. Australia sees the TSD as a means to indicate to Beijing that Canberra's close ties to Washington and Tokyo 'are non-negotiable' despite rapidly growing economic ties. The United States sees the trilateral effort as a natural extension of enhanced bilateral alliances with Japan and Australia to address new threats around the world.
- Recent nuclear and missile testing by the Democratic People's Republic of Korea (DPRK) has intensified the Australian, Japanese and American collective security interest in a stable Korean peninsula. TSD collaboration on sanctions policies, WMD non-proliferation measures and other steps targeting the DPRK, however, will need to be balanced against longer-range factors, including Chinese and South Korean interests and sensitivities concerning unnecessarily provoking escalated North Korean belligerence.
- The perspectives of the three TSD participants to what might be gained in terms of the key areas of alliance management, regional multilateralism and bilateral relations are captured in Table 0.1.
- All three countries see benefits in practical cooperation on issues ranging from counterterrorism, piracy, energy security, and other transnational threats. There is also some interest in contributing to democracy promotion and regional capacity-building.

Table 0.1 National perspectives on alliance management, regional multilateralism and bilateral relations

	Alliance management	*Regional multilateralism*	*Bilateral relations*
United States	Buttresses existing alliances and engages Australia and Japan as prospective willing partners	Hedges against the development of multilateral architectures excluding the United States	Enhanced networking with no loss to existing bilateral relationships
Japan	Adds another facet and increased relevance to United States–Japan alliance	Maintains US engagement in region while allowing Japan to pursue other regional forum like the East Asia Summit	Enhances basis and opportunities for Japan's bilateral activities in the region
Australia	Adds another facet and increased relevance to United States–Australia alliance	Maintains US engagement in region while enhancing Australia's credentials as a member of Asian community	Opportunity to further broaden Japan–Australia relationship into security arena

- China represents the most complex policy management challenge for the TSD. The essence of the challenge is to calibrate efforts aimed at engaging China with those aimed at responding to the failure of China to become a responsible stakeholder.
- Regional multilateralism and community-building must also be calibrated with the TSD. TSD members share an interest in inclusive rather than exclusive regionalism, and the TSD serves to blunt China's efforts to create an East Asian economic community that marginalizes the United States. TSD members appreciate that regional multilateralism cannot substitute for strong bilateral relationships – not only among allies, but also new partnerships such as between Japan and Australia.
- The TSD also has the means to facilitate and coordinate relationships with other important regional actors including the Association of Southeast Asian Nations (ASEAN), the Republic of Korea (ROK), and India. The TSD is hence not intended to be itself exclusive, but to provide yet another mechanism for dialogue and cooperation with other players in the Asia-Pacific region.
- Other future challenges to the sustainability of the TSD include political leadership changes, United States preoccupation with events in the Middle East, and uncertainty about bureaucratic commitment to specific acts of cooperation and coordination.
- Still, the TSD represents an important, novel element of the evolving security architecture.

Acknowledgements

This project originated as a continuation of a benchmark study undertaken in 2004–5 and led by the Research Institute for Peace and Security (RIPS) in Tokyo. That review, involving Japanese, Australian and American scholars and policy experts, generated a policy recommendations document that coincided with announcements by their respective governments that bilateral security dialogues conducted between them would be upgraded and that trilateral consultations at the full ministerial level were pending. Given such prospects, it seemed entirely appropriate to explore the possible intensification and ramifications of the trilateral dimension. In July 2005, RIPS agreed to proceed to the next research phase with funding support from the Japan Foundation's Center for Global Partnership. The most significant RIPS players in reaching and sustaining this commitment have been Professor Akio Watanabe, Professor Yoshinobu Yamamoto, Mr Daisuke Hayashi and Mr Yasutomo Tanaka. We are particularly grateful to Mr Hayashi for seeing through this venture at a time when RIPS was undertaking some time-consuming and complex administrative changes.

The study benefited from other important collaborators. The Griffith Asia Institute (GAI) at Griffith University in Brisbane and the Institute for Defense Analysis (IDA) in Alexandria, VA assumed the role of institutional counterparts to RIPS for project oversight. Michael Wesley, GAI's Director, and Satu Limaye who was then at IDA and a participant in the original RIPS project as well as this one deserve special mention for their participation and support. The Department of International Relations at the Australian National University's Research School of Asia and Pacific Studies was sufficiently sensitive to the value of the project's policy analysis to afford William Tow the time needed to coordinate much of the ongoing editorial process. He is grateful to his Departmental colleagues and to his postgraduate students for taking an interest in this project and for their continued encouragement as it unfolded.

This volume is largely the product of RIPS foresight but other noteworthy actors facilitated the transformation of research into what appears between these pages. Peter Jennings, then Director of Research Programs for the Australian Strategic Policy Institute (ASPI), approached Routledge with the idea that this volume could be a 'co-branded' product of ASPI and Routledge's Asian Security Studies programme. Peter left ASPI before this vision was fulfilled but his place was ably filled by Mark Thomson, ASPI's Director for Defence Budgeting and Management Research, and by his boss and ASPI's Director, Major General Peter Abigail (Retd). Mark quickly and cheerfully assumed the role of co-editing this book and his talents for project organization and his overall conceptual guidance proved critical to bringing it to completion. ASPI also provided much appreciated financial support for the project. So too did the Australian Department of Defence which recognized early on the potential significance of this issue for Australia's own future security planning. Particular thanks are extended to Marc Ablong and Vikki Templeman for their material and moral support at the project's critical juncture.

In regard to the book's editorial phase, Ms Robin Ward proved to be an engaged and patient copyeditor while Jacob Townsend was invaluable in preparing this book's index. Great credit must also be conferred to Andrew Humphrys, Editor, Military and Strategic Studies, Routledge, and to his Editorial Assistant, Ms Katie Gordon, for seeing this enterprise through to its culmination despite it incurring some last minute challenges. Again, without their help and understanding the book would never have been completed.

Finally, the co-editors would like to thank all of those colleagues and others within the public policy arena consulted during this study on its various components. Their encouragement on the project's overall salience gave us the heart to stay the course and to offer our readership assessments of what promises to be a key Asia-Pacific security issue for the three countries directly involved, and for the entire region.

Abbreviations

ABAC	APEC's Business Advisory Committee
ABM	anti-ballistic missile
ACSAs	Acquisition Cross-Servicing Agreements
ADB	Asian Development Bank
ADF	Australian Defence Force
AMS	Agreement for Maintaining Security (Australia and Indonesia)
ANZUS	Australia, New Zealand and the United States
APEC	Asia Pacific Economic Cooperation
APT	ASEAN + 3
ARF	ASEAN Regional Forum
ASDF	[Japanese] Air Self-Defence Force
ASEAN	Association of Southeast Asian Nations
ASG	Abu Sayif Group
ATSML	Anti-Terrorism Special Measures law
AUSMIN	Australian–American Ministerial Consultations
AWDs	air warfare destroyers
BMD	ballistic missile defence
BWC	Biological and Toxin Weapons Convention
C4I	command, control, communications, computing and intelligence
CTAG	[G8] Counter-Terrorism Action Group
CTBT	Comprehensive Test Ban Treaty
CTTF	Counter-Terrorism Task Force
CWC	Chemical Weapons Convention
DAC	[OECD] Development Assistance Committee
DPRI	Defense Policy Review Initiative
DPRK	Democratic People's Republic of Korea
DSP	Defence Support Program
EAEC	East Asian Economic Caucus
EAEG	East Asian Economic Group
EAS	East Asia Summit
EEZs	Exclusive Economic Zones
EPG	[APEC's] Eminent Person's Group
ERPD	[APT] Economic Review and Policy Dialogue

ESCAP	[UN] Economic and Social Commission for Asia and the Pacific
FMCT	Fissile Material Cut-off Treaty
FTA	free trade area/agreement
GDP	Gross Domestic Product
GNI	Gross National Income
GPR	Global Posture Review
IAEA	International Atomic Energy Agency
INTERFET	International Force East Timor
JCTC	Joint Combined Training Center
JGSDF	Japanese Ground Self-Defence Force
JI	Jemaah Islamiyah
JORN	*Jindalee* over-the-horizon radar network
JSDF	Japanese Self-Defence Forces
JSP	Japanese Socialist Party
KEDO	Korean Peninsula Energy Development Organization
LCSMHRA	Law Concerning Special Measures on Humanitarian and Reconstruction Assistance
LDP	[Japanese] Liberal Democratic Party
LEAP	Lightweight Exo-Atmospheric Projectile
MANPADS	Man Portable Air Defence Systems
MD	missile defence
METI	[Japan's] Ministry of the Economy, Trade and Industry
MILF	Moro Islamic Liberation Front
MOU	memorandum of understanding
MSDF	[Japanese] Maritime Self-Defence Forces
MTCR	Missile Technology Control Regime
NATO	North Atlantic Treaty Organization
NBC	Nuclear, Biological, Chemical
NPT	Non-Proliferation Treaty
NSG	Nuclear Suppliers Group
NSS	National Security Strategy
ODA	Overseas Development Assistance
OECD	Organization for Economic Cooperation and Development
OPTAD	Organization for Pacific Trade and Development
PALM	Pacific Islands Leaders' Meeting
PECC	Pacific Economic Cooperation Council
PKO	[UN] Peacekeeping Operations
PSI	Proliferation Security Initiative
PSOs	Peace Support Operations
PTBT	Partial Test Ban Treaty
QDR	Quadrennial Defense Review
RAMSI	Regional Assistance Mission to the Solomon Islands
RAN	Royal Australian Navy
R&D	research and development
RIMPAC	Rim of the Pacific [Exercise]

RMA	Revolution in Military Affairs
SBIRS	Space-Based Infrared System
SCO	Shanghai Cooperation Organization
SDF	See JSDF
SEATO	Southeast Asia Treaty Organization
SIP	Statement of Interdiction Principles
SLOCs	sea lanes of communication
SMD	Sea-based Midcourse Defense [system]
TAC	[ASEAN's] Treaty of Amity and Cooperation
TCOG	Trilateral Coordination and Oversight Group
TSD	[Australia–Japan–United States] Trilateral Strategic Dialogue
UAVs	unmanned aerial vehicles
UNCTC	UN Counter-Terrorism Committee
UNSC	United Nations Security Council
UNTAC	UN Transitional Authority in Cambodia
USTR	[Office of the] US Trade Representative
WMD	weapons of mass destruction
WTO	World Trade Organization

1 Introduction

William T. Tow

Well after the end of the Cold War the shape and meaning of ongoing structural change in the Asia-Pacific region remains unclear. Early predictions that the United States would exercise uncontested hegemony there have been overtaken by that country's preoccupation with such emerging asymmetrical threats as international terrorism and the proliferation of weapons of mass destruction (WMD) to 'states of concern' and, potentially, to hostile non-state entities. The rise of China and its implications for regional order are not yet understood, even by the Chinese, much less by other regional and extra-regional actors. Asia-Pacific 'community-building' is proceeding, although in only painstaking ways. Regional security dilemmas or 'flashpoints' in the Korean peninsula, the Taiwan Strait and Kashmir remain capable of exploding rapidly and with global ramifications. The politics of energy security has assumed centre-stage as Asia's rapidly growing economies become increasingly competitive in their quest for access to fossil fuels and other commodities. Other 'non-traditional security' challenges have intensified in such areas as environment, health and human rights. Too little consensus still exists, however, over how such developments are best confronted.

That the postwar US-led bilateral alliances in this region remain largely intact during such a period of change constitutes a major surprise in international security relations. Alliance theorists had argued that such relationships would dissolve if the threat that instigated their creation disappeared.[1] The United States' alliances with Japan, and Washington's equally enduring security relationship with Australia, survive as viable icons of strategic stability, increasingly involved in US global strategies as well as constantly relevant to US agendas in Asia. This is the case notwithstanding Japan increasingly coming to terms with its own national identity as a security actor and Australia's geographic distance from the Middle East and Central Asia areas which most preoccupy contemporary American policy-planners.[2] There is currently no equivalent threat to American global primacy such as the Soviet Union during the Cold War. United States policy-makers have publicly expressed a preference for engaging with China as a 'responsible stake-holder' to build a stable international order rather than contesting China's growing power in Asia and beyond.[3]

Given this stability and these circumstances, and the recent worsening of Sino-Japanese relations over historical and strategic issues, critics of the decision by

Australia, Japan and the United States to enter into a 'Trilateral Strategic Dialogue' (TSD) have questioned why two long-standing alliances that have served their purposes of containing Soviet power, and, more recently, allowed a viable US balancing role in the region, are now adding a distinct three-way dimension to their security collaboration. In early May 2005, US Secretary of State Condoleezza Rice and Australian Foreign Minister Alexander Downer announced that trilateral strategic discussions previously convened by Australia, Japan and the United States at a vice-ministerial level would be upgraded to full ministerial status.[4] By doing so, they insisted that 'more direct discussions' of key political elements would lead to more systematic coordination between the three allies on a wide range of regional security issues. However, critics of this decision asserted that the inaugural TSD meeting in March 2006 was 'shrouded in speculation and opacity' to conceal a visible difference between Australia's relatively benign outlook on China from Japan's and the United States' more hardline postures. They also observed that while the United States had invited China to collaborate in building an enduring security order in Asia, it simultaneously had criticized China's increased defence spending as a sign that that country could become a 'negative force' for regional security. The TSD, they concluded, would undermine the burgeoning but positive multilateral dialogue processes conducted within the ASEAN Regional Forum (ARF). It would instead convert the traditional Japanese and Australian 'spokes' in the American-led network of regional bilateral alliances into a de facto 'little NATO'.[5] Chinese foreign policy experts meanwhile warned that the dialogue should not view Chinese defence spending and other aspects of Chinese foreign policy with a 'Cold War mentality'.[6]

Notwithstanding such reservations, the TSD's communiqué issued after its first ministerial session projected China's regional security role in a surprisingly positive light: Dialogue participants 'welcomed China's constructive engagement in the region and concurred on the value of enhanced cooperation with other parties such as ASEAN and the Republic of Korea'.[7] It became quickly apparent that a more central focus for the Sydney discussions was how the three long-time Pacific allies would conceptualize and respond to *global* security issues as they affect the Asia-Pacific's security environment. These included the potential erosion of WMD non-proliferation norms in 'states of concern' such as North Korea and Iran, international counterterrorism measures and broader 'human security' concerns such as disaster relief and pandemic controls.[8] The TSD was posited by its proponents as a regionally 'inclusive' initiative designed to effect closer Australia–Japan security consultations and policy coordination on a wide range of traditional and non-traditional security issues. The TSD's initial evolution appeared to conform to such expectations, incorporating what has been termed a 'bilateralism-plus' formula: 'A more distinctive and active Australia–Japan component of security collaboration on a range of traditional and human security issues, TSD advocates maintain, could gradually modify Chinese threat perceptions and concerns that those two countries were merely acting as proxies for a new American containment posture directed against Beijing.'[9] This proposition was further tested when Australia's Prime Minister John Howard and his Japanese counterpart, Shinzo

Abe, signed the Australia–Japan Joint Declaration on Security Cooperation in Tokyo on 13 March 2007. [10]

What is beyond question is that the Australia–Japan–United States security relationship is gaining increasing attention in the Asia-Pacific region by both policy-makers and independent observers and has potentially important implications for the security architecture of the region. The TSD is an important development in a region that has reached an historical crossroads in determining what type of security order will emerge in the Asia-Pacific. Obviously, China's security interests, along with those of other regional security actors, will be directly affected by any viable evolution of 'trilateralism' between the three long-time Pacific allies. Two major questions materialize in this context. Can future Australia–Japan–United States trilateral consultations and interactions become viewed by other regional actors as an element of 'strategic reassurance' by allowing the United States and its two traditional postwar maritime allies to better synchronize their mutual approaches to an evolving East Asia Community (EAC)? Or will the TSD evolve into a rival power base to other regional security entities, intent on containing Chinese power and reinforcing US strategic predominance in the region?

The latter question appears especially pertinent with the US Defense Department's February 2006 release of the 'Quadrennial Defense Review' identifying China as a future 'peer competitor' of the United States at both the regional and global levels of geopolitical rivalry. [11] In the absence of careful alliance management, traditional Chinese fears of an American-led 'neo-containment' strategy directed against itself could be aggravated by Washington transforming its separate bilateral security relationships with Japan and Australia into a more integrated security arrangement. Other Asian states – especially South Korea (also a US ally) – could also become apprehensive of an ill-managed TSD initiative at a time when the Korean peninsula is at a crossroads in its politico-strategic identity and when the nuclear non-proliferation issue is alienating North Korea from much of the international community. This remains problematic despite the Six Party Talks negotiating breakthrough attained on 13 February 2007.

Australia and Japan could also unintentionally create or increase domestic and regional perceptions that they are acting as American strategic proxies or 'deputy sheriffs' in Northeast Asia and Southeast Asia, respectively, by affiliating with US 'coalitions of the willing' peace-building ventures too readily or without making clear how their independent national security interests are served by such coalitions.

The aim of this book is to explore the implications of the recent upgrading of security interactions among these three countries and to analyse to what extent the TSD compares favourably or otherwise with other regional security mechanisms as a means to pursue conflict avoidance or to achieve conflict resolution in Asia. It therefore goes beyond the recent and authoritative study edited by Brad Williams and Andrew Newman (also published by Routledge) on the widening of Australian and Japanese security ties occurring since the 1970s. It sees focus on the regional and international security problems and opportunities presaged by the

Australia–Japan–United States strategic triad.[12] Incorporating extensive analysis by Japanese contributors, this study includes discussions of the 'China dimension' of TSD politics and of critical 'non-traditional' Asia-Pacific security issues such as energy security and maritime security. These issues are becoming increasingly central to the Asia-Pacific strategic environment and to the United States, Japan and Australia as regionally prominent maritime powers.[13]

This volume is also concerned with how the TSD affects the development of other new multilateral instrumentalities for Asia-Pacific regional order-building such as the ARF, the East Asia Summit and *ad hoc* instrumentalities such as the Six Party Talks on the Korean peninsula. Within this framework, it considers the theoretical and empirical context of 'trilateralism'; the evolving history of the Australia–Japan–United States trilateral security relationship; its connection to and impact on the US bilateral alliance network in Asia; how domestic politics in each country relates to regional security politics; the growing 'economic–security nexus' linking alliance related issues; and recent initiatives by the United States to incorporate Japan and Australia as valued 'Pacific partners' to NATO and in US global strategy.

The study's framework

This study is divided into three major parts: (1) assessments of the TSD's evolution and possible theoretical and domestic policy explanations; (2) analysis of regional security dimensions and implications of the TSD initiative; and (3) considerations of selected key issue-areas that will be directly affected by that initiative. A conclusion will then offer some policy recommendations emanating from the analyses contained in these three parts.

Part I offers four chapters that develop the theme of trilateralism in Australia–Japan–United States security relations and trace the historical and domestic imperatives shaping it. In Chapter 2, Brendan Taylor and Desmond Ball provide an overarching historical framework for considering the possible advantages and drawbacks for the three allies. They describe common regional threat perceptions, policy accountability, technology transfers and how strategic orientations have matured over successive postwar decades. William Tow develops several theoretical perspectives on trilateral security politics in Chapter 3. He focuses on how triliteralism 'fits' with the different modes of security cooperation contending for primacy as a mechanism for Asia-Pacific security community-building, and revisits the concept of threat in contemporary alliance politics to assess why the traditional US-led bilateral security strategy of 'hub and spokes' alliance management is changing. In Chapter 4, Michael Wesley demarcates which elements of the Australian, Japanese and American governments will be most important in sustaining or advancing the TSD, and what domestic factors are most likely to shape their TSD agendas. Along with Taylor and Ball, Wesley underscores the importance of elite commitment to making triliteral mechanisms succeed and overcome the policy logjams that otherwise tend to mire bureaucracies in allied countries and prevent them from achieving the institutional consistencies required for policy credibility in regional security politics. Finally, in Chapter 5 Mark Thomson offers an important 'bridging chapter', relating the theoretical and empirical rationales underlying TSD formulation to the actual expectations and limitations of the processes and results of this security mechanism. He observes that the TSD cannot be assumed to immediately or completely replace the traditional US asymmetrical bilateral alliance system that has been in place for over half a century. It can, however, provide a cohesive basis for Australian, Japanese and American coordination of their policies towards China and in ways that can be regarded as non-threatening by Beijing.

Part II of the book concentrates on the 'regional dimensions' of TSD concern. In Chapter 6 Yoshinobu Yamamoto weighs how recent changes in the United States–Japan bilateral alliance have influenced the development of the TSD. He notes that US Asia-Pacific force postures have been reduced since the Cold War and that Japan has been required to adjust its own defence policies in line with this hard reality; that Japan's overall process of defence normalization can be managed more efficiently in a framework of close allied consultation. He posits that the United States and Australia, as the Asia-Pacific's other maritime powers that have collaborated closely with Tokyo throughout the postwar era, are Japan's two most logical strategic associates during this time of rapid transition in regional and global geopolitics. In Chapter 7 this view is at least partially or implicitly contested by Yoshihide Soeya who argues in his assessment of 'Trilateralism and Northeast Asia' that Japanese security normalization must be tempered by a greater sensitivity towards China's rise and towards the flashpoints of North Korea and Taiwan than has thus far been displayed by Tokyo. His view is that Japan must apply 'middle power diplomacy' to defuse both of these crises and to what extent the TSD can facilitate this outcome will determine its overall relevance and constructiveness over the next few years. Hugh White, in Chapter 8, is more openly critical of the TSD's probable utility as a 'stabilizer' in regional security. Arguing that there is little other real business for this trilateral configuration than to coordinate responses to Chinese power and influence, White notes that Australia's interests directed towards China are sufficiently diverse from those of Japan and the United States to render future TSD agendas largely unworkable; that this could change, however, if Australia is able to use the TSD forum to moderate American and Japanese threat perceptions of China.

In Chapter 9 Susan Windybank expands the purview of TSD 'regionalism' by appraising the geopolitical relevance of the South Pacific to Australia–Japan–United States security relations. Recent Australian interventions to prevent state failure in this sub-region are reminiscent of the West's 'strategic denial' posture applied there against the Soviet Union during the Cold War. China is economically active in various South Pacific economies. However, there does not seem to be any sentiment within the TSD that Beijing's activities in the South Pacific context warrant a similar containment posture, although Australian policy leaders share a concern with their Japanese and American counterparts that Chinese economic competition with Taiwan for the loyalties of South Pacific microstates must not be allowed to spin out of control. In Chapter 10 Taizo Watanabe and William Tow employ a similar argument in regard to TSD relations with the ASEAN sub-region. In order to be an effective contributor to Southeast Asian stability and prosperity, TSD affiliates must complement rather than compete with existing multilateral organizations to overcome intensifying traditional challenges such as arms racing and maritime security as well as such non-traditional security challenges as terrorism and 'human security' contingencies. Japan will need to work assiduously with Australia and the United States to overcome a long-standing hostility to its historical and cultural legacies within ASEAN and to neutralize any possible exploitation of such animosity by other external powers. Finally, the TSD must work diligently to ensure that the United States remains a full regional 'player'. Expanding on the book's Executive Summary, in Chapter 11 Satu Limaye weighs how Japan and Australia can work and have worked together to involve the United States in regional security politics by adopting inclusive strategies for institutional formation and development. Trilateral consultations ease the task of synchronizing inclusivism and its implementation.

Part III of this volume concentrates on three key issue-areas that could largely determine the TSD's relative importance. Charles Morrison in Chapter 12 looks at the 'economic drivers' that a viable TSD must incorporate into those collective policies it engenders: China's economic growth, globalization and technological development, and other transnational economic activities with security ramifications. He identifies coordination with the Asia-Pacific region's 'cooperative architectures' in the economic arena (APEC, the ASEAN + 3 or APT and the East Asia Summit) as critical. This, Morrison concludes, justifies the participation of trade ministers as well as foreign and defence ministers in future TSD deliberations.

In Chapter 13 Thomas Wilkins introduces the notion of how terrorism and WMD proliferation to states of concern have evolved as threats to the TSD partners' collective security interests. He concludes that the TSD process should enhance 'overarching coordination of policies and initiatives that were already in close synchronization' established by the three allies when the events of 11 September 2001 reconstituted international security relations. In Chapter 14 Richard Bitzinger provides an instructive case study of one such collective security response, tracing Australia–United States and Japan–United States collaboration on missile defence technology. A fine line exists between exploiting such technology for clearly defensive purposes and developing it in ways that may seem too pre-emptive to China and to other actors within the Asia-Pacific region. The TSD's success in formulating and managing a missile defence posture that is sufficiently balanced to avoid the emergence of an acute security dilemma between its members and the Chinese will be an important test relative to its overall ability to act as a stabilizing element in regional security politics. Getting this delicate balance right has been made more important, but not any easier, by the recent North Korean nuclear test. Japan especially will want to move as quickly as it can to counter the threat posed by emerging North Korean nuclear and missile technology. Such action, however, does not include the acquisition of its own nuclear force, which Japan's Prime Minister Abe has already ruled out.[14]

Significantly, Beijing's response to the evolution of Australia–Japan–United States relations has thus far been comparatively innocuous, signalling a preliminary inclination by Beijing to adopt a 'wait and see' posture on the TSD's implications for China's security. South Korean policy-makers and analysts remain deeply concerned about what they view as a rise of militarist nationalism in Japan, but are consumed with adjusting their own bilateral security alliance with the Americans. They have yet to devote extensive attention to the TSD. ASEAN, too, is largely preoccupied with making its own burgeoning institutional architectures more viable. This low-key situation could change, however, if TSD policy-makers neglect the task of carefully calibrating both the policy advantages and the dangers relating to trilateralism's purview and constraints. This volume is an effort to facilitate such calibration.

Notes

1 See, for example, George Liska (1962), *Nations in Alliance: The Limits of Interdependence*, Baltimore, MD: Johns Hopkins University Press; Glenn Snyder (1997), *Alliance Politics*, Ithaca, NY: Cornell University Press; and Stephen M. Walt (1997), 'Why alliances endure or collapse', *Survival*, vol. 39, no. 1, especially pp. 158–59.

2 Japan's march towards becoming a fully 'normalized' state is particularly interesting. On 1 September 2006, Shintaro Abe, frontrunner for the Japanese prime ministership scheduled to change hands from incumbent Junichiro Koizumi later that month, declared that it was time to change his country's constitution to clarify the capability of the Japan Self-Defence Force (SDF) to 'engage in normal military activity overseas'. Abe also announced he had made 'enhanced strategic dialogue' with Australia and India a plank of his platform for the presidency of the Liberal Democratic Party (LDP) from whose ranks the next Japanese prime minister would be selected. See Peter Alford (2006), 'Japan's next PM to redraw constitution', *The Australian*, 2–3 September.

3 United States Department of State, International Information Programs (2005), 'United States urges China to be responsible world citizen', 22 September, available at: http://usinfo.state.gov/eap/Archive/2005/Sep/22-290478.html (accessed 21 October 2006).

4 The Hon. Alexander Downer, MP, Minister for Foreign Affairs, Australia (2005), 'Joint Press Conference with Secretary of State Condoleezza Rice – Washington', 5 May, available at: www.foreignminister.gov.au/transcripts/2005/050505_rice.html (accessed 21 October 2006).

5 'Dubious dialogue', *Providence Journal*, 5 April 2006, as reprinted in 'Daniel Widome Natural Selection' blog at: www.watsonblogs.org/dwidome/archives/2006/04/dubious_dialogu.html (accessed 21 October 2006); Gautaman Bhaskaran (2006), 'Trilateral stratagem to slow China's growth', *Seoul Times*, 1 September, available at: http://theseoultimes.com/ST/?url=/ST/db/read.php?idx=3184 (accessed 21 October 2006); and Pernundra Jain (2006), 'A "little NATO" against China', *Asia Times Online*, March 18, available at: www.atimes.com/atimes/China/HC18Ad01.html (accessed 21 October 2006).

6 Cao Desheng (2006), 'Look at military spending objectively', *China Daily*, March 17, available at: www.chinadaily.com.cn/english/doc/2006-03/17/content_542020.htm (accessed 21 October 2006).

7 The Ministry of Foreign Affairs of Japan, 'Trilateral Strategic Dialogue Joint Statement: Australia–Japan–United States' (2006), 18 March, available at: www.mofa.go.jp/region/asia-paci/australia/joint0603-2.html (accessed 21 October 2006).

8 Ibid. This focus was predicted in the 'Policy Recommendations' section of a report

prepared by the Research Institute for Peace and Security (Tokyo), the Asia-Pacific Center for Security Studies (Honolulu) and Griffith Asia Institute (Brisbane) (2005), *Japan, US and Australia: In Search of a New Strategic Framework in the Post 9–11 Era*, July 29, available at: http://66.102.7.104/search?q=cache:UfiWFk7_Gu4J:www.rips.or.jp/ Project/policy_recommendation_E.pdf+trilateral+strategic+dialogue+australia+japa n+U.S.&hl=en&gl=au&ct=clnk&cd=10 (accessed 21 October 2006).

9 Ibid., p. 3.
10 See Australian Government, Department of Foreign Affairs and Trade, 'Australia–Japan Joint Declaration on Security Cooperation', 13 March 2007 at http://www.dfat. gov.au/geo/japan/aus_jap_security_dec.html. Accessed on 9 April 2007. (See page 7 below.)
11 A full text of the February 2006 QDR can be found at: www.globalsecurity.org/ military/library/policy/dod/qdr-2006-report.pdf (accessed 21 October 2006).
12 Brad Williams and Andrew Newman (eds) (2006), *Japan, Australia and Asia-Pacific Security*, London: Routledge.
13 A definitive survey of maritime and energy security related questions is: Michael Wesley (ed.) (2006), *Energy Security in Asia*, London: Routledge.
14 Joseph Coleman (2006), 'PM says Japan won't build atomic weapons', *Washington Post*, 18 October.

Part I

Setting the context

2 Historical overview

Brendan Taylor and Desmond Ball

In September 1967, an eminent group of economists and International Relations scholars gathered in Canberra, Australia to discuss the prospects for another triangular relationship – one comprising Australia, India and Japan. The papers from this conference were subsequently published in a volume edited by J. D. B. Miller, who was at the time Professor of International Relations at the Australian National University.[1] In the volume's concluding chapter Miller identified five factors which, according to historical experience, facilitate cooperation of a meaningful and continuous nature between states. These factors were similarity of cultural background, economic equality (or lack of economic inequality), the habit of association in past international enterprises, a sense of common danger, and pressure from a greater power.[2] This chapter applies Miller's five 'conditions for cooperation' to the Trilateral Strategic Dialogue (TSD) partners. It finds that, while the United States, Japan and Australia have much in common and are in many respects 'natural allies', the obstacles to any further intensification of their trilateral endeavours remain significant. In line with Miller's prescient predictions of 1968 regarding the Australia–Japan–India triangular relationship, therefore, the chapter concludes that these obstacles to collaboration should not be underestimated.

Cultural similarity

Miller's first 'condition for cooperation' is cultural similarity, which he defines in terms of common language, history, values and social systems. He cites the examples of Scandinavian and English-speaking countries, Latin Americans, and Arab states as illustrative of groupings exhibiting such similarities. Miller observes, however, that it is often the absence – as opposed to the presence – of cultural similarity which is of greater relative importance in explaining political cooperation (or the lack thereof) between states. In his terms 'if countries have to learn new languages, get to know one another's histories as totally new exercises, comprehend social systems quite different from their own, and take account of systems of values which at first sight do not make sense, they are obviously presented with obstacles to cooperation'.[3] Consistent with this, Miller also concludes that similarity of cultural background alone cannot serve as a basis for political cooperation, not least because no one group of states will typically exhibit a level of cultural commonality sufficient to prevail over the dictates of their respective national interests.[4]

Their geographical separation notwithstanding, it could be argued that Australia, Japan and the United States have developed at least a modicum of cultural contiguity in the postwar era. In the United States–Japan alliance, the 'normative context' of alliance policy is underwritten by both countries' mutual commitment to democratic values rather than by any distinct sense of collective identity. They are each liberal democracies, espousing broadly similar economic and political values. This represents an explicit and shared cultural preference that translates into alliance affinity.[5] As one Japanese analyst has recently observed, 'the [Japanese] generation which experienced a poor and hungry childhood developed in awe of the US ... [t]his experience encouraged the intellectual class of this new generation to become strong adherents of American ways'.[6] Similarly, cultural and normative factors have combined to underwrite the Australian–American alliance. Various observers of this security relationship have argued that they are at least as important as short-term interest calculation as barometers of alliance viability and persistence.[7]

Consistent with this, Australia and Japan maintained robust formal alliance relationships with the United States during the Cold War. These alliances, while ostensibly directed against the ideological and military challenge posed by the Soviet Union, have survived the dissipation of that challenge surprisingly well. Indeed, the cultural, ideological and historical commonalities between them provide one rationale for why these respective bilateral alliances have not only outlasted the Soviet threat, but have – contrary to the expectations of mainstream theories of alliance politics[8] – actually attained an even greater level of cohesion and intensity during the period since.

A further commonality between Australia, Japan and the United States stems from the fact that they are each regarded – albeit to varying degrees – essentially as 'outsiders' in Asia. This ostracism is not only a product of how the region views these three countries, but also one of how Australians, Japanese and Americans perceive themselves and their place in this part of the world. The American political scientist Samuel Huntington, for instance, has described Australia as a 'torn country', a people who, in his words, are 'divided over whether their society belongs to one civilization or another'.[9] Despite its geographical location in East Asia, Huntington also describes Japan as 'a society and civilization unique to itself', before proceeding to observe that 'however strong the trade and investment links Japan may develop with other East Asian countries, its cultural differences with these countries inhibit and perhaps preclude its promoting regional economic integration like that in Europe and North America'.[10] However, whereas ongoing regional concerns deriving from Japan's wartime militaristic past have played a role in reinforcing Tokyo's sense of detachment from the rest of Asia, this is certainly not so in the case of America – whose deep economic engagement and postwar military presence has generally been welcomed. Nevertheless, the United States too continues to be viewed as an 'outsider' by most if not all Asian countries, as epitomized by its exclusion from the inaugural East Asia Summit of December 2005.

When contemplating the similarity of cultural background between Australia,

Japan and the United States, it is important to acknowledge the extent to which the personal chemistry between President Bush and Prime Ministers Junichiro Koizumi and John Howard respectively has served to underwrite the sense of commonality in the United States–Japan and United States–Australia relationships. Certainly not since the so-called 'Ron-Yasu' friendship of the 1980s between President Reagan and Japanese Prime Minister Nakasone Yasuhiro have such strong personal ties existed between the leaders of America and Japan. Like Bush and Koizumi (and, indeed, Howard for that matter), Reagan and Nakasone were conservative leaders who were ideologically compatible by virtue of their vehemently anti-communist outlooks. They met an unprecedented twelve times during their respective terms in office, elevating the United States–Japan alliance to new heights in the process through expanded intelligence exchanges, the initiation of joint military exercises and increased Japanese host nation support for US forces.[11]

The Bush–Koizumi and Bush–Howard personal friendships certainly go some way towards accounting for the tightening in the United States–Japan and United States–Australia alliances which has taken place during the five years since the 11 September attacks on the World Trade Center and the Pentagon. President Bush is known to value personal friendships with his foreign counterparts and reportedly holds Howard and Koizumi in the highest regard of all, along with British Prime Minister Tony Blair.[12] This raises an interesting question as to the future of the TSD, however, specifically in terms of whether it can survive and prosper beyond these close personal synergies. One envisages, for instance, that the dynamics of the United States–Australia alliance would have been markedly different had the Labour Opposition leader Mark Latham won the Australian federal election of October 2004. Latham was highly equivocal in his support for the alliance and, recalling American–Australian cultural commonalities of days gone by, at one point actually referred to the relationship as 'the last manifestation of the White Australia mentality'.[13]

Economic equality

One of the outcomes Latham claimed to be seeking through the espousal of such sentiments was a more equal alliance relationship with the United States. Equality is also one of the conditions for cooperation to which Miller refers. Although Miller refers to 'economic' equality, it is clear that what he has in mind is something much broader than just trading and financial relationships. He does identify economic strength as an area where equality (or its absence) is important between states. However, Miller gives greater emphasis to disparities between them in terms of resources. Brief mention is made of population as one such resource – in which Australia is obviously regarded as the weakest relative to Japan and India – but Miller devotes most attention to military resources, including the respective capacities of these three countries to 'provide naval, [land], and air contingents to a joint operation somewhere is Asia', as well as in terms of their 'capacity to produce substantial manpower'.[14]

In terms of their military resources, the United States, Japan and Australia do enjoy some compatibilities, particularly when considered relative to other countries in the region. With the obvious exception of Singapore, for instance, the United States, Japan and Australia are the only three countries in the Asia-Pacific with the capacity to meaningfully engage in the so-called 'Revolution in Military Affairs'. The armed forces of these three countries are also relatively interoperable. Beyond this, however, stark resource inequalities exist that are likely to place real constraints on the expansion of cooperative activity between the three.

It is important to bear in mind, for instance, that the United States remains the dominant power in the region (and indeed the world) by all material indicators. This dominance is most apparent in terms of the military assets it has at its disposal. Contemplate the fact, for instance, that the United States possesses not only the most powerful air force in the world, but also the second most powerful air force in the form of the US Navy's air wing. The Bush administration has certainly made no secret of its ambitions to cement and possibly even extend this dominance, with a view to dissuading potential adversaries from pursuing military build-ups aimed at equalling or surpassing the United States.

Even a comparison between the Japanese and Australian defence forces, however, reveals that there are also very real constraints to the expansion of cooperative activity on the Australian side. The Australian Defence Force (ADF), for instance, is only a small force – perhaps about a fifth of the size of the Japanese Self-Defence Force (JSDF). Australia's defence budget (US$17.4 billion in 2005) is about a third of Japan's (US$44.7 billion). Australia's total active defence force is 52,872, compared to the JSDF's 239,900. The Australian Army has 26,035 personnel while the Japanese Ground Self-Defence Force (JGSDF) has 148,200. The Royal Australian Navy (RAN) has six submarines and only ten principal surface combatants (destroyers and frigates).[15] Australia's annual expenditure on defence cooperation averages about A$230 million (about US$150 million) – covering the costs of combined exercises, training programmes, overseas visits and various forms of defence assistance, and focused mainly on the ASEAN and Southwest Pacific areas. It also includes the cost of regional maritime surveillance operations by Australia's P-3C long-range maritime patrol aircraft.[16] The ADF has been operating at an extraordinary tempo since 1999, with both platforms and personnel fully committed.

Habits of association

These obvious resource inequalities between the United States, Japan and Australia notwithstanding, the three countries have, in recent years, been developing an impressive record of association in international enterprises. Miller identifies this condition for cooperation as one of the most powerful amongst the five – a condition that is self-reinforcing to the extent that, according to Miller, 'states which have been together in past endeavours can always recall these when they wish to mobilise support for new ones'.[17] Miller goes on to observe that 'if the past association has been recent, purposes and procedures which applied in one set of international difficulties can form the mode of approach to new problems'.[18] When considered against the backdrop of the burgeoning cooperation that has been occurring between the United States, Japan and Australia in recent years – in a whole host of military, technological and humanitarian endeavours – this would appear to augur well for the future of their trilateral relationship.

The 11 September terrorist attacks and the subsequent onset of the US-led war on terror (or recently dubbed 'long war') has generated a myriad of opportunities for expanded United States–Japan–Australia cooperation – in US-led 'coalitions of the willing', regional multilateral forums, as well as the TSD itself. On the defence side, this has meant expanding dialogues and intelligence exchanges, inten- sified cooperation with regard to maritime surveillance activities, and increasing joint exercise activities. For example, in September 2003, military and law enforce- ment personnel from Australia, Japan, the United States (and France) conducted Exercise *Pacific Protector* in the Coral Sea, in which a vessel 'suspected' (for training purposes) of carrying weapons of mass destruction (WMD) was interdicted, boarded and inspected as part of the Proliferation Security Initiative (PSI). The exercise was widely regarded as being aimed at North Korea. Following its success- ful completion, Australia hosted a second *Pacific Protector* exercise in early April 2006, again as part of the PSI. Held around Darwin in the far north of Australia, the 2006 exercise focused on an air interception scenario, coupled with ground- based activities. In addition to the involvement of personnel and assets from the United States, Japan and Australia, New Zealand, Singapore and the United Kingdom also participated.[19]

Cooperation in operational situations between the United States, Japan and Australia has also increased during the period in question, not only with respect to the provision of intelligence and logistic support, but also in actual combat oper- ations. Australia and Japan were the only countries in the region to provide a military contribution to Operation *Enduring Freedom*, for instance, although only the Australian forces participated in combat operations. Nevertheless, Japan's support for the war in Afghanistan was particularly significant in terms of breaking the constraints on overseas deployments of the JSDF.

In the case of the war in Iraq, actual Japanese support for Operation *Iraqi Freedom* was very limited. The *Kirishima*, one of Japan's Aegis destroyers, was sent to the Indian Ocean in December 2002 to protect Japanese supply ships that were refuelling US and British naval vessels, and to conduct surveillance activities in the area, in accordance with another special anti-terrorist law passed in November 2002.[20] It was widely (if only tacitly) understood that this was an indirect contribution to the forthcoming war in Iraq in that it relieved a US Aegis destroyer from Afghanistan operations to move into the Gulf.[21]

Following the declared end of the war in Iraq on 1 May 2003, and the passage by the Diet of the Iraq Humanitarian Reconstruction Support Special Measures Law in July, JSDF forces were sent to Iraq to assist the US-led coalition forces 'recon- structing' the country – the first time that JSDF units have served abroad outside the UN Peacekeeping Operations (PKO) framework.[22] Between January 2004 and June 2006, approximately 5,500 JSDF personnel were despatched to the Iraqi city of Samawah, in the southern Al Muthanna province.[23] In February 2005, the Howard government deployed 450 ADF personnel to Iraq (in addition to the 850 already stationed there) specifically to guard the JSDF personnel engaged in reconstruction work, as well as to help train new Iraqi Army Units in Al Muthanna province. The Al Muthanna deployment cost Australia some A$200 million in the 2005–6 fiscal year, compared to a total of approximately A$270 million for all ADF activities in Iraq in 2004–5, but was justified in terms of ensuring that the Japanese stayed in Iraq and the strengthening of the Australia–Japan security relationship.[24]

United States–Japan–Australia cooperation in Afghanistan and Iraq builds on a longer history of collaboration between the three countries in various peacekeeping operations and humanitarian missions. Japan's first military contribution to a UN PKO, for example, was its involvement in the UN Transitional Authority in Cambodia (UNTAC) in 1992–93. Australia and the United States also contributed personnel to this mission. The three countries again worked closely together in responding to the East Timor crisis of 1999. Australia led the international intervention and Japan, while initially declining military participation, ultimately decided to send JSDF personnel to East Timor in 1999. Likewise, although Washington did not provide ground troops, it did give critically important intelligence, planning, transport, logistics and communication support.[25] Along with India, the United States, Japan and Australia were also members of the coalition which coordinated assistance efforts in the immediate aftermath of the December 2004 Indian Ocean tsunami.[26]

The decisions by Australia and Japan in December 2003 to participate in US ballistic missile defence (BMD) programmes also raise collaborative possibilities. In June 2002, the United States officially withdrew from the Anti-Ballistic Missile (ABM) Treaty and embarked on a wide-ranging programme to develop and deploy both theatre and strategic/national BMD systems, but this really only codified commitments made by the Bush administration before 11 September. Both Australia and Japan had also been interested in different aspects of missile defence well before 11 September. However, the war on terror has provided new justifications, with the United States explaining its need for defences in terms of the proliferation of WMD among 'rogue states', and, potentially, international terrorist organizations – with North Korea being prominent in this milieu.

Common danger

There is no doubt that current and prospective geopolitical trends have the potential to lead to a further strengthening of security cooperation between the United States, Japan and Australia. Given the growing probability of their common involvement in the 'long war', counter-proliferation initiatives and peacekeeping operations (with and without UN mandates), as well as their mutual interest in BMD developments, it is becoming increasingly likely that elements of the American, Australian and Japanese armed forces will serve together in operational situations, including not only combat support activities but also actual combat. It is not difficult to envisage, for instance, Australian, American and Japanese units committed to the same theatre, being embroiled in firefights in which they fight, and survive, together.

The realization of such scenarios, however, will remain heavily contingent upon whether Washington, Tokyo and Canberra share relatively compatible threat perceptions. Indeed, according to Miller, it is the 'sense of common danger [that] is usually regarded as the most powerful incentive to co-operation'.[27] To illustrate this point, Miller draws upon the well-worn and somewhat simplistic suggestion made by science fiction writers, that if the earth were to confront an extra-terrestrial threat – an invasion from Mars is a scenario commonly portrayed in such writings[28] – that this would occasion most if not all states to cast aside their earthly differences and unite against the common threat.[29] While it is true that a common danger often does make strange bedfellows, Miller also goes on to concede, however, that a sense of common danger may only be temporary and, moreover, that states may not agree upon the best way to confront it.[30] This latter observation is especially pertinent when contemplating the future of trilateral cooperation between the United States, Japan and Australia.

The foregoing analysis illustrates that there is no shortage of common security concerns weighing on the minds of policy-makers in Washington, Tokyo and Canberra. Terrorism, WMD proliferation and, increasingly, the threat of political marginalization from East Asia appear to be at the top of that list. Notwithstanding these extensive areas of mutual interest and common threat perception, it is important to bear in mind that the United States, Japan and Australia have very different strategic interests, driven in part by the fact that they are each physically located in parts of the world with very different strategic dynamics. From the point of view of the defence of Australia, for instance, Japan lies far outside Australia's 'sphere of primary strategic interest'.[31] Likewise, despite suggestions that Australia is in the process of becoming (if it has not already become) a truly 'global' ally of the United States,[32] there is a risk that the increasing emphasis being accorded to coalition operations and interoperable capabilities will lead to the diversion of resources and distortions in force structure development. The total cost of the Al Muthanna deployment to guard the JSDF personnel in Iraq, for instance, could amount to some A$300 million.[33] This is roughly equivalent to the cost of two Wedgetail airborne warning and control aircraft, or five Global Hawk unmanned aerial vehicles (UAVs), or a dedicated multi-transponder geostationary communications satellite for the ADF.

It is in relation to the issue of China's (re)emergence, however, that the divergence in threat perceptions between Washington, Tokyo and Canberra is most acute. Amongst the three, Canberra is clearly the more sanguine on this issue. For Australia, China is seen as such a commercial opportunity that the Howard government appears to have spent little time (publicly at least) considering, for instance, some of the potential geopolitical implications of Australia's growing energy ties with China.[34] Instead, it has consistently come out with statements such as that recently issued by the Australian Ambassador to the United States, Dennis Richardson, who in January 2006 suggested that 'the question for Australia is not whether China's growth is innately good or bad; Australia made up its mind long ago that it was a good thing. China's growth is unambiguously good for Asia and the United States.'[35]

Washington, on the other hand, sees China's economic rise as both a blessing and potentially as a threat. American consumers, of course, benefit tremendously from the flood of cheap Chinese imports. However, the effect of these on US labour, coupled with China's reluctance to undertake any meaningful revaluation of the yuan and America's growing trade deficit with China, has, in recent times, stoked anti-China sentiment in the US Congress, which even resulted in legislative efforts to impose blanket 27 per cent sanctions on all Chinese imports.

These differences between the United States and Australia regarding China's (re)emergence have been evident in other areas. During a visit to China in June 2005, for instance, the then Australian Defence Minister Robert Hill indicated that he saw China's expanding military expenditure as a process of 'modernisation, not destabilisation'.[36] Such a statement stood in stark contrast to those consistently issued by his American counterpart, Donald Rumsfeld, suggesting that 'Beijing's military spending threatens the delicate security balance in Asia'.[37] Such differences are also apparent over human rights. During a joint press conference in June 2005, for example, President Bush alluded to differences between the United States and China over issues of values – particularly in relation to freedom of worship – to which Prime Minister Howard replied that the Sino-Australian relationship was 'mature enough' to ride through 'temporary arguments' over human rights and that he remained 'unashamed' in developing Australia's relations with China.[38]

The divergence between Japanese threat perceptions of China's (re)emergence and those of Australia is even more pronounced. Deep-seated animosities between Beijing and Tokyo have certainly intensified in recent times. By way of example, Japan's December 2004 National Defence Program Outline, which provides guidelines and sets the direction for future Japanese military capabilities, for the first time explicitly identified China as a significant military threat. Consistent with this, Sino-Japanese tensions have spiked during the period since over a host of historical, economic, resource, political, societal and strategic issues.[39] In many respects this worrisome trend is unsurprising given that, as the two historical great powers of East Asia, both countries have aspirations for leadership and influence over the region. We have seen this most clearly in ongoing debates regarding the notion of East Asian Community. The problem from the perspective of Sino-American relations, however, is that the growing intimacy which is occurring in an already close United States–Japan alliance increases the risk of the United States being pulled into a security dilemma that it would probably rather not enter, should Sino-Japanese relations continue along their current downwards trajectory. The dilemma for Australia is a slightly different, but equally serious one, bearing in mind that Japan and China remain Australia's number one and number two trading partners respectively. The outbreak of open hostilities between them would clearly be catastrophic from Canberra's perspective.

These diverging threat perceptions were certainly apparent in the lead up to the first ministerial-level meeting of the TSD, which was held in Sydney in March

2006. In the days prior to the meeting, Secretary of State Condoleezza Rice indicated during media interviews that the United States, Japan and Australia had to be mindful of the pace and reach of Beijing's military build-up. She also raised the prospect of China becoming 'a negative force'.[40] The Australian Foreign Minister Alexander Downer promptly distanced himself from these comments, indicating that 'a policy of containment of China would be a very big mistake'[41] and suggesting that Australia's desire was for 'successful engagement with China'.[42] In welcoming China's constructive engagement in the region, the joint statement which ultimately came out of the TSD was much closer to the Australian line.[43]

There remains a possibility, of course, that Australia remains just as apprehensive as the United States and Japan regarding China's rise but that (consistent with Miller's prescription) it is simply adopting a different approach – one emphasizing the engagement (as opposed to the soft balancing) elements of a 'hedging' strategy as a means towards meeting this 'common' danger.[44] Based on the publicly available information regarding the lead-up to the first ministerial-level TSD, however, this possibility seems a remote one. Hence, Miller's observation regarding the Australia–India–Japan triangular relationship – that 'if anything can bring the three countries together in continuous co-operation, it is concern about China'[45] – appears some way off when applied to the triangular relationship which is the focus of the current study.

Greater power pressure

The final condition for cooperation which Miller identifies is pressure from a greater power. Such pressure can come in many forms. As Miller observes it can be 'strong or subtle, open or concealed, military, political, or economic in character'.[46] He cites the examples of French influence over parts of Eastern Europe during the 1920s, Russian influence over Eastern Europe and American influence over Western Europe during the Cold War, as well as periodic US influence over Latin America as indicative. Miller does not, however, appear to attach the same significance to this particular condition for cooperation as he does to the others. In his terms, 'if conditions are favourable, the benevolent interest of a major power will probably consolidate co-operative arrangements between lesser states, especially if they are given concrete benefits'.[47] From this perspective, pressure from a greater power might perhaps best be seen as a factor reinforcing existing cooperation, rather than one necessary for its existence in the first instance.

In the case of the United States–Japan–Australia triangular relationship, there is mixed evidence as to whether pressure from a greater power even exists. As alluded to previously, Washington is in the process of executing a 'transformation' of its Asia-Pacific alliance relationships from originally region-specific mechanisms to increasingly 'global' arrangements. For Australia and Japan, however, this process has very much been undertaken via their respective bilateral alliance relationships with the United States, rather than through TSD channels. To be sure, calls have emanated from the United States for a more effective integration of America's Asia-Pacific alliances.[48] Publicly at least, however, the primary impetus for initiating and driving forward the TSD seems to have come from the Australians and the Japanese. It was the Australian Foreign Minister Alexander Downer, after all, who first publicly raised the possibility of closer United States–Japan–Australia security dialogue during a press conference following the July 2001 Australia–US Ministerial (AUSMIN) meeting.[49] The TSD was then formally announced by Japanese Prime Minister Koizumi during a visit to Canberra in August 2002.[50] Added to this, Secretary of State Rice's January 2006 postponement of her attendance at the scheduled meeting of the TSD in Sydney[51] would appear to suggest that if Washington is indeed exerting 'greater power pressure to drive this process forward', then it is doing so in the most subtle of ways.

Conclusions

The recent past – when viewed through the prism of Miller's analytical framework – shows that Australia, Japan and the United States are, in many respects, 'natural allies'. They are each liberal democracies, sharing broadly similar economic and political values. They are also building an impressive history of association through their collaborations in the war on terror (Afghanistan and Iraq), peacekeeping operations (Cambodia and East Timor), humanitarian assistance efforts (Indian Ocean tsunami relief) and military exercises (PSI). However, Miller's prescient observation regarding the Australia–Japan–India triangular relationship – that 'In general, the obstacles to co-operation seem to be more influential at present than the aids to it'[52] – also resonates deeply when applied to the TSD partners.

Australia, Japan and the United States exhibit substantial resource inequalities – most notably on the Australian side – which seems likely to preclude any significant expansion of collaborative activity between them. Added to this, each country has disparate strategic interests, driven in part by the fact that they are all physically located in parts of the world with very different strategic dynamics. This divergence is most apparent in relation to the issue of China's (re)emergence, where Australia appears to have adopted a highly optimistic approach, in contrast to American ambivalence and Japan's heightened sense of vulnerability. Added to these obstacles to cooperation, it also remains unclear just how contingent the current halcyon period in trilateral cooperation between the United States, Japan and Australia will be upon the unique personal synergies between their respective national leaders.

In the final analysis, history suggests that the Asia-Pacific has not provided fertile ground for the cultivation of trilateral security arrangements. The most famous example of trilateralism gone awry would have to be the ANZUS alliance, which essentially collapsed in the mid-1980s under the weight of New Zealand's anti-nuclear policies. During the 1990s, fears of an anti-American strategic triangle comprising China, India and Russia failed to materialize. More recently, proposals for a United States–Japan–South Korea strategic triangle have been hindered by seemingly irreconcilable differences over how to deal with the continuing North Korean nuclear problem, in addition to revived historical animosities between Seoul and Tokyo. Against that backdrop, the findings of this chapter suggest that, if indeed the TSD partners are to buck this trend, then the challenges associated with the further advancement of trilateral collaboration between them should not be underestimated.

Notes

1 The authors are grateful to Satu Limaye for drawing their attention to this volume.
2 J. D. B. Miller (1968), 'The conditions for co-operation', in J. D. B. Miller (ed.), *India, Japan, Australia: Partners in Asia?*, Canberra: Australian National University Press, p. 200.
3 Ibid.
4 Ibid.
5 See Peter J. Katzenstein (1996), *Cultural Norms & National Security: Police and Military in Postwar Japan*, Ithaca, NY: Cornell University Press, pp. 131–32.
6 Naoko Sajima (1999), 'Japan: strategic culture at a crossroads', in Ken Booth and Russell Trood (eds), *Strategic Culture in the Asia-Pacific Region*, Basingstoke: Macmillan, p. 84.
7 William Tow and Henry Albinski (2002), 'ANZUS – alive and well after fifty years', *Australian Journal of Politics and History*, vol. 48, no. 2, pp. 154–55.
8 See, for example, Stephen M. Walt (1987), *The Origins of Alliances*, Ithaca, NY: Cornell University Press.
9 Samuel P. Huntington (1993), 'The clash of civilizations?', *Foreign Affairs*, vol. 72, no. 3, p. 42; and Huntington (1995), *The Clash of Civilizations and the Remaking of World Order*, New York: Simon & Schuster, pp. 151–54.
10 Ibid., pp. 27–28.
11 Victor Cha (1999), *Alignment Despite Antagonism: The United States–Korea–Japan Security Triangle*, Stanford, CA: Stanford University Press, pp. 177–78.
12 Peter Baker (2006), 'Bush reinforces friendship with Australia', *Washington Post*, 17 May, p. A04.
13 Cited in Peter Edwards (2005), *Permanent Friends? Historical Reflections on the Australian–American Alliance*, Lowy Institute Paper 08, Sydney: Lowy Institute for International Policy, p. 54.
14 Miller (1968), 'The conditions for co-operation', p. 204.
15 The International Institute for Strategic Studies (2005), *The Military Balance 2005–2006*, London: Routledge, pp. 266–67, 279.
16 Desmond Ball and Pauline Kerr (1996), *Presumptive Engagement: Australia's Asia-Pacific Security Policy in the 1990s*, Sydney, NSW: Allen & Unwin, p. 63.
17 Miller (1968), 'The conditions for co-operation', p. 201.
18 Ibid.
19 Australian Department of Defence (2006), 'Exercise Pacific Protector 06 overview', available at: www.defence.gov.au/PSI/expp06.htm (accessed 25 September 2006).
20 Axel Berkofsky (2002), 'Aid and comfort: Japan's Aegis sets sail', *Asia Times Online*, 19 December, available at: www.atimes.com/atimes/Japan/DL19Dh01.html (accessed 25 September 2006).
21 Yoichiro Sato (2003), 'The GSDF will go to Iraq without a blue helmet', *PacNet* 31, 31 July.
22 Gordon Fairclough and Charles Hutzler (2004), 'Japan: marching on to a new role', *Far Eastern Economic Review*, 15 January, pp. 18–21.
23 *Daily Yomiuri* (2006), 'GSDF contribution hailed', 21 June, p. 2.
24 Patrick Walters (2005), 'Spreading freedom is expensive', *Australian*, 11 May, p. 11.
25 See David Dickens (2002), 'Can East Timor be a blueprint for burdensharing?', *Washington Quarterly*, vol. 25, no. 3, pp. 29–40.
26 Tim Huxley (2005), 'The tsunami and security: Asia's 9/11?', *Survival*, vol. 47, no. 1, pp. 123–32.

27 Miller (1968), 'The conditions for co-operation', p. 201.
28 See, for example, H. G. Wells (1898), *The War of the Worlds*, London: William Heinemann.
29 Miller (1968), 'The conditions for co-operation', p. 201.
30 Ibid.
31 Paul Dibb (1986), *Review of Australia's Defence Capabilities: Report to the Minister for Defence*, Canberra: Australian Government Printing Service, pp. 3–4.
32 See, for example, Greg Sheridan (2006), 'US sees us as a global ally, a vision well worth sharing', *Australian*, 29 June, p. 10.
33 Walters (2005), 'Spreading freedom is expensive', p. 11.
34 For further reading see David Hale (2004), 'China's growing appetites', *The National Interest*, Issue 76, pp. 137–47.
35 Geoff Elliott (2006), 'Stay cool on China, Ambassador tells US', *Australian*, 30 January, p. 1.
36 Cited in Paul Dibb (2005), 'Don't get too close to Beijing', *Australian*, 2 August, p. 12.
37 Ibid.
38 Transcript of the Prime Minister The Hon. John Howard MP, Joint Press Conference with The President of the United States of America George W. Bush, The White House, Washington, DC, 19 July 2005.
39 For further reading see Denny Roy (2005), 'The sources and limits of Sino-Japanese tensions', *Survival*, vol. 47, no. 2, pp. 191–214.
40 Patrick Walters (2006), 'Containing China a big mistake: Downer', *Australian*, 16 March, p. 1.
41 Ibid.
42 Geoffrey Barker (2006), 'Search for common ground on China', *Australian Financial Review*, 1 March, p. 4.
43 Patrick Walters (2006), 'Tri-nation forum's potential excites participants', *Australian*, 20 March, p. 2.
44 For further reading on 'hedging' strategies see Evan S. Medeiros (2005–6), 'Strategic hedging and the future of Asia-Pacific stability', *Washington Quarterly*, vol. 29, no. 1, pp. 145–67; and Evelyn Goh (2006), 'Understanding "hedging" in Asia-Pacific security', *PacNet* 43, 31 August.
45 Miller (1968), 'The conditions for co-operation', p. 206.
46 Ibid., p. 202.
47 Ibid.
48 See, for example, Robert Blackwill (2000), 'An action agenda to strengthen America's alliances in the Asia-Pacific region', in Robert Blackwill and Paul Dibb (eds), *America's Asian Alliances*, Cambridge, MA: MIT Press, pp. 126–34.
49 Purnendra Jain and John Bruni (2006), 'American acolytes: Tokyo, Canberra and Washington's emerging "Pacific Axis"', in Brad Williams and Andrew Newman (eds), *Japan, Australia and Asia-Pacific Security*, Oxford: Routledge, p. 95.
50 William Tow and Russell Trood (2006), 'The "anchors" – collaborative security, substance or smokescreen?', in Williams and Newman (eds), *Japan, Australia and Asia-Pacific Security*, p. 78.
51 Paul Dibb (2006), 'The decline of American sway', *Australian*, 11 January, p. 12.
52 Miller (1968), 'The conditions for co-operation', p. 209.

3 'Contingent trilateralism'

Applications for the Trilateral Security Dialogue

William T. Tow

For over half a century, the predominant means for organizing security cooperation in the Asia-Pacific region has been through the creation and maintenance of bilateral defence arrangements. The United States' network of bilateral security alliances with Japan, Australia, South Korea, Thailand and the Philippines – often referred to collectively as the 'San Francisco System' – and Washington's more recent intensification of its bilateral security relations with Singapore has been and remains the most conspicuous example of this trend. It reflected a conscious choice by key regional security actors (especially maritime powers) to 'bandwagon' with American power and prosperity at the Cold War's outset.[1]

The American 'hub and spokes' system of bilateral security, however, is by no means the only case of bilateralism's prevalence in Asian security politics. The Sino-Soviet Treaty of Friendship, Alliance and Mutual Assistance signed in February 1950 initially promised to rival the American network yet soon floundered on the shoals of intensifying tensions between Moscow and Beijing as the Cold War evolved (a modified security treaty was later negotiated between Russia and China in 2001 but it contains no real commitment for the parties to defend each other). Both the Soviet Union and China negotiated separate treaties with North Korea (in 1961) and the Soviets subsequently engineered significant bilateral accords with India (August 1971) and Vietnam (February 1978); Vietnam signed similar treaties with Laos (1977) and Cambodia (1979) and Australia signed a short-lived Agreement for Maintaining Security (AMS) with Indonesia (1995–99). Numerous bilateral defence memoranda of understandings and friendship accords were also negotiated and many still remain in force.

Why have bilateral forms of collective defence remained predominant as an ordering strategy for Asia-Pacific security politics? Apart from the somewhat amorphous Shanghai Cooperation Organization (SCO), multilateral collective defence treaties are non-existent in the region. Reasons why an 'Asian NATO' never emerged have been assessed in depth; many in the region were either only decolonized after World War II or, in the cases of South Korea and Taiwan, were still contested sovereignties as the Cold War hardened.[2] Most projected lower levels of shared collective identity than did NATO Europe's member-states and the characteristic of 'exclusiveness' inherent to bilateral security relations was tailor-made for postwar US policy-makers to exert high levels of control in an occupied Japan or, following the Korean War, to contain such Asian leaders as South Korea's Syngman Rhee or Taiwan's Chiang Kai-shek from deliberating escalating crises in ways that would entrap the United States into defending these contested polities against their communist adversaries.[3] The key point here is that bilateralism has been and remains most prevalent in a region where states are highly diverse in historical, cultural and geopolitical composition.

What is 'trilateralism'?

Given bilateralism's durability, the recent intensification of 'trilateralism' as a potential element of Asia-Pacific security politics commands greater attention, especially in the context of the Australia–Japan–United States Trilateral Strategic Dialogue (TSD). The concept of 'trilateralism' has often been used interchangeably with another international relations structural concept, 'triangularity'. Yet each concept is distinct from the other, notwithstanding their diverse applications within the broader international security literature. A brief review of these variations is offered here to help establish a clearer theoretical context for explaining the emergence of the TSD.

Trilateralism usually suggests cooperative security behaviour between three states or strategic polities (that is, the European Community is a distinct strategic polity comprised of different states) to promote specific values and orders. The condition describes strategic affinity by these three polities at both the regional and global levels of analysis. Internationally, traditional postwar interpretations of trilateralism related to the notion of influential policy and business leaders in the United States, Europe and Japan uniting, through the 'Trilateral Commission', to propose and implement solutions to 'common problems of international society'. This concept, which was first implemented during the early 1970s, focused on 'symmetry' and 'homogeneity'. The United States would act as a pivot power for coordinating free market economic initiatives, promoting democracy on a global scale and acting as a conduit for both NATO and Japanese defence concerns.[4] Overtaken by events such as the demise of the Soviet Union and 11 September 2001, this form of trilateralism still applies to limited forms of security interaction: for instance, the George W. Bush administration's recent initiative (early 2006) to assign Japan, Australia and other Pacific democracies more 'formal' status within NATO. As will be discussed below, this has some relevance to the Australia–Japan–United States Trilateral Strategic Dialogue's identity and agendas. However, the prospect of Japan and Australia taking part in a still largely undefined NATO-centric 'global policeman' initiative is less central to the Asia-Pacific's security environment and the major problems that shape it. It is also one that engenders sharp resistance from various European quarters who have little desire to be associated with a NATO that ascribes to the role of 'global policeman'.[5]

Another form of trilateralism that appears more relevant to the Trilateral Strategic Dialogue is the Trilateral Coordination and Oversight Group (TCOG), involving Japan, South Korea and the United States to coordinate policies towards

North Korea. Formed in 1999 to coordinate the 'Perry Process' of diplomatic initiatives towards Pyongyang, the TCOG was not designed to convert the two existing US bilateral alliances with Japan and South Korea, respectively, into a trilateral one. It was, however, initiated to reassure both Japan and South Korea that the United States would not 'abandon' either ally in return for both Japan and South Korea responding to US defence burden-sharing pressures against the North Korean threat.[6] Meeting under TCOG auspices until late 2003 when the acronym was dropped from describing increasingly less frequent formal trilateral consultations, American, Japanese and South Korean diplomats found that they often entertained as many differences as common interests in perceiving and orchestrating their North Korean policies.

While there are some parallels between the TCOG and the TSD, more differences than similarities emerge when they are compared. Like South Korea, Australia finds itself increasingly at odds with the United States and Japan over the question of a 'China threat'. To a greater extent than their recent South Korean counterparts, however, Australian policy-makers have sustained threat perceptions of a North Korea armed with weapons of mass destruction (WMD) and ballistic missile capabilities that are quite analogous with those held by their American and Japanese counterparts. They have responded to such concerns by supporting the Proliferation Security Initiative (PSI) without qualification (South Korea has only been an 'observer' of PSI initiatives and operations). Australia has also entered into missile defence research with the United States and Japan. Like the TCOG, the momentum and durability of the Trilateral Strategic Dialogue rests upon a process that James Schoff argues is meant 'to facilitate cooperation when planning for and responding to a variety of regional crisis … strengthen[ing] the two bilateral alliances and help[ing] build connecting threads between them'.[7] Ultimately, however, this has not occurred in a TCOG context. Trilateralism has been pre-empted by the Six Party Talks involving North Korea or has succumbed to shifting imperatives of South Korean domestic politics. There is no commensurate domestic political consensus in Australia or Japan that would support multilateral regional security initiatives supplanting traditional bilateral alliance ties with the United States. Overall, the 'ties that bind' the Australian–American and Japanese–American security dyads remain far more robust than those constituting bilateral Japanese–South Korean politico-security ties or even (more recently) American–South Korean geopolitical relations.

Trilateralism versus triangularity

To establish greater clarity when referring to 'triangles' in international security relations, the ideas of 'trilateralism' and 'triangularity' must be differentiated. As noted above, trilateralism connotes strategic cooperation based on adherence to common values or visions of regional and international order. Triangularity is less about ideals and more about balancing interests.

Triangularity usually occurs in one of two forms: as an anti-hegemony strategy, or as a conflict avoidance mechanism. There is overlap in the strategic rationales underlying both of these approaches but they remain sufficiently distinct to warrant separate analysis.

Triangularity in an anti-hegemony context is a signalling strategy designed to maintain a relatively stable synergy between three powers engaged in a regional or global balancing process. During the 1970s, a plethora of Western assessments were generated about the 'strategic triangle' between China, the Soviet Union and the United States.[8] The 'triangularity' process was generally understood as when three large powers manoeuvre to gain advantageous or 'pivot' status within their triangular relationship. This variation of triangularity has been described as 'the logical, quasi-geometrical relationship among political actors in the international arena' and is characterized by three key pre-conditions: (1) it circumscribes the possible relationships among three rational, autonomous actors; (2) the bilateral relationship among any two of these actors is contingent on their relationship with the third; and (3) each actor actively seeks to engage one or the other or both to forestall its defection or hostile collusion and advance its own interests. The Sino–Soviet–American 'triangle' that emerged during the Cold War conforms to this version of triangularity.[9] Another version of an anti-hegemonic triangularity is one featuring a form of containment strategy in a regional or international power-balancing system. In the late 1970s, some Western strategists envisioned an Australian–Indian–Japanese consortium forming to coordinate a 'local containment' strategy against rising Chinese power.[10]

Conflict avoidance-oriented triangularity can operate in different ways. One variant occurs when a powerful country pursues systemic stability relative to two less powerful states by working to forestall conflict between them. It can do so by allying separately with both of the smaller states in ways that its potential defection from one alliance or the other is sufficiently threatening to both that their strategic behaviour can be controlled by the most powerful state. The United States' maintenance of separate alliances with Japan and South Korea during the Cold War is an example of this approach. Or the powerful country can intervene short of alliance commitment to ensure conflict prevention between the two smaller states. This is the idea that conflict materializing in a relationship between two states (a 'dyad') can be minimized by the intervention of an outside great power playing the role of a central authority in various ways: for instance, exercising patronage, setting norms or enforcing agreements. Recent US mediation efforts in the Middle East exemplify this form of triangularity.[11]

Although the United States–Japan–South Korea case constituted part of Washington's postwar collective defence model that was predominant in Asia during the Cold War, the overall American style of generating and/or relating to dyads in the Asia-Pacific was hierarchical, not intercessional, and designed to deter or contain security threats external to all its Pacific allies rather than to mediate or defuse tensions between them. Nor has collective defence in this region usually been conditioned by fluidity or posturing amongst allies to seek short-term advantage (the Sino-Soviet rift that materialized in the early 1960s was the major exception). The San Francisco System has been remarkably stable notwithstanding immense structural changes that challenged its original rationales during the 1990s and the first years of this century.[12] Most other protracted bilateral security relationships in Asia have likewise adhered to their original rationales (that is, containing or balancing American power in East Asia or stabilizing key regional maritime straits and chokepoints).

Contingent trilateralism and alliance politics

The characteristics underwriting the Australia–Japan–United States trilateral alliance relations assessed in this volume therefore posit a unique theoretical challenge for explaining trilateral security cooperation. Japan and Australia have been long-standing and genuinely loyal allies of the United States at the regional level of operations. Neither has been restricted by the United States from pursuing 'aberrant' strategic behaviour to the extent that South Korea or Taiwan were constrained by Washington during the height of the Cold War, or that South Korea now appears to be considering towards its Northeast Asian neighbours. Neither Australia nor Japan, moreover, has projected strategic animosity towards the other since reaching the Agreement on Commerce between the Commonwealth of Australia and Japan in July 1957. Indeed, within the half century since that accord was signed, their strategic ties have become stronger, in tandem with their substantial economic relations. Such trends set them apart from both the trilateralism and triangularity prototypes cited above.

These benign circumstances lead to a new model of trilateral security cooperation that might be termed 'contingent trilateralism'. Security cooperation between a major power and two close allies can intensify trilaterally when one or more of the following conditions are present: (1) when that major power's traditional hegemony at either the regional or global level of international security politics is sufficiently challenged by a rising strategic competitor that it responds by attempting to bind its other two allies closer together in an effort to restore a power balance more favourable to itself; (2) when all three allies have enough complementary geopolitical attributes that drive them towards greater strategic collaboration against forces that would otherwise undercut their collective strategic positionality; and (3) when one or both of the two smaller allies is able to balance against potential rivalries involving its larger ally in ways that stabilize regional or global politics. Contingent trilateralism is most likely to occur when potential rivals to the three allies are not yet so threatening as to preclude confidence-building and other forms of cooperative security behaviour developing between the triad and strategic rivals and when small allies are still able to exercise sufficient independence from their hegemonic guardian to attempt defusing security dilemmas without risking alliance defection.

To what extent are these three conditions present in the contemporary Asia-Pacific security environment? If they do underwrite the emerging Australia–Japan–United States trilateral cooperation, can they be applied in enduring and meaningful ways within that environment? China's so-called 'peaceful rise' has instigated concerns about an imbalance of power emerging in East Asia at a time when the United States, postwar East Asia's offshore hegemon, has been preoccupied with the Persian Gulf and Central Asia. Agents of interdiction (terrorists, pirates or developing states enforcing territorial claims) against energy supplies transversing Asia-Pacific's sea lanes of communication (SLOCs) and WMD proliferation have certainly strengthened the imperative for the United States, Japan and Australia to coordinate their maritime power and high technology capabilities more closely and systematically.

Despite these imperatives for greater trilateral collaboration, however, counter-vailing forces against the intensification of trilateralism are also at play. The potential for alliance policy miscalculations emanating from trilateralism is signifi-cant because China, ASEAN and even South Korea could interpret the newly established TSD as nothing more than Cold War 'containment revisited'. More-over, cautionary notes are warranted even within the TSD construct. Without sustained and careful policy management, the TSD could precipitate the erosion of alliance cooperation either if the major ally's (United States') agenda to check the power of a rising Chinese competitor led to feelings of alliance 'entrapment' by one of its smaller allies (in this case, Australia) or one of the two smaller allies (Japan) was unable to control its own worsening relations with China thereby entrapping the United States and Australia into a future confrontation in the East China Sea. These possibilities and their implications must be assessed more extensively below.

China's rise and the TSD

American strategic outlooks on and postures directed towards China remain ambivalent well into the second decade beyond the end of the Cold War. Tacit 'hedging strategy' is currently favoured by American policy-planners as the most optimum approach in response to growing Chinese power: 'pursuing policies that, on one hand, stress engagement and integration mechanisms and, on the other, emphasize realist-style balancing in the form of external security cooperation with Asian states and national military modernization programs'.[13]

This strategic orientation has shaped the evolution of what was originally labelled the Australia–Japan–United States Trilateral Security Dialogue in 2003 – a consultative group primarily designed to complement the TCOG in responding to the North Korean nuclear threat – to the 'Trilateral Strategic Dialogue' that convened in Sydney in March 2006 with China primarily on its mind.[14] United States State Department spokespersons accompanying US Secretary of State Condoleezza Rice to Indonesia and to Australia for the March 2006 inaugural TSD Ministerial Meeting reportedly disclosed to journalists that the Secretary's intent was to 'make China a [more] positive force in the region' by encouraging it to contribute to regional security and while signalling that the United States was not advocating a containment strategy against Beijing. Even so, Rice complained to both Indonesian and Australian media about China's lack of transparency over its defence spending, its economic policies relating to patents and currency controls, and its human rights record. Observers could hardly be blamed for being confused over a very mixed batch of messages.[15]

American strategy at the inaugural TSD met the first criterion for 'contingent trilateralism': a major power attempting to bind two smaller but critical allies (Australia and Japan are the most important United States allies in the Asia-Pacific) to its own interests and policies in response to a strategic rival's growing power. 'Hedging strategy' has been adopted by the United States to circumvent the risks and costs of entering into an all-out arms race or into direct conflict with China. If Beijing can be induced to gradually liberalize its political system, modify its irredentist and territorial claims in the region and observe reasonable limits to its defence build-up it will conform to the role of 'responsible stakeholder' in the international system that the United States has envisioned for it. Given this outcome, future Sino-American collaboration could spearhead a more stable and prosperous international order.[16] Critics of this view, however, embrace a more competitive interpretation of Chinese objectives. The Congressionally funded and bipartisan United States–China Economic and Security Review Commission released a lengthy report in November 2005 that the current Chinese leadership remains implacably hostile to the United States and to its strategic objectives. China, according to this report, is pursuing trade and energy security policies that are clearly targeted to denying the United States critical natural resources and undercutting its wealth, while it covertly pursues its own military modernization programmes.[17] This view has also been embraced by the Pentagon, as reflected in its annual reports to the US Congress on the growth of Chinese military power.[18]

Washington's recent efforts to tighten alliance bonds with Tokyo and Canberra have engendered positive results. As Japan's own relations with China have deteriorated in recent years, its responsiveness to American initiatives for strengthening the United States–Japan defence alliance have intensified. This includes a tacit process of widening that alliance's geographic scope of concern to encompass East Asian flashpoints beyond the Korean peninsula. Most notably, American Secretary of State Condoleezza Rice and US Secretary of Defense Donald Rumsfeld, along with their Japanese counterparts, embraced Taiwan as a legitimate purview of the alliance in the joint communiqué released by the United States–Japan Security Consultative Committee in February 2005, calling for 'the peaceful resolution of issues concerning the Taiwan Strait through dialogue'.[19] In May 2006, the same committee approved the 'United States–Japan Roadmap for Realignment Implementation' that mandates substantial Japanese financial support for building up a US strategic presence in Guam, shared facilities and command centres for the US forces remaining in Japan and Japanese Self-Defence Forces and upgraded bilateral missile defence collaboration.[20] United States defence collaboration with Australia has also been recently stepped up, with the signing of a memorandum of understanding (MOU) that promotes closer counterterrorism collaboration between the two countries in May 2006, and a similar agreement signed during the July 2004 Australian–American Ministerial Consultations (AUSMIN) that solidified American–Australian cooperation on missile defence and joint combined training to achieve greater force interoperability.[21]

Notwithstanding these arrangements, however, if Washington's preference is to realize completely seamless trilateral security cooperation with its Japanese and Australian allies as a hedge against growing Chinese regional influence it must still overcome some major challenges in its alliance relations with both Japan and Australia. Both allies' relations with China are viewed by the Bush administration as potentially complicating the development of trilateral security cooperation. Japan's worsening ties with China are clearly viewed by many within Washington's policy-making circles as a strategic liability. Michael Green, former director of Asian affairs at the National Security Council during the Bush administration, has speculated that if Sino-Japanese ties fail to improve by 2008 many American policy officials will begin to question a diplomatically isolated Japan's long-term usefulness vis-à-vis Washington's own efforts to achieve a stable balance in Sino-American relations.[22] In his September 2005 testimony to the US Senate Foreign Relations Committee, Assistant Secretary of State for East Asian and Pacific Affairs Christopher Hill observed that continuing Sino-Japanese tensions generate 'unfortunate obstacles to taking full advantage of the tremendous [economic] opportunities that exist in the region'.[23]

Recent public opinion polls in Australia have revealed the Australian public's greater affinity with China's 'charm offensive' than with US strategy demanding Australian loyalty and contributions of Australian manpower and resources for distant and potentially divisive military interventions against insurgencies and terrorist movements. Such factors have combined with the Howard government's rejection of the Bush administration's strategy to link Chinese human rights practices with economic and strategic relations, and with Australia's clear enthusiasm to export uranium and other critical natural resources to China, to raise suspicions among some critics in Washington that Australia could be a 'soft ally' engaging in its own great power manoeuvring game between China and the United States.[24]

Such divisions existing within the trilateral alliance framework should not be overrated. What they indicate is that the United States is entering into more varied security relationships with its allies, particularly on such 'transregional' issues as energy politics, the closer integration of economics and both 'traditional' and 'non-traditional' regional and international security problems as multilateral diplomacy, and humanitarian contingencies. However, US bilateral alliances remain for now the foundation of Western security politics in the Asia-Pacific region and the starting point for whatever strategic coalitions are developing there in a post-9/11 context. If Japan and Australia are no longer relying exclusively on catering to US strategic preferences, it is because they well understand that the security provided by their traditional alliances with Washington allows them to expand their range of economic, diplomatic and security contacts. Without the San Francisco System's existence, regional security would be more volatile in the absence of an offshore US balancer. Given that reality, contemporary bilateral alliances involving the United States and other great powers in the Asia-Pacific are more (although never completely) symmetrical; alliance exclusiveness is no longer a dominant feature in Asian security politics. With few exceptions, everyone is hedging their bets – encouraging peaceful evolution, hoping to get rich in the China market, and protecting against downside risks. Yet without an American alliance-based commitment to the region, there may be no effective hedge against China, leading to worsening security dilemmas between Northeast Asian states and to more geopolitical polarization in Southeast Asia and Oceania.[25]

Contingent trilateralism and geopolitics

A second prerequisite for contingent trilateralism is for the three allies' common geopolitical attributes to come under greater threat. Saul Cohen's classical definition of geopolitics is applied here: 'the study of the political and strategic relevance of geography to the pursuit of international power ... closely related to strategic geography, which is concerned with the control of, or access to, spatial areas that have an impact on the security and prosperity of nations'.[26] Critics of the geopolitical perspective argue it adds little to understanding international relations, particularly in an age of globalization and at a time when non-state actors are assuming greater importance over state-centric agents who normally contend for primacy in structural and spatial terms.[27] But spatial 'pivotal binaries' remain critical to how power is perceived and operationalized in the strategic policy-maker's world: 'sea power' and 'land power', 'maritime' and 'continental', 'heartland' and 'rimland', and 'core areas' and peripheral 'shatterbelts'. Mental constructs or (to use the constructivist terminology) 'intersubjective understandings' they may be; but strategic thinking is still 'directly related to perceptions about the geographic attributes that configure the global space in which conflict occurs'.[28]

The United States is the world's dominant maritime power whose traditional geopolitical imperative is to prevent the rise of a contending hegemon that dominates Eurasia. Australia and Japan are both part of a 'maritime outer crescent' with the former geographically proximate to some of the world's key littorals and chokepoints (the straits areas of Southeast Asia) and the latter contiguous to the great industrial sectors of the Chinese land mass (that is, Manchuria). George Kennan's 'strongpoint containment' posture derived nearly sixty years ago argued that a Japan in any condition (even as a defeated wartime power) was geopolitically more valuable to the United States than was any Sino-American entente because China had no real integrated industrial base (except along its eastern seaboard) while Japan's industrial infrastructure was highly advanced, even in the aftermath of its wartime defeat.[29] Early in the twenty-first century, Japan remains the world's second wealthiest country.

Well into the twenty-first century, Kennan's observations remain valid. Despite China's recent spectacular economic growth, its lingering internal socio-economic problems, its lack of energy security (and its failure to grasp the necessary technologies for managing energy consumption relative to environmental challenges) and even its inability to project military power beyond very small distances of its own boundaries are all clear impediments for it to become a truly global power. By contrast, Japan has 'arguably the second best navy in the Pacific' with 4 helicopter carrying destroyers, 9 guided-missile destroyers, 34 destroyers, and 18 diesel-electric submarines. A substantial number of these ships (2 of the guided-missile destroyers, 13 of the destroyers, and 9 of the submarines) have entered service since

1995, underscoring the modernity of Japanese naval deployment. Japan's rate of ship construction equals that of China's (which has added 8 destroyers, 12 frigates, and 10 submarines in that time frame), 'and this is with Japan arguably holding back'.[30] Japan's extensive fast-breeder civil nuclear power programme and missile launching activities make it capable of becoming a formidable nuclear weapons power within a year. In summary, Japanese power has been restrained by a combination of domestic political factors and alliance guarantees offered by the United States. If it were so inclined, it could convert its economic prowess and technological proficiency into a world-class military capability over a very short period of time. Acutely sensitive to this factor, China has applied political and diplomatic pressure against Japan at every opportunity to preclude a 'breakout' of Japanese military prowess.

Washington's other 'maritime crescent' Pacific ally, Australia, has the seventeenth largest economy in the world but expends only about 1.9 per cent of it on defence. Like Japan, it has abstained from developing and deploying its own nuclear weapons capability. It has, however, maintained substantial naval and air capabilities for a country of its size, to operationalize its self-proclaimed role as guardian of the long sea lanes of communication emanating from its own substantial eastern coastline into the wider South Pacific (that is, the band of straits of islands constituting Melanesia that has recently been designated an 'arc of instability').[31] Although distant from the region's industrial power centres (and from the concentration of US military power surrounding them), its economic and, ultimately, its strategic survival is predicated on Northeast Asia's balance of power and its ability to keep its 'great and powerful friend', the United States, engaged in that sub-region.[32] While it is in Australia's interest to engage in an activist multilateral foreign policy throughout the region – and to enmesh China into a regional 'community-building' process as part of that policy – any notion of an evolving Sino-Australian 'alliance' that would eventually replace ANZUS is geopolitically misguided.

This remains true despite intermittent Australian tendencies to placate Chinese strategic preferences in ways that generate confusion and tension in various great power capitals. Foreign Minister Alexander Downer's cavalier speculation about ANZUS possibly not applying to a future Taiwan crisis during his August 2004 visit to Beijing was illustrative: following his discussion of Sino-Australian strategic relations with Chinese Foreign Minister Li Zhaoxing, his Chinese counterpart, Downer announced that Li had 'given him the lead to say that Australia is now a "strategic partner"'. By itself, this terminology was not alarming (the Clinton administration had used the same descriptor following the Clinton–Jiang summits in 1998 and 1999). Coupled with Downer's speculation about possible Australian restraint in backing the United States against China on Taiwan, however, the Australian posture appeared distinctly unsupportive to Bush administration officials.

Rapid and pointed 'reminders' about ANZUS interpretations and responsibilities flowed from the US Embassy in Canberra and from the State Department, precipitating a 'clarification' from the Prime Minister's office and later from Downer himself.[33] Japan remained publicly silent over this episode, however, and has generally adopted a lower-key strategy on developing a maritime coalition in specific response to China's growing power as opposed to applying it to more 'comprehensive security'-oriented issues in the human security area and in region-wide diplomatic arenas.[34] Only when Sino-Japanese relations visibly deteriorated during 2005–6 did Japan begin to view trilateralism as a direct remedy for the 'China threat' problem, and even then with careful qualifications. Pointedly the Japanese press viewed the inaugural TSD Ministerial Meeting as an opportunity to rediscover alliance unity on the China question rather than to contain Chinese power directly:

> China is, and will continue to be, a focus of regional interest and concern ... Its military modernization program seems disproportionate to any regional threat ... the convocation of trilateral talks has inspired feverish speculation about a new alliance to contain China. That will not happen ... The governments in Tokyo, Washington and Canberra look to build constructive relations with Beijing and recognize that several issues have to be confronted before that is possible. Speaking with one voice about their concerns increases the chances that they will be heard and their warnings heeded.[35]

The geopolitical dimension of contingent trilateralism is the most ambiguous criterion of the three considered in this chapter. Two out of three of the maritime powers are hedging strategically against China while cultivating that country's vast markets. The third (Japan) still pursues substantial economic ties with Beijing even as its worsening politico-security relations with the Chinese have clearly become more central in shaping the overall context of Sino-Japanese ties. For geopolitics to drive future TSD agendas, China would need to move more rapidly and more efficiently to supplement its traditional land power with a truly formidable (blue water) maritime force, be even more effective in alleviating traditional threat perceptions concerning China among the key ASEAN peninsular states (Indonesia and Malaysia) and more effectively finesse its presently crude bilateral economic competition with Taiwan for influence in the South Pacific islands region. (A frustrated Australian Foreign Minister recently issued a warning to both China and Taiwan to stop interfering in the domestic affairs of the Solomon Islands and other vulnerable Pacific microstates as an offshoot of their own irredentist dispute.)[36] In the absence of a more concerted Chinese effort to project maritime power beyond its peripheries and a complete eradication of 'China threat' sentiment by its neighbours, this element of contingent trilateralism will remain the most elusive to track and to operationalize.

Can TSD allies 'balance' regional and global security?

Evaluating the Trilateral Strategic Dialogue's application to other forms of collective defence operating within and beyond the Asia-Pacific relates to the 'balancing' component of contingent trilateralism. It will also illuminate the overall relevance of the TSD initiative to contemporary regional and global security politics.

If the TSD is not an instrument of 'containment' directed against China, it remains for its architects to define and shape a compelling general purpose for its existence. If it is to be a mechanism for determining how US power will be applied to future Asia-Pacific contingencies, the extent to which Australian and Japanese interests help shape the American role will set it apart from the San Francisco System of US bilateral alliances where 'hub and spokes' hierarchy and alliance exclusivism have normally prevailed. A larger allied role in the TSD would be further evidence of Washington's growing propensity to accord its regional allies more serious weight in forging US regional security postures at a time when structural and normative factors underlying Asia-Pacific security politics are becoming increasingly fluid. One could envision, for example, the TSD adopting a specific agenda to support ASEAN's *Vision 2020* by working with that grouping to promote that document's human security stipulations.[37] Or it could also be employed to supplement the ASEAN Regional Forum's 'comprehensive security' agenda (identifying and implementing regional confidence-building and 'preventative diplomacy') in specific policy sectors such as regional arms control.

The problem of 'general purpose' in the TSD's case may well pervade additional levels of implementation to that covering only regional security issues. As noted previously, the US initiative to fuse Pacific democracies to NATO deliberations more systematically may have been premature. European resistance to this initiative could be attributed to a response against the Bush administration's campaign to impose its own ideological brand of geopolitics upon an Atlantic Alliance still recovering from alliance divisions precipitated by the Iraq War. Other, more delicately formulated and specifically 'extra-regional' initiatives, however, could engender greater appeal. Future NATO–Pacific coordination on counterterrorist and maritime security imperatives could fill an existing transregional security gap in European and Asian maritime crescent powers without unduly alienating Beijing in the process. NATO coordination with Japan and Australia on certain arms control issues may also be feasible, given that US missile defence has both a Europe-centric and an Asia-Pacific component. If broadened beyond its currently punitive rationales and missions, the Proliferation Security Initiative might also act as a catalyst for greater inter-regional coordination on WMD proliferation politics if embraced by a TSD that already has supplemented American and Japanese efforts to address the North Korean nuclear issue.

How does the balancing component of contingent trilateralism relate to the above scenarios? Despite intermittent gaffes experienced in its efforts to balance its relations between China and the United States, Australia is in the best position to lead any TSD balancing role within both regional and global security politics because it has achieved 'room to manoeuvre' between its separate bilateral ties with China and the United States in ways that Japan has not. It was invited to participate in the East Asia Summit (EAS), for example, as a regional partner rather than an American proxy. It did so without compromising its ANZUS credentials and emerged from what proved to be a largely inconsequential organizational meeting with its politico-security credentials intact and with the prospect of hosting a more meaningful Asia Pacific Economic Cooperation (APEC) summit in Sydney during 2007. This situation contrasts sharply with that of Japan, as Japanese diplomats reportedly engaged in vigorous infighting during the EAS conclave with their Chinese counterparts over the content of the summit's communiqué.[38] Australia has also become increasingly viewed in Beijing as a complementary resource provider for China's future energy needs rather than as a contentious, unpredictable and difficult, albeit highly interdependent economic partner, which is how Chinese leaders often see the United States.

Globally, Australia also enjoys more flexibility than does Japan for conceptualizing and promoting the TSD's identity and policy objectives. That Australian forces have protected Japanese Self-Defence Forces involved with reconstruction projects in southern Iraq speaks volumes about the two countries' relative strategic profile beyond Asia. Apart from the United Kingdom, Australia under John Howard has become regarded by Washington as the United States' closest ally, notwithstanding occasional American concerns about Australia's China posture. This highlights Australia's capacity to project its diplomatic and strategic objectives as an 'entrepreneurial middle power' in ways that Japan cannot, due to the latter country's historical legacy and ongoing problems in reconciling that image with its ambitions for raising Japan's international diplomatic profile (that is, permanent voting status in the UN Security Council).[39] Australia constitutes the most logical policy conduit between the processes of Asian community-building and American global alliance management where they may intersect over the remainder of this decade and beyond.

Conclusion

If such is the case, it was entirely appropriate for the inaugural Trilateral Strategic Dialogue to convene in Australia. It could not have met in Washington or Tokyo without having raised more suspicions in China and regionally about its ultimate purpose and it is reasonable to assume that Australian diplomats had much to do with softening the TSD communiqué by ensuring that it praised China's efforts in regional security. The question remains to what extent Australia can work with China to condition that country towards adopting more transparent explanations of its own regional security postures that will alleviate American and Japanese threat perceptions. An equally critical question is to what degree the United States and Japan can be induced by Australia within a TSD context to develop a long-term mutual security posture that ultimately appears less threatening to China than is currently the case. Urgent attention in this context needs to be directed towards defusing Taiwan as a regional flashpoint, identifying tangible initiatives for regional arms control and modifying growing Sino-Japanese tensions over questions of history and identity. A longer-term imperative is to better integrate various and (in some cases) contending regional economic and security architectures within a viable process of Asia-Pacific order-building.

This last imperative constitutes the most fundamental test of contingent trilateralism's value as an approach to regional and international security. All three of its components discussed above – facing Chinese power, shaping maritime alliance politics and orchestrating intra-alliance balancing – incorporate both highly promising and clearly dangerous elements of alliance management. Avoiding alliance policy miscalculations while fusing new approaches to alliance collaboration represents one of the key policy challenges now confronting Australian, American and Japanese decision-makers. How well they meet this test could well determine how stable and peaceful their region and the world will be for years to come.

Notes

All websites accessed 19 September 2006.

1 Robert Jervis and Jack Snyder (eds) (1991), *Dominoes and Bandwagons: Strategic Beliefs and Superpower Competition in the Asian Rimland*, New York: Columbia University Press, provides comprehensive theoretical perspectives on postwar bandwagoning motives and policies.
2 The two seminal articles on why no NATO equivalent was established in Asia during the Cold War are Christopher Hemmer and Peter J. Katzenstein (2002), 'Why is there no NATO in Asia? Collective identity, regionalism and the origins of multilateralism', *International Organization*, vol. 56, no. 3, pp. 575–607 and John Duffield (2001), 'Why is there no APTO? Why is there no OSCAP? Asia-Pacific security institutions in comparative perspective', *Contemporary Security Policy*, vol. 22, no. 2, pp. 69–95.
3 Alliance 'exclusivism' as a component of bilateral security politics is developed by William Tow (2003), 'US bilateral security alliances in the Asia-Pacific: moving beyond "hubs and spokes"', paper presented at the Australasian Political Studies Association Conference, Hobart, Australia, 29 September–1 October, available at: www.utas.edu. au/government/APSA/WTowfinal.pdf
4 See Richard H. Ullman (1976), 'Trilateralism: "partnership for what?"', *Foreign Affairs*, vol. 55, no. 1, pp. 1–19; and Hisashi Owada (1980/81), 'Trilateralism: a Japanese perspective', *International Security*, vol. 5, no. 3, pp. 14–24.
5 See an Australian Associated Press report reprinted by the International Institute for Strategic Studies on its website, 28 April 2006, available at: www.iiss.org/whats-new/ iiss-in-the-press/april-2006/nato-debates-australian-partnership
6 James L. Schoff (2005), *Tools for Trilateralism: Improving US–Japan–Korea Cooperation to Manage Complex Contingencies*, Medford, MA: Institute for Foreign Policy Analysis in Association with the Fletcher School, Tufts University. Historical background is provided by Victor Cha (1999), *Alignment Despite Antagonism: The US–Korea–Japan Security Triangle*, Stanford, CA: Stanford University Press, especially pp. 200–201. The classic work on the 'entrapment–abandonment' dilemma in alliance politics remains Glenn Snyder (1984), 'The security dilemma in alliance politics', *World Politics*, vol. 36, no. 4, pp. 461–96.
7 Schoff, *Tools for Trilateralism* (2005), p. viii.
8 Among the most cited are Lowell Dittmer (1981), 'The strategic triangle: an elementary game theoretical analysis', *World Politics*, vol. 33, no. 4, pp. 485–515; William E. Griffith (1973), *Peking, Moscow and Beyond: The Sino-Soviet American Triangle*, The Washington Papers no. 6, Washington, DC: Center for Strategic and International Studies, Georgetown University; Kenneth Lieberthal (1978), *Sino-Soviet Conflict in the 1970s: Its Evolution and Implications for the Strategic Triangle*, Santa Monica, CA: The RAND Corporation; Ilpyong Kim (ed.) (1987), *Strategic Triangle: China, the United States and the Soviet Union*, New York: Paragon House; Gerald Segal (ed.) (1982), *The China Factor: Peking and the Superpowers*, New York: Holmes & Meier; and Richard H. Solomon (ed.) (1981), *The China Factor: Sino-American Relations and the Global Scene*, New York: American Assembly and Council of Foreign Relations.

9 Michael Tatu (1970), *The Great Power Triangle: Washington, Moscow, Paris*, Paris: Atlantic Institute; David Kerr (2005), 'The Sino-Russian partnership and US policy toward North Korea: from hegemony to concert in Northeast Asia', *International Studies Quarterly*, vol. 49, no. 3, pp. 411–38; Dittmer (1981), 'The strategic triangle'; and Dittmer (2005), 'The Sino–Russian–Japanese triangle', *Journal of Chinese Political Science*, vol. 10, no. 1, pp. 1–21. The quote in the text is extracted from Dittmer (2005), 'The Sino–Russian–Japanese triangle', p. 1.

10 See, for example, the remarks of Alastair Buchan, Director of the Institute for Strategic Studies (later the IISS) in London, and of Paul Hasluck, the Australian Minister for External Affairs, as cited in J. D. B. Miller (ed.) (1968), *India, Japan, Australia: Partners in Asia?*, Canberra: Australian National University Press, pp. 195–96.

11 The best quantitative study using triangularity in this context is by Joshua Goldstein, John C. Pevehouse, Deborah J. Gerner and Shibley Telhami (2001), 'Reciprocity, triangularity and cooperation in the Middle East, 1979–97', *Journal of Conflict Resolution*, vol. 45, no. 5, pp. 594–620. This assessment concluded that triangular responses to US intervention were few but, when present, were also significant.

12 Kent E. Calder (2004), 'Securing security through prosperity: the San Francisco System in comparative perspective', *Pacific Review*, vol. 17, no. 1, pp. 135–57; and Michael Lankowski (2003), 'America's Asian alliances in a changing world', *Australian Journal of International Affairs*, vol. 57, no. 1, pp. 113–24.

13 Evan S. Medeiros (2005/2006), 'Strategic hedging and the future of Asia-Pacific stability', *Washington Quarterly*, vol. 29, no. 1, p. 145.

14 Background on the Trilateral Security Dialogue process is provided by the Research Institute for Peace and Security (Tokyo); Asia-Pacific Center for Security Studies (APCSS), Honolulu; and Griffith Asia Institute (GAI), Brisbane, Australia (July 2005), *Japan, US and Australia: In Search of a New Strategic Framework in the Post 9–11 Era*; and by Anna Searle and Ippei Kamae (2004), 'Anchoring trilateralism: can Australia–Japan–US security relations work?', *Australian Journal of International Affairs*, vol. 58, no. 4, pp. 464–78.

15 Steven R. Wiseman (2006), 'Rice seeks to balance China's power', and 'Australia, US, Japan praise China, seek to enhance Asian cooperation', *New York Times*, March 19.

16 The term 'responsible stakeholder' was used by US Deputy Secretary of State Robert Zoellick, 'Whither China: from membership to responsibility?', remarks to National Committee on US–China Relations, New York City, 21 September 2005, available at: www.ncuscr.org/articlesandspeeches/Zoellick.htm

17 US–China Economic and Security Review Commission, Annual Report 2005, available at: www.uscc.gov/annual_report/2005/annual_report_full_05.pdf

18 US Department of Defense, Office of the Secretary of Defense (2006), *Annual Report to Congress: Military Power of the People's Republic of China 2006*, Washington, DC: USGPO, available at: www.dod.mil/pubs/pdfs/China%20Report%202006.pdf

19 Ministry of Foreign Affairs, Japan (2005), 'Joint Statement: US–Japan Security Consultative Committee', Washington, DC, 19 February, available at: www.mofa.go.jp/region/n-america/us/security/scc/joint0502.html

20 See US Department of State, Office of the Spokesman, 'Media Note' (2006), 1 May, available at: www.globalsecurity.org/military/library/news/2006/05/d20060501realign-implement.pdf

21 Donna Miles (2006), 'US–Australia Agree to Increase Counterterrorism Cooperation', American Forces Information Service, 17 May, available at: www.defenselink.mil/news/May2006/20060517_5150.html; and US Department of State (2004), 'Text: US–Australia Joint Communiqué Outlines Areas of Cooperation', Washington File, EPF406 07/08/2004, available at: http://usembassy-australia.state.gov/hyper/2004/0708/epf406.htm

22 Cited in Norimitsu Onishi (2006), 'Race to lead Japan may turn on Asia ties', *New York Times*, 4 June.

23 Christopher R. Hill, Assistant Secretary for East Asian and Pacific Affairs (2005), 'US relations with Japan', remarks to the Senate Foreign Relations Committee, Washington, DC, 29 September, available at: www.state.gov/p/eap/rls/rm/2005/54110.htm

24 Lowy Institute for International Policy (2005), *Australians Speak 2005: Public Opinion and Foreign Policy*, March, available at: www.lowyinstitute.org/Publication.asp?pid=236; David Shambaugh (2005), 'Beijing charms its neighbors', *International Herald Tribune*, 14 May, available at: www.iht.com/articles/2005/05/13/opinion/edshambaugh.php; and Mohan Malik (2005), 'The China factor in US–Australia relations', *China Brief* (The Jamestown Foundation), vol. 5, no. 8, 12 April, available at: www.jamestown.org/publications_details.php?volume_id=408&issue_id=3298&article_id=2369588. On the Australia uranium sale to China see remarks by Henry Sokolski, executive director of the Nonproliferation Policy Education Center based in Washington, DC, on Worldpress.org, 26 April 2006, available at: www.worldpress.org/Asia/2327.cfm

25 The author is indebted to James Przystup for refining these observations in various discussions.

26 Saul B. Cohen (1973), *Geography and Politics in a World Divided*, 2nd edn, New York: Oxford University Press, p. 29.

27 Mackubin Thomas Owens (1999), 'In defense of classical geopolitics', *Naval War College Review*, vol. 52, no. 4, p. 62.

28 Ibid., p. 63.

29 For a comprehensive overview of the US containment strategy as shaped by Kennan and others at the time, see John Lewis Gaddis (1982), *Strategies of Containment: A Critical Appraisal of Postwar American National Security Policy*, New York: Oxford University Press, pp. 25–53. For a critical assessment of Kennan's geopolitical interpretation of China, see Bruce Cumings (1999), 'China through the looking glass', *Bulletin of the Atomic Scientists*, vol. 55, no. 5, pp. 30–37.

30 Harold C. Hutchison (2005), 'Japan's superpower potential', *Strategy Page*, 12 May, available at: www.strategypage.com/dls/articles/2005512213835.asp

31 Paul Dibb (2003), 'The arc of instability and the north of Australia: are they still relevant to Australia's new defence posture?', Strategic and Defence Studies Centre, The Australian National University, 1 October, available at: http://rspas.anu.edu.au/papers/sdsc/viewpoint/paper_031002.pdf

32 Australian Strategic Policy Institute (2004), *Power Shift: Challenges for Australia in Northeast Asia*, prepared by William Tow and Russell Trood with assistance from Brendan McRandle, Canberra: ASPI; and Robyn Lim (2003), *The Geopolitics of East Asia*, London: Routledge, p. 48.

33 Catherine Armitage (2004), 'Message in a muddle', *Weekend Australian*, 21–22 August.

34 For a Japanese perspective on this point, see Naoko Sajima (2006), 'Japanese security perceptions of Australia', in Bradley Williams and Andrew Newman (eds), *Japan, Australia and Asia-Pacific Security*, London: Routledge, pp. 47–69.

35 'Trilateral breakthrough down under' (Editorial), *Japan Times*, 23 March 2006, available at: http://search.japantimes.co.jp/cgi-bin/ed20060323a1.html

36 'Government warns China, Taiwan on Solomons', *Sydney Morning Herald*, 26 April 2006, available at: www.smh.com.au/news/NATIONAL/Govt-warns-China-Taiwan-on-Solomons/2006/04/26/1145861412201.html

37 The ASEAN Heads of Government summit adopted this agenda at their summit in Kuala Lumpur convened in December 1997. The document can be found at the ASEAN Secretariat's website at: www.aseansec.org/1814.htm

38 See an assessment by Mohan Malik (2006), 'The East Asia Summit', *Australian Journal of International Affairs*, vol. 60, no. 2, especially pp. 210–11.

39 For analysis on Australia's entrepreneurial diplomacy, see William T. Tow and Richard Gray (1995), 'Asian-Pacific security regimes: conditions and constraints', *Australian Journal of Political Science*, vol. 30, no. 3, pp. 436–51.

4 The Trilateral Strategic Dialogue's institutional politics

Michael Wesley

The Trilateral Strategic Dialogue (TSD) represents, at the institutional level, the most sustained attempt yet to operationalize the concept of 'expansive bilateralism', an idea with considerable intuitive appeal but which has largely remained in the realm of ideas until now.[1] That the TSD process came together in 2002, met regularly at the officials' level thereafter, and reached the ministerial level in 2006 is due to the remarkable confluence of events and interests at the international and institutional levels. More specifically, international events interacted with, and to some extent drove, the evolution of institutional structures and politics in the United States, Japan and Australia, resulting in a strong convergence of interests among the three countries to begin and sustain the TSD process. The argument in this chapter is that the momentum and direction of the TSD process has until now been, and will continue to be, driven primarily by confluences of international and institutional developments affecting its three participating countries. At the political–bureaucratic level, the evolution of the TSD process faces a combination of short-term limits and long-term drivers.

This chapter has three sections. The first examines the origins of the TSD at the institutional level. This is intended to set the scene for the second section, which explores in greater detail the ways in which international events coincided with, and partly shaped, alterations in institutional structures and outlooks in each of the three countries, to result in the confluence of interests that has driven the TSD. Examination of the institutional politics of each of the countries also examines how further developments at the institutional level in each of the countries create either positive or negative inertia towards the advancement of the process. The third section moves to a general examination of the dynamics of the TSD process: how it works, and the major considerations and interests at the level of institutional politics. The chapter concludes by revisiting the elements at the bureaucratic level that are likely to influence the evolution of the TSD process.

The TSD: institutional origins

The most important development within the political–institutional realm for the inauguration of the TSD occurred at the level of prime minister and president in each of the three countries. George W. Bush, Junichiro Koizumi and John Howard share very similar, conservative approaches to international relations, and close personal bonds have developed among the three leaders. The Howard government had identified Bush as a possible future president and begun building a relationship with him long before the 2000 presidential elections in the United States, and was delighted when Bush scraped home in that poll. Howard and Bush developed a close friendship, based on shared conservative values and a common contractualist, interest-based approach to international affairs.[2] Most crucial, however, was Australia's support for the United States after the 11 September 2001 attacks and during the war in Iraq. Canberra's solidarity in the face of opposition, especially as the enunciated pre-war case for invasion unravelled, was a gesture that resonated strongly in Washington. As Tom Schieffer, the American Ambassador to Australia, described it, 'You had a deepening of the relationship. Adversity creates a bond. And particularly with George Bush, he is a person who responds to people who are friends when it is harder to be a friend, because he knows there's more friendship there.'[3] Howard and Bush saw in the arrival of Koizumi another outsider, with an idiosyncratic approach to politics, to which he held strongly despite criticism, and finely honed political skills. Each of the three leaders has emphasized the importance of solidarity among democratic societies in the context of the post-September 11 world.

The Bush team that took office in early 2001 brought with it a strong, Republican-nationalist commitment to rebalance what it saw as its predecessor's preoccupation with Europe, with a new and mature devotion of greater resources to Asia and the Pacific. A key thread of Republican criticism of Clinton administration foreign policy was that, on the rare occasions that it did pay attention to Asia, it focused on China at the expense of the United States' long-standing, democratic allies such as Japan. A crucial member of the Bush team was Richard Armitage, who took the position of Deputy Secretary of State. Armitage was a strong believer in the importance of the Asia-Pacific to the United States, and in the importance of America's alliances in the region as the anchors of United States policy and influence there. He had made key statements on Washington's alliances with Japan and Australia just prior to taking office. Over the spring and summer of 2000, he co-chaired a group of policy professionals to discuss developing the United States–Japan alliance as part of a new, Asia-centric defence policy for the United States. The Nye–Armitage Report, published just weeks before the 2000 presidential elections, advocated a much more equal, balanced United States–Japan alliance, and strong support for the process of Japanese defence 'normalization'.[4] Through his regular participation in the Australian–American Leadership Dialogue, Armitage was aware of the growing preoccupation of Australians with the possible tensions between the Australia–United States alliance and Australia's growing commercial intimacy with China. In 1999, he made an uncompromising statement on the American view of the alliance to his Australian interlocutors: 'if Washington found itself in conflict with China over Taiwan it would expect Australia's support. If it didn't get that support, that would mean the end of the US–Australia alliance.'[5]

In the early months of his tenure as Deputy Secretary of State, Armitage found himself sitting opposite an old friend, the Japanese Deputy Minister of Foreign

Affairs, Ryozo Kato, at a regular United States–Japan officials meeting. Kato raised the concept of trilateral officials talks between the United States, Japan and Australia. Armitage had realized that there was no regular sub-Cabinet dialogue between the United States and Australia, similar to that between the United States and Japan, and had planned to rectify that. Kato's proposal struck him as an opportunity to do that, and at the same time bring greater coordination between two of the United States' key relationships in the Pacific. After talks between American, Japanese and Australian officials at the July 2001 ASEAN Regional Forum meeting in Hanoi, Armitage told reporters in August 2001:

> I've noted Australia has a very close – primarily political and economic – relationship with Japan. The United States has a very close economic and political, military and security relationship with Japan. It seems to me we are all liberal democracies, we're all concerned with the fate of Asia and it seems to me a perfectly reasonable proposition that we ought to get together and talk.[6]

The principal drivers of the early stages of the process were Armitage, Japanese Vice-Foreign Minister Yukio Takeuchi and the Secretary of Australia's Department of Foreign Affairs and Trade, Ashton Calvert. Once again, personal chemistry was crucial, as these three principals had known each other for a quarter of a century. Calvert, who had been Secretary since 1997, was imbued with the Howard government's emphasis on the American alliance, and had served as Ambassador to Japan. A process of consultations among the US State Department, the Japanese Foreign Ministry, and the Australian Department of Foreign Affairs and Trade, and involving the relevant embassies, was well under way by the time the US Secretary of State Colin Powell and Australian Foreign Minister Alexander Downer discussed the advantages of trilateral talks in response to a question at the press conference following the July 2001 AUSMIN meeting in Canberra. Reflecting their officials' discussions, Powell and Downer assured journalists that they were talking about a process that would be much less formalized than a trilateral alliance structure. The TSD, which by 2006 had gone through five Senior Officials' Meetings and one Ministerial Meeting, gained initial momentum from a confluence of interests and institutional alignments in each of the countries, but due to further institutional developments may struggle to consolidate these gains through a regular and increasingly meaningful dialogue process.

Institutional politics in the member-states

The United States

The two abiding preoccupations of US foreign policy during the first years of the twenty-first century, terrorism and the rise of China, contributed to interest alignments and institutional evolutions supportive of the TSD process. The 11 September attacks functioned as 'a purifier of alliances'[7] in the minds of the Bush administration, in which alliances were no longer seen as defensive assets to be maintained and deferred to, but as potentially perishable arrangements that needed to be justified according to their usefulness. Japan, within the limits of its pacifist constitution, and Australia, emerged in the post-September 11 period as staunch 'systemic supporters' of the United States – allies prepared to endorse and help defend the American vision for regional and global order.[8] Tokyo and Canberra subscribed to Washington's view that alliances were no longer to be narrowly defined and geographically prescribed; through their contributions to the conflict in Afghanistan, Iraq and the Proliferation Security Initiative, Japan and Australia endorsed Washington's vision of alliances as flexible arrangements with multiple objectives and a global remit. Over time, policy-makers in the United States have increasingly come to see the connections among America's alliances, and moves have been made to establish closer connections between NATO and the United States' Pacific alliances.[9] To American officials, alliance arrangements provide a toolbox of responses to security crises, necessitating much greater attention to inter-alliance understandings than were previously thought necessary. In a world of greater contention over American security interpretations and commitments, the value of regular security dialogues with and among Washington's closest allies was compelling.

The other preoccupation for Washington is the rise of China and its implications for America's regional position. The Bush administration came to power rejecting its predecessor's characterization of China as a 'strategic partner' in favour of the more uncompromising interpretation of China as a 'strategic competitor'. The 11 September attacks brought an alignment of Sino-American interests against sub-national groups, but this submerged, rather than dissipated, the structural competition that had developed between Washington and Beijing during the course of the 1990s. At the end of that decade, Beijing had changed foreign policy tack, embarking on a multilateralist charm offensive in Southeast Asia in a bid to assure regional countries that they had nothing to fear from the rise of China. Beijing advocates a 'new security concept', built around the principles of non-intrusive relations, building on common interests while shelving differences, and the 'democratization of international relations', in clear differentiation from American standards and demands associated with the war on terror. It is a formula that has made great diplomatic gains in Southeast Asia. A key plank in Beijing's strategy is to use the 'new security concept' in combination with the lure of its dynamic economic growth to attenuate the institutional anchors underpinning US dominance in the region.

It is against this background that the United States, and to some extent Japan, has watched the burgeoning Sino-Australian relationship with growing consternation. By 2005, China was Australia's second largest trading partner, overtaking the United States as its second largest merchandise export market, and Japan as its second largest source of merchandise imports. The tax cuts given to Australians in 2006 were made possible by the tax receipts from booming commodities exports to China. According to one observer, 'China is now as critical for Australia's economic security and prosperity as the US is in terms of Australia's military'.[10] In October 2003, the Howard government made much symbolic mileage from a coincidence in the visits of President Bush and Chinese President Hu Jintao, by inviting Hu to address a joint sitting of the Houses of Parliament the day after Bush had done so. Alexander Downer further cemented the message of China's importance to Australia when, on a visit to Beijing in August 2004, he announced that he and Chinese Premier Wen Jiabao had 'agreed that Australia and China would build up a bilateral strategic relationship, that we would strengthen our economic relationship and we would work together closely on Asia-Pacific issues, be they economic or security issues'.[11] On the same visit, when asked whether the ANZUS alliance would commit Australia to join the United States in supporting Taiwan in the event of an outbreak of Sino-Taiwanese hostilities, Downer replied:

> The ANZUS is invoked in the event of one of our two countries, Australia or the United States, being attacked. So some other military activity elsewhere in the world ... does not automatically invoke the ANZUS Treaty. It is important to remember that we only invoked the ANZUS Treaty once, that is after the events of 9/11, because there was an attack on the territory of the United States. It is very important to remember that in the context of question.[12]

Such statements have led to concern among officials in Washington that Australia has succumbed to 'China fever',[13] a susceptibility to China's particular form of soft power, which – sometimes explicitly but most times implicitly – makes current and future relations, including trading relations, dependent on Beijing's approval of a country's conduct towards China. For some American policy-makers, Australia's unwillingness to antagonize China has made it a 'bellweather' of how extensive a United States coalition in opposition to Chinese interests will be.[14] There was great concern in Washington over Downer's interpretation of ANZUS, which was believed to have only encouraged Beijing in its efforts to attenuate US alliances. Downer's statement was interpreted by American policy-makers to have sent a signal of 'anything goes' to Beijing in relation to US security partnerships in the Pacific.[15] For the Japanese, engaged in an intensifying game of competitive regionalism with China, there is a concern that Australia is following the pattern of countries with close, mutually beneficial ties to Tokyo that are increasingly succumbing to China's regional game. Furthermore, 'Japanese strategists fear a strong Beijing–Canberra link could hurt Japan in competition for commodity exports – even food, of which Australia is Japan's main foreign supplier'.[16] For the United States and Japan, which have seen their bilateral relationship drawn ever closer by increasingly convergent perceptions of China, a dialogue with Australia that offers them the opportunity to counteract Beijing's apparently inexorable gravitational pull on Canberra was and continues to be important.

These considerations, allied with Armitage's enthusiasm for the concept, drove US involvement in successive TSDs between 2002 and 2004. Armitage, Takeuchi and Calvert were the principals in the first Dialogues. But by 2004 and 2005, international events and institutional change within the US government had begun to distract Washington. The United States became increasingly preoccupied with events in the Middle East – in relation to Iraq, Iran and Israel – and the small amount of attention that could be spared for Asia and the Pacific was focused on the situation in North Korea. Even within a system as vast as the foreign policy–security bureaucracy of the United States, an information-authority 'funnel' operates, where on all issues of importance the United States has as few senior decision-makers as any other state – and the American ones are beset by a broader range of issues. As the first Bush administration came to a close, elements of the bureaucracy working on Asia and the Pacific were finding that both resources and the oxygen of relevance were flowing towards their counterparts working on the Middle East and North Korea.

Then in January 2005, Armitage and Powell left the Bush administration, to be replaced by Condoleezza Rice as Secretary of State and Robert Zoellick as Deputy Secretary of State. The role of senior policy-makers and their focus of expertise and enthusiasm is especially important in the Bush administration. Bush is the first President whose highest qualification is an MBA, and who came to office having run a large corporation. His presidential style is that of a CEO, and he relies on, among other things, the principle of single point accounting – that is, being able to look to one person with expertise and responsibility for each major set of issues. In such a system, if the Deputy Secretary of State is the Japan/Australia person, those relationships receive resources and attention. Armitage's replacement, Zoellick, became the China person, reflecting a long history of interest in and engagement with China, and to some extent the bruises of dealing with Japan and Australia as US Trade Representative in the 1990s. Responsibility for Japan and Australia devolved downwards onto Undersecretary of State for Political Affairs Nicholas Burns. From October 2005, at the official level, the TSD was downgraded from a 'D-level' (meaning Deputy Secretary level) to a 'P-level' (Undersecretary level) dialogue in the US system, even though Japan sent its Deputy Foreign Minister Suneo Nishida and Australia was represented by the Secretary of the Department of Foreign Affairs and Trade, Michael L'Estrange. Although the Department of Political Affairs is responsible for the geographic branches and drives policy in the US system, the moving of the carriage of the TSD process to the 'P-level' represents a significant loss of momentum on the American part. The departure of Zoellick in June 2006 illustrates another factor of negative bureaucratic inertia in the United States: that the Bush team is increasingly being seen as a 'lame duck' administration beset by the seemingly intractable problems in the Middle East/Persian Gulf and, more recently, in North Korea. On historical patterns, an administration tarred with this perception will continue to lose talented officials and will fail to attract replacements with the energy or authority to reanimate US policy in any particular area. So while there are glimmers of positive inertia – such as the appointments of Ryozo Kato, the originator of the Dialogue idea, as Japan's Ambassador to Washington, and of Tom Schieffer, Bush confidant and former Ambassador to Australia as Ambassador to Tokyo – most institutional developments within the US government indicate a slowing of bureaucratic momentum.

Japan

The 1990s saw the emergence of ominous developments in Japan's immediate security environment which led to important changes in its security outlook, its internal politics, and the balance of influence in its foreign policy bureaucracy. An increasingly antagonistic relationship developed between Japan and China, reflecting Japanese alarm at Beijing's belligerence over Taiwan, its nuclear weapons testing, clashes over territorial disputes and the airing of Chinese nationalist antipathies towards Japan. China's new regionalism also emerged as a diplomatic threat to Japan's regional influence. As a result, Japan has emerged as the only regional country other than Taiwan that is prepared to antagonize China in standing up for what it sees as its own interests: 'Japan is not about to accept subordinate status in a future Chinese-dominated hegemonic order in East Asia. It will resist Chinese attempts to weaken its influence as a substantial power in the region.'[17] Over the same period, North Korea had emerged as dangerous, unpredictable and seemingly unable to be socialized or restrained by diplomatic dialogue, agreements or institutions. A series of missile launches, maritime incursions and controversies over the kidnapping of Japanese citizens by North Korea indicated a particular malevolence directed towards Japan.[18] These developments produced a change in public attitudes towards foreign policy, inclining majority support for the 'normalization' of Japan's security posture within the framework of a closer alliance with the United States.

This evolution in attitudes has affected electoral politics in Japan. The end of the Cold War's influence on party politics and reforms to the electoral system have resulted in greater influence and authority for the Japanese Prime Minister, at the same time that public opinion has given influence to more nationalist, security-minded elements within the ruling Liberal Democratic Party.[19] These trends in the executive have flowed through to the bureaucracy. After the end of the Cold War a predominance of opinion within the Foreign Ministry believed that the US alliance system needed to be supplemented by conflict resolution and confidence-building institutions to bring comprehensive security to the region. In 1993, the Foreign Policy Bureau was created within the Foreign Ministry to drive Japan's institutional engagement in APEC and the nascent ASEAN Regional Forum. But over time, with the disappointing progress of the ASEAN Regional Forum and the increasingly antagonistic postures of China and North Korea, the multilateralist–internationalist position lost adherents. Within the Foreign Ministry the hawkish North American Affairs Bureau, which was devoted to the United States–Japan relationship, argued that investing in the stagnant ASEAN Regional Forum process was a waste of scarce bureaucratic resources.[20] The Foreign Ministry's shift from liberal internationalism to alliance bilateralism was also driven by the increasing assertiveness of the Liberal Democratic Party's hawkish Foreign Affairs Division, which over time forced the Foreign Ministry towards policies more in line with increasingly nationalist public opinion in order to protect its policy-making autonomy and bureaucratic interests.[21]

From the mid-1990s, Japan retreated into the US alliance as the most dependable foundation on which to deal with its security challenges. In this context trilateralism emerged as a promising diplomatic framework for Japan. It unsuccessfully proposed a TSD with the United States and China as a mechanism for dealing with Sino-Japanese tensions during Chinese Premier Li Peng's visit to Tokyo in October 1997.[22] It has also gravitated over time towards the position of a group of APEC states, including the United States, Australia, Canada and Singapore, that are impatient with that body's lowest-common-denominator, consensual approach to trade reform. Tokyo has recently proposed reforms to APEC that will boost its policy-making functions.[23] Japan's refocusing on the US alliance coincided with Australia's shift of attention in the same direction. Both were encouraged by the election of the Bush administration, with its avowed intention of devoting more resources to its Asia-Pacific alliances, concentrating on practical matters and giving less attention than its predecessor to normative issues in the region. As the United States has become more distracted by the Middle East/Persian Gulf, terrorism and nuclear proliferation, Tokyo and Canberra have found an increasingly convergent interest in trying to draw Washington's attention back to the Asia-Pacific. A strong symbol of American inattention was that in her first year as Secretary of State, Condoleezza Rice visited the Asia-Pacific once.[24] Japan's commitment to the TSD process has been driven by the perceived advantages of having Australia as an ally in trying to counteract Washington's Pacific attention deficit disorder. Early concerns in some parts of the Foreign Ministry that the TSD process would detract from the substance of Japan's bilateral relationship with the United States have been allayed, and there is strong institutional and political backing for the process in Tokyo.

However, as with the US system, the Japanese bureaucracy has its own aspects that may hold back progress in the TSD process from being as rapid as it might be. Carriage of the Dialogues rests with the geographic bureaux of the Foreign Ministry, primarily the Bureau of North American Affairs and the Bureau of Asian and Oceanic Affairs. A rigid principle of non-interference operates within the Foreign Ministry, which means that policy bureaux which may give the process a broader vision than the geographic bureaux' preoccupation with issues in the respective bilateral relationships are unable to influence the process. Some officials believe that greater momentum may be given to the TSD process if it were to be transferred to the Foreign Policy Bureau. However, in the near term there is little prospect of this, due to bureaucratic protocols and intense rivalry between the heads of the Foreign Policy Bureau and the North American Affairs Bureau.

Another source of negative momentum is the delicate politics of constitutional interpretation and reform in Japan. Article 9 of the Japanese Constitution has hitherto been interpreted narrowly as allowing Japan to provide for its own defence, but not to engage in any collective security or collective defence arrangements. The alliance with the United States and joint United States–Japan defence exercises are permitted under the justification that they relate to Japan's self-defence. Japanese Self-Defence Force participation in RIMPAC (Rim of the Pacific) exercises (major multinational naval exercises involving US allies and friends held every two years) is justified as being bilateral United States–Japan manoeuvres within the broader exercise. This places real limits on the extent and nature of

Japanese participation in the operational aspects of the TSD, which are discussed below. Despite both major parties in Japan supporting the process of constitutional revision, the bureaucracy is under clear instructions not to push the bounds of what the Constitution will permit. If the current constitutional arrangements appear flexible enough to allow Japan to participate with ease in an expanding range of defence cooperation, it will provide the opponents of constitutional change with a powerful argument in favour of constitutional inertia. So major advances in Japan's ability to play a greater operational role will need to await its political process of constitutional change.

Australia

In Australia, the election of the Howard government in March 1996 brought to power a government committed to bilateralism and strong investment in the US alliance, in contrast to its predecessor's commitment to multilateralism and regionalism. Foreign affairs is, in Howard's words, too 'messy and uncertain',[25] and the Asian region too diverse, to be pushed or cajoled into grand multilateral constructs. From its 1996 pre-election foreign policy statement, *A Confident Australia*, through both of its foreign and trade policy White Papers, the Coalition has insisted that its foreign policy approach to the Asian region will be primarily bilateral, with concern for regional and global institutional structures coming a distant second and third. It has established bilateral political–military talks with most regional states and embarked on a sustained programme of negotiating bilateral free trade agreements. Howard also signalled that on coming to office his government would 'reinvigorate' the alliance with the United States. In 1996, the US economy was in the midst of an information technology driven growth spurt, its military prowess and confidence were resurgent and diplomatically it had become, in the words of its then Secretary of State, 'the indispensable nation'. Furthermore, the tie with the United States was one of the few of Australia's external relationships that yielded tangible benefits: military equipment and technology, access to a global intelligence gathering network, and shelter under the American nuclear umbrella. These appealed intuitively to John Howard's preference for tangible returns and practical benefits.

The Howard government's approach to regional diplomacy relies heavily on convergences of interests rather than 'emotional' or normative ties.[26] Over its decade in office, it has found at times to its discomfort that different convergences of interest can imply some difficult choices. Australia's increasingly interdependent relationship with China potentially places it in a difficult position in the event of serious tensions between China and Australia's other two key Pacific partnerships, the United States and Japan. And as Australia's economic relationship with India grows, and Indo-American strategic cooperation intensifies, this potentially adds further complication to the Sino-Australian relationship.[27] Canberra has come to realize that Beijing's strategy involves attenuating US alliances in the Pacific. China has been delighted to encourage Australia to think of their bilateral relationship in 'strategic' terms. After Downer's temporizing statement on whether ANZUS would apply in the event of a Sino-American conflict over Taiwan (see above), the Director-General of the North American and Oceanic Affairs Bureau in China's Foreign Ministry told Australian reporters:

> We all know Taiwan is part of China, and we do not want to see in any way the Taiwan issue become one of the elements that will be taken up by bilateral military alliances, be it Australia–US or Japan–US. If there were any move by Australia and the US in terms of that alliance [ANZUS] that is detrimental to peace and stability in Asia then [Australia] has to be very careful.[28]

Australia has developed two basic strategies for managing these tensions. The first is to try to remove the roots of Sino-American and Sino-Japanese tensions by attempting to 'socialize' China to current regional norms. According to Alexander Downer: 'We … believe that China has to understand that as it grows more powerful and more influential in the region that can arouse sensitivities and so it itself has to make a very constructive contribution to the affairs of the region.'[29] But the evidence is still ambiguous about how successful this strategy has been. China has become an enthusiastic multilateralist, but it is not at all clear that this entails it subscribing to current regional norms, or whether China's multilateralism is a mechanism for challenging those regional norms.

The second strategy is to attempt to decouple the Sino-Australian from the Sino-American relationship. By simultaneously strengthening its relationships with Beijing and Washington, the Howard government has sent signals to both that it expects each to respect Australia's right to deal with the other on its own terms. For Canberra, the TSD represents a chance to send a message to Beijing that Australia's relationships with the United States and Japan are non-negotiable. In a major foreign policy speech in March 2005, Howard called Australia, Japan and the United States the 'three great Asia Pacific democracies' with a unique role to play in upholding regional stability.[30] When Koizumi telephoned Howard in February 2005 to request that Australian troops guard engineers from Japan's Self-Defence Forces repairing infrastructure in southern Iraq, it was crucial in resolving the issue of whether Australia would recommit troops to Iraq.[31] For the Australian government, the Iraq deployment became a symbol of the growing intimacy of the Australia–Japan security relationship and of the new global scope of that partnership.

Within the Australian bureaucracy, the TSD is run out of the International Security Division of the Department of Foreign Affairs and Trade. The International Security Division lost personnel and prestige in the early post-Cold War years as Australia's foreign policy focus shifted from geopolitics to geoeconomics and multilateralism. With Gareth Evans as Foreign Minister, resources, prestige and the most ambitious staff flowed towards the Trade Development Division, International Organisations and Legal Division, and especially the Trade Negotiation Division (now Office of Trade Negotiation). The events of 11 September 2001 brought security roaring back to prominence. The Howard government realized quickly that the terrorist attacks, along with the issue of asylum seekers, would promote the stewardship of national security to the topmost rung, alongside management of the national economy, as the key measure of a party's governing credentials in the mind of the electorate. The International Security Division saw its branches managing terrorism, people smuggling, intelligence policy and proliferation gain resources, prestige and personnel. In parallel, a new National Security Division was created alongside a better resourced International Policy Division within the powerful Department of Prime Minister and Cabinet.

The Australian foreign policy bureaucracy is in general smaller, more collegial and more nimble than its American and Japanese counterparts.[32] The geographic divisions – the Americas and Europe Division and North Asia Division – interact naturally with International Security Division on the TSD process. Australian officials worry more about maintaining the Dialogues' traction within their counterpart bureaucracies than any internal rivalries or blockages in their own. Despite the departure of Ashton Calvert as Secretary in 2005, the TSDs still have considerable positive inertia within Australian institutions of government.

Conclusion: the dynamics of the Dialogues

A key determinant of the ongoing viability of the TSDs is whether each of the participating countries believes that they deliver outcomes and opportunities not available in other formats. Observers of the Dialogues to date have suggested that the trilateral format of talks differs significantly from bilateral meetings. On the one hand, the trilateral setting is more formal and 'multilateral' than the freer discussions possible within bilateral settings. Agreements and disagreements have a third party 'audience' in the trilateral setting, making national positions on issues much more thought-out and choreographed. On the other hand, the TSDs are freed from the formal alliance management business that dominates the United States–Japan Two-Plus-Two meetings and the United States–Australia AUSMIN meetings. This allows more conceptual discussions about aspects of the global and regional security environments, and greater attention to be paid to the coordination of diplomacy and policy around key issues. The TSDs provide the possibility to use 'minilateralism' to build support for specific policies in broader settings by first coordinating the positions of the United States, Japan and Australia.[33] Within the TSDs, the format allows for issue-based alignments, where any two of the participants can work collectively on the third to bring it around to their preferred position.

The inauguration of ministerial-level meetings to complement officials' meetings represents a major step forward. But it also intensifies an element of negative inertia in the process. Officials report that some of the most intensive and demanding parts of the Dialogues involve finding dates on which the principals are free to hold meetings. Amidst a crowded agenda of global and regional meetings, this is a challenge for senior officials; for ministers, the challenge is multiplied.

The main challenge for the TSDs lies, on the one hand, in demonstrating to its participants that it is more than the sterile 'talk shop' in the way that each country views the ASEAN Regional Forum; while on the other hand not making it so active as to trigger China's containment paranoia. In its initial phases, officials have focused on building in 'deliverables', results that satisfy the sceptical that this is a process with substance. Beyond 'sharing strategic assessments',[34] something the three countries do extensively anyway, the Dialogues have promoted practical, operational cooperation on counterterrorism, energy security, and trilateral interoperability on transnational threats. Such transnational security issues have the virtue of being front-of-mind issues and less antagonizing to China. The Dialogues also discuss specific challenges, from Burma and North Korea to Iraq and Iran, and how to reinvigorate the ASEAN Regional Forum.

The key litmus test for the TSDs will be the issue of China. On this issue, Australia is isolated from an increasingly aligned American–Japanese view. Before the March 2006 Ministerial Meeting, Rice made hawkish statements on China's military spending, and Aso caused controversy by calling Taiwan a 'country', whereas Downer was much more conciliatory.[35] The blandness of the communiqué on China – 'We welcomed China's constructive engagement in the region' – represents a compromise between Australia's insistence on not allowing a hawkish statement on China and the United States' success in popularizing Zoellick's 'responsible stakeholder' framework for engaging China.[36] Where the Dialogue has failed was in early 2005, when the United States and Japan attempted to convince Australia to sign on to their joint position lobbying the European Union not to end its arms embargo on China. American officials 'had hoped they would do this lobbying in the company of both Japan and Australia, the three Pacific democracies together lobbying heavily against lifting the embargo'.[37] Faced with a flat Australian refusal, US and Japanese officials lobbied European capitals in a double act. It was, according to one observer, a humiliating defeat for the United States: 'You can see how it looks to the Europeans. They are inclined now to say to the Americans: even your closest and most conservative ally in the Pacific, Australia, is relaxed about us ending the embargo; you Americans are just paranoid.'[38]

Thus far, the reaction of Beijing to the TSD has been muted – 'We hope that the countries in the Asia Pacific region will increase mutual trust, co-operation and consultation to jointly maintain regional security and stability'[39] – and particularly so in comparison with a now nuclear North Korea's response to this initiative.[40] But whether the Dialogue can weather a serious bout of Sino-American confrontation or Sino-Japanese confrontation, remains to be seen. Canberra may find that the TSD process, which once served as a mechanism for decoupling the Sino-Australian from the Sino-American relationship, turns rapidly into a context within which both Beijing and Washington can test Canberra's loyalty between its two 'strategic' relationships.

Notes

1 Over time, there have been numerous proposals to connect the United States' San Francisco System of bilateral alliances in the Asia-Pacific but until recently, these have remained in the realm of proposals.

  The term 'expansive bilateralism' is developed by Brian L. Job (1997), 'Multilateralism in the Asia Pacific region', in William Tow, Russell Trood and Toshiyta Hoshino (eds),

Bilateralism in a Multilateral Era: The Future of the San Francisco Alliance System in the Asia-Pacific, Tokyo and Nathan, QLD: The Japan Institute of International Affairs and the Centre for the Study of Australia–Asia Relations, p. 162.

2 Michael Wesley (2002), 'Perspective on Australian foreign policy, 2001', *Australian Journal of International Affairs*, vol. 56, no. 1, pp. 47–63.

3 Quoted in Robert Garran (2004), *True Believer: John Howard, George Bush and the American Alliance*, Sydney: Allen & Unwin, p. 138.

4 Institute for National Strategic Studies (2000), *The United States and Japan: Toward a Mature Partnership*, Washington, DC: National Defense University, October, available at: www.ndu.edu/inss/strforum/SR_01/SR_Japan.htm (accessed 28 September 2006).

5 Quoted in Peter Edwards (2005), *Permanent Friends? Historical Reflections on the Australian–American Alliance*, Lowy Institute Paper 08, Sydney: Lowy Institute for International Policy, p. 45.

6 'Armitage backs US–Australia–Japan security talks', *Kyodo News*, 17 August 2001.

7 Jacques Almaric (2001), 'Purifier les alliances', *Liberation*, 17 September, p. 4, quoted in Bruno Tertrais (2004), 'The changing nature of military alliances', *Washington Quarterly*, vol. 27, no. 2, pp. 135–47.

8 Takashi Inoguchi and Paul Bacon (2006), 'Japan's emerging role as a "global ordinary power"', *International Relations of the Asia Pacific*, vol. 6, no. 1, p. 3.

9 'NATO to expand cooperation with Asian nations: US official', *Jiji Press English News Service*, 25 April 2006.

10 Mohan Malik (2005), 'Australia and the United States 2004–5: all the way with the USA?', *Special Assessment Series*, Hawaii: Asia-Pacific Center for Security Studies, February, p. 7.

11 Alexander Downer, Media Conference Transcript, Beijing, 17 August 2004.

12 Ibid.

13 Sue Pleming (2006), 'Rice to discuss China, Iraq in Australia', *Reuters News*, 15 March.

14 Greg Sheridan (2005), 'PM defies Bush over China arms', *Australian*, 12 February.

15 Ibid.

16 Peter Alford (2006), 'Australia enters jealous threesome', *Australian*, 26 June.

17 Aurelia George Mulgan (2005), 'Why Japan still matters', *Asia Pacific Review*, vol. 12, no. 2, p. 111.

18 Tomohiko Taniguchi (2005), 'A cold peace: the changing security equation in Northeast Asia', *Orbis*, vol. 49, no. 3, pp. 445–57.

19 Robert Pekkanen and Ellis S. Krauss (2005), 'Japan's "coalition of the willing" on security policies', *Orbis*, vol. 49, no. 3, pp. 429–44.

20 Takeshi Yuzawa (2005), 'Japan's changing conception of the ASEAN Regional Forum: from an optimistic liberal to a pessimistic realist perspective', *Pacific Review*, vol. 18, no. 4, p. 483.

21 Tsukasa Takamine (2005), 'A new dynamism in Sino-Japanese security relations: Japan's strategic use of foreign aid', *Pacific Review*, vol. 18, no. 4, p. 456.

22 'Japan wants security dialogue accord with China', *Japan Economic Newswire*, 5 October 1997.

23 'Japan, US, Australia, Singapore to aim for APEC reform', *Kyodo News*, 2 June 2006.

24 'Keeping China onside', *Australian*, 13 March 2006.

25 John Howard (2004), address to the Australian Strategic Policy Institute, Sydney, 18 June.

26 Michael Wesley (2007), *The Howard Paradox: Australian Diplomacy in Asia, 1996–2007*, Sydney: ABC Books.

27 Philip Bowring (2006), 'Australia's delicate dance on the global stage', *International Herald Tribune*, 3 April.

28 Quoted in John Kerin (2005), 'Beijing's ANZUS warning', *Australian*, 8 March.

29 Quoted in 'Call for China to play constructive role in Asia Pacific region', *Asia Pulse*, 30 March 2006.

30 John Howard (2005), 'Australia and the World', speech to the Lowy Institute for International Policy, Sydney, 31 March.
31 Patrick Walters (2005), 'A bigger target', *Australian*, 26 February.
32 Allan Gyngell and Michael Wesley (2003), *Making Australian Foreign Policy*, Melbourne: Cambridge University Press.
33 Miles Kahler (1992), 'Multilateralism with small and large numbers', *International Organization*, vol. 46, no. 3, pp. 681–708.
34 *Joint Statement Australia–Japan–United States, Trilateral Strategic Dialogue*, Sydney, 18 March 2006, available at: www.foreignminister.gov.au/releases/2006/joint_statement-aus-japan_usa_180306.html (accessed 19 October 2006).
35 'US, Japan, Australia diplomats to meet for security talks', *Dow Jones International News*, 15 March 2006.
36 *Joint Statement Australia–Japan–United States, Trilateral Strategic Dialogue*.
37 Greg Sheridan (2005), 'Howard steers between giants', *Australian*, 12 February.
38 Ibid.
39 'China hopes US, Japan, Australia promote stability in Asia Pacific', BBC, 17 March 2006.
40 'North Korea News Agency blasts US–Japan–Australia security dialogue', BBC, 27 March 2006.

5   The power of three

Mark J. Thomson

Introduction

What do Australia, Japan and the United States hope to achieve through their emerging Trilateral Strategic Dialogue (TSD)? Ultimately, the goal must be to achieve a meaningful level of security policy coordination among the three parties. But what is it that the three countries judge they cannot achieve through either bilateral or broader multilateral means? For the moment, it is hard to say. The inaugural ministerial-level dialogue in March 2006 resulted in a joint communiqué that did little more than check off a predictable list of generic topics without proposing specific policy action on how to approach or pursue them.[1]

Clearly it is early days yet, and it would be wrong to suggest that the 2006 ministerial dialogue heralded the start of a substantive three-way strategic relationship between the three countries. Indeed, the existing system of US bilateral alliances in the Asia-Pacific is likely to remain the dominant regional security framework for some time. Nonetheless, the mere convening of the dialogue showed that the three parties have overlapping strategic agendas they wish to pursue through employing a more coordinated approach. This may include forging a common stance relative to a rising China, bolstering maritime security in the region and confronting international terrorism through a more 'globalized' Western alliance system.

Still, any trilateral strategic relationship between Australia, Japan and the United States remains nascent and this should not be a surprise. There is a manifest asymmetry between the three bilateral sides of the triangle. While the United States has strong military alliances with both Australia and Japan, the Australia–Japan post-World War II relationship is almost entirely economic with only a very recent history of military cooperation. Arguably, it has been the absence of common ground on security issues between Australia and Japan that has prevented the emergence of a strategic trilateral relationship in the past. What then would motivate either nation to involve itself more closely in each other's strategic affairs beyond that mediated through their respective US alliances? Moreover, what is it that would encourage the United States to complicate a pair of bilateral strategic alliances that has served it well for over fifty years?

The purpose of this chapter is to try and answer these questions. To do so, the chapter surveys – in deliberately quantitative terms – the three countries' key attributes in terms of geography, population, economics, trade, energy, development assistance, security policy and military capability. In each case, the aim is to understand what the three nations can offer each other strategically and what they might be able to achieve collectively. This entails looking for shared and divergent interests while examining the individual and collective strategic weight that the three countries can muster.

In a number of areas, this chapter surveys issues that are explored in more depth elsewhere in this volume. Accordingly, the emphasis here is on presenting facts and identifying overarching issues. The chapter concludes with a preliminary assessment of the prospects for a deepening trilateral relationship between Australia, Japan and the United States.

Geography

Australia, Japan and the mainland United States sit on the rim of the Pacific Ocean. They are anything but proximate. The city of San Francisco on the US west coast is almost 8,300 km from Tokyo and more than 12,200 km from Australia's capital, Canberra. Tokyo and Canberra are themselves separated by just under 9,000 km.

Australia is an island continent of 7.6 million square kilometres on the southern periphery of Asia. To its northeast are arrayed a string of small Western Pacific island states, the largest being Papua New Guinea which was a UN protectorate under Australian control until 1975. To Australia's northwest is Southeast Asia. Aside from the problematic and tiny East Timor, Australia's closest Asian neighbour is

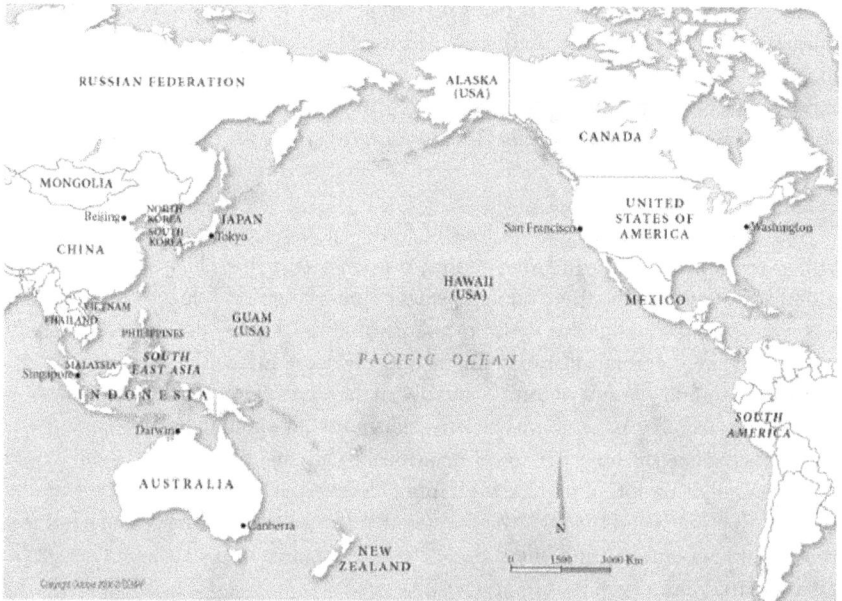

Figure 5.1 The Asia-Pacific.

Indonesia with a population of more than 220 million spread across 6,000 inhabited islands. Australia–Indonesia relations are usually constructive but rarely warm. To the southeast lies Australia's historical friend and ally New Zealand.

Japan is a string of four main islands occupying 377 thousand square kilometres in the heart of North Asia. To Japan's direct west are the two Koreas. At the point of closest approach, there is less than 200 km between the Korean peninsula and Japan. To the north lie the eastern-most territories of the Russian Federation. To the west and southwest lies the People's Republic of China. Some distance to the southwest is Taiwan. Despite strong and growing economic interdependence with its immediate neighbours, Japan's relationships are complicated by historical tensions dating back to World War II and a series of unresolved territorial disputes in valuable fishing and prospective energy fields.

With an area of 9.6 million square kilometres, the United States is the largest of the three countries. Located due east of Japan across the expanse of the Pacific, the mainland of the United States sits astride the western hemisphere. Nestled between Canada in the north and Mexico in the south, the United States occupies the majority of profitably arable land in North America. Closer to both Australia and Japan is the mid-Pacific US state of Hawaii, home to the Pearl Harbor naval base. Closer still is the US territory (and military base) of Guam only 2,500 km south of Tokyo and 3,200 km north of Australia's northern-most city, Darwin. The United States maintains sizable military forces in both Japan and South Korea, and small but strategically important joint facilities in Australia.

The key dimension to 'TSD geography' is that Australia, Japan and the United States are three interlocking maritime powers. And although they are distant from each other, they have a common interest in maintaining freedom of action across the maritime Asia-Pacific. Only by doing so can they guarantee the flow of trade that underscores their prosperity and, where necessary, the projection of power to safeguard their approaches and protect their security interests further afield.

Population

The size and composition of a country's population constrains its economic weight, and in extremis, its direct capacity to mobilize armed force. Currently, the United States and Japan rank first and second by size of population within the OECD and Australia ranks thirteenth.[2] A different picture emerges, however, in comparison with key Asian countries. As Table 5.1 shows, even the almost 300 million-strong US population pales in comparison with the billion-plus people in China and India, and both the Russian Federation and Indonesia are more populous than Japan. As for Australia, it has one of the smallest populations in the region and ranks fifty-second globally.[3]

Like most other industrialized countries, Australia, Japan and the United States have relatively older populations than developing countries. This is clear from the aged dependency ratio (the ratio of the population aged 65 years or over, to the population aged 15 to 64 years) listed in Table 5.1 for the three countries and other Asian states.

Table 5.1 Projected population growth and aging

	Population (millions)		Aged dependency (%)	
	2005	*2050*	*2005*	*2050*
Australia	20.2	27.9	19	40
Japan	128.1	112.2	30	71
United States	298.2	395.0	18	33
China	1,315.8	1,392.3	11	39
India	1,103.4	1,592.7	8	22
Indonesia	222.8	284.6	8	27
Malaysia	25.3	38.9	7	21
Philippines	83.1	127.1	12	56
South Korea	47.8	44.6	13	65
Russia	143.2	111.8	22	27
Singapore	4.3	5.2	10	35
Thailand	64.2	74.6	10	35
Vietnam	84.2	116.7	8	29

Source: United Nations Department of Economic and Social Affairs, UN World Population Prospects, Population Database, 2004 Revision. Available at: www.esa.un.org/unpp (accessed 15 September 2006).

Interestingly, while the United States and Australia have an aged dependency ratio of around 18 to 19 per cent, Japan's sits at 30 per cent. This reflects Japan's relatively low fertility rate of 1.38 children per woman which is substantially below Australia's 1.76 and the US figure of 2.04. Compounding this disparity are the rates of net migration to the three countries. Between 1980 and 2000, Australia averaged 5.7 net migrants per thousand residents each year, while the United States achieved 3.6. The corresponding average figure for Japan over the same period was 0.[4]

On current trends, these differential rates of fertility and migration will see the population of Japan evolve quite differently to that of Australia, the United States and many of the other countries in the region. While the populations of Australia and the United States will grow by more than 30 per cent between now and mid-century – thereby more-or-less keeping up in proportional terms with other regional states – Japan's population will decline by around 12 per cent. At the same time, the proportion of elderly people in all three countries will grow, especially in the case of Japan which is projected to have an aged dependency ratio of 71 per cent by mid-century.

In the three countries, aging populations will constrain economic growth (through falling workforce participation rates) and add steadily to the fiscal burden of health and aged care. From a purely military perspective, changing demographics will have little or no impact on the availability of individuals for military service. The armed forces of Australia, Japan and the United States only account for a tiny proportion of their populations, all three having long ago moved from a strategy of massed personnel to reliance on high-tech equipment.

Economics

In gross structural terms, the Australian, Japanese and the US economies are similar (see Table 5.2). The notable exception is that Australia's agriculture sector occupies a two to three times larger slice of its economy than that of Japan or the United States – albeit still a small proportion of the whole. (This does not stop the agriculture lobbies in both Japan and the United States from exerting significant influence on trade policy.)

The Australian economy also differs from that of Japan and the United States when it comes to innovation. As a percentage of Gross Domestic Product (GDP), the United States and Japan spend 63 per cent and 85 per cent more respectively on R&D than Australia.[5] This translates into significantly fewer international patents per head of population; less than one-fifth as many as Japan and less than one-third as many as the United States.[6] In the long term, this may hinder Australia's ability to find niches of comparative advantage as traditional manufacturing shifts to developing economies like China.

Over the twenty-year period from 1985 to 2004, annual economic growth[7] in Australia and the United States averaged 3.3 per cent and 3.0 per cent respectively. Although recent growth has been stronger, the corresponding figure for Japan is only 2.5 per cent due to slow growth through much of the 1990s. In the recent past, all three countries have managed to keep unemployment at around a healthy 5 per cent while containing inflation to manageable levels. Over the past twenty years, multi-factor productivity growth in all three countries has outstripped the OECD average.[8]

At present, the United States and Japan are the two largest economies on earth and, as Table 5.3 shows, Australia is a significant second-tier economy in the region. However, over the next several decades, the economic ranking of regional countries will change as demographics and economic development take effect. Indicative projections appear in Table 5.3.

Three trends are apparent from the data in this table. First, the decline and aging of Japan's population will see its economy grow much more slowly than the economies of Australia and the United States. Second, developing countries will grow relatively more quickly than developed nations including Australia and the United States. This will likely see China overtake Japan as the world's second largest economy around 2025 and India become an increasingly important economic power. At the same time, the economic gap between Australia and its Southeast Asian neighbours will close significantly. Third, the United States will

Table 5.2 Economic value-add by activity 2003

	Agriculture (%)	Industry (%)	Services (%)
Australia	3.4	25.7	70.9
Japan	1.3	30.5	68.2
United States	1.2	22.3	75.5

Source: World Bank Country Profiles. Available at: www.worldbank.org (accessed 7 September 2006).

Table 5.3 Projected gross domestic product

	GDP ($US billion)		
	2005	*2015*	*2030*
Australia	652	826	1,180
Japan	4,734	5,603	6,505
United States	12,134	16,465	25,282
China	2,109	3,997	8,550
India	738	1,261	2,659
Indonesia	272	438	824
Malaysia	125	201	378
Philippines	89	144	271
Singapore	113	182	342
South Korea	707	1,119	1,693
Russia	617	931	1,515
Thailand	172	278	523
Vietnam	48	77	145

Sources: Baseline figures taken from World Bank Country Profiles. Available at: www.worldbank.org (accessed 7 September 2006). Projected figures calculated using estimated future growth rates contained in the US Energy Information Administration, International Energy Outlook 2006. Available at: www.eia.doe.gov (accessed 7 September 2006).

Note
All figures calculated at market exchange rates.

remain the pre-eminent global economic power – and if it chooses, military power – for at least the next twenty or thirty years.

Because a country's strategic weight is ultimately proportional to its economic weight, these changing economic rankings will have important implications. For Australia and Japan, whose relative economic standing in the region will erode in the coming years, the value of maintaining an alliance with the United States will grow. Conversely, as the economic weight of other major powers approaches that of the United States, the value of alliances with Japan and Australia increases to the United States.

Trade

According to data collected by the World Trade Organization between 1985 and 2005, the value of global trade in merchandise increased five-fold, and trade in services six-fold.[9] Australia, Japan and the United States have all benefited from these increases. Nonetheless, by international standards, trade represents a comparatively small proportion of the economic activity of the three countries (Table 5.4).

The pattern of trade for Australia, Japan and the United States is set out in Table 5.5, along with that for China which has been included because of its strong trade linkages with the other three. Not surprisingly, Australia accounts for only a very small proportion of trade as measured by the larger countries. In contrast,

Table 5.4 Exports and imports 2003

	Exports (% GDP)	Imports (% GDP)
Australia	17.6	20.6
Japan	11.8	10.2
United States	9.6	14.1
China	29.6	27.4
European Union	35.2	33.1
India	14.9	16.4
South Korea	37.9	35.6
Russia	35.2	23.8

Source: World Bank Country Profiles. Available at: www.worldbank.org (accessed 7 September 2006).

Japan, China and the United States all figure amongst each other's top-five export/import partners. In the future, the importance of China as a trading partner is likely to grow as its economic growth outpaces that of other nations.

It is important to note that for Australia, Japan and the United States, bilateral trade with China is commensurate in scale with imports and exports amongst themselves. The overall diversity of trade is similarly noteworthy; there are very few instances of trade with a single country exceeding 20 per cent of another's total. On recent experience, these characteristics are unlikely to change even if further bilateral free trade agreements are reached between the countries. Not that any such agreements are likely; although all three countries profess a commitment to free trade, they have failed to negotiate truly comprehensive bilateral free trade agreements between themselves despite appearances to the contrary.

Combining the data in Tables 5.4 and 5.5 leads to an important conclusion. While trade between Australia, Japan and the United States is important, it ultimately represents a small fraction of each country's economic activity, which, moreover, is similar to that due to trade with China. As intimated above, trade appears to be neither valuable enough, nor unique enough, to form a basis for a three-way strategic partnership. Nor, it must be said, is the value of trade with China large enough, or asymmetric enough, to constitute a potential wedge between the region's three traditional maritime allies as is sometimes implied. In particular, the proposition that Australia's trade links with China are so large as to imperil its strategic relations with the United States[10] (or even Japan) is not supported by the data. It is difficult to see how this would change even given the projected rise in China's economy.

An important consequence of the current pattern of trade is the long-term development of financial interdependence due to trade imbalances. According to the OECD, in 2004 Australia and the United States ran current account deficits of 6.2 per cent and 5.7 per cent of GDP respectively.[11] This adds to the mounting private debt in both countries and in the case of the United States to its 64 per cent of GDP government debt (of which China holds more than a trillion dollars of credit). How these imbalances will be resolved is unclear, although the potential for friction between the United States and China is already apparent. Certainly there

Table 5.5 Merchandise trade 2005

	Exports			Imports		
	Rank		*%*	*Rank*		*%*
Australia						
	1	Japan	20.4	1	China	14.6
	2	China	13.5	2	United States	13.7
	3	South Korea	7.9	3	Japan	11.0
	4	United States	6.7	4	Germany	5.6
	5	New Zealand	6.5	5	Singapore	5.6
United States						
	1	Canada	23.4	1	Canada	17.2
	2	Mexico	13.3	2	China	14.6
	3	Japan	6.1	3	Mexico	10.2
	4	China	4.6	4	Japan	8.3
	5	United Kingdom	4.3	5	Germany	5.1
	14	Australia	1.7	35	Australia	0.04
Japan						
	1	United States	22.5	1	China	21.3
	2	China	19.5	2	United States	12.4
	3	South Korea	7.8	3	Saudi Arabia	5.5
	4	Taiwan	7.3	4	UAE	4.9
	5	Thailand	3.8	5	Australia	4.7
	12	Australia	2.1			
China						
	1	United States	21.4	1	Japan	17.9
	2	Japan	11.0	2	South Korea	13.7
	3	South Korea	4.6	3	Taiwan	13.3
	4	Germany	4.3	4	United States	8.7
	5	Netherlands	3.4	5	Germany	5.5
	14	Australia	1.5	8	Australia	2.9

Sources: World Bank Country Profiles. Available at: www.worldbank.org (accessed 7 September 2006); Australian Government, Department of Foreign Affairs and Trade, Country Fact Sheets. Available at: www.dfat.gov.au/geo/fs (accessed 9 September 2006); The United States–China Business Council, China's World Trade Statistics. Available at: www.uschina.org (accessed 9 September 2006); Japan External Trade Organization, Statistics & Surveys. Available at: www.jetro.go.jp/en/stats (accessed 9 September 2006).

is nothing that Australia, Japan and the United States can do among themselves to fix the problem.

Energy

As developed industrial nations, Australia, Japan and the United States have high per-capita energy consumption rates (Table 5.6). As a consequence, the three countries account for around 27 per cent of global energy consumption, even though they only make up less than 6 per cent of the world's population.

Table 5.7 details the net energy dependency of the three countries. Australia has the highest level of energy independence (notwithstanding that the *net* figure quoted

Table 5.6 Net energy consumption 2003

	Million tonnes of oil equivalent	%	Per capita tonnes of oil equivalent
Australia	113	1	5.6
Japan	517	5	4.0
United States	2,281	21	7.8
China	1,409	13	1.1
India	553	5	0.5
South Korea	205	2	4.3
Russia	640	6	4.5
Other	5,005	47	1.0
Total	10,723	100	1.7

Source: Organization for Economic Co-operation and Development (2006), *OECD Factbook 2006*, Paris: OECD, pp. 84–85.

Table 5.7 Net energy import dependency 2000

	Oil (%)	Coal (%)	Gas (%)
Australia	8	0	0
Japan	100	97	95
United States	58	0	16

Source: Australian Government (2004), *Securing Australia's Energy Future*, p. 119.

conceals significant oil imports that are counterbalanced by exports of different fuel types). Moreover, Australia's largest commodity export is coal and its third largest is crude petroleum. Japan, on the other hand, is almost entirely dependent upon imports for its energy, while the United States sits somewhere in between with 58 per cent of oil coming from offshore.

For the next several decades at least, Australia will remain a net energy exporter, Japan will remain almost entirely dependent on imports, and the United States will become increasingly dependent on foreign energy. According to the US Energy Information Administration, rising demand and falling production will see the United States importing 75 per cent of its oil by 2020, with gas imports rising to 39 per cent of demand over the same period.[12]

Australia holds 40 per cent of the world's uranium reserves, and exports uranium to a number of countries including Japan, the United States, South Korea and the European Union (and soon also to China). Japan produces 30 per cent, and the United States 20 per cent, of their electricity from nuclear power.[13] Notwithstanding Australia's energy exports to Japan and the United States, these only go a small way towards meeting the latter's requirements. Far more significant is reliance on Persian Gulf energy, with Japan importing 75 per cent and the United States 21 per cent of their oil from there (the United States also imports from western hemisphere sources including Venezuela).[14]

As is the case with trade more generally, Australia, Japan and the United States have a shared interest in guarding against disruptions to energy supply. But this is an interest that is shared equally with others in the international community.

Official development assistance

As a proportion of the 24-member OECD Development Assistance Committee (DAC), the three countries together account for over 37 per cent of official bilateral development assistance (Table 5.8). Note that both Japan and the United States contribute a significantly smaller proportion of Gross National Income (GNI) to bilateral aid than the DAC average of 0.26 per cent, and all three countries are well below that of European countries such as Norway (87 per cent), Denmark (0.87 per cent), Sweden (0.78 per cent) and even Portugal (0.63 per cent). Nonetheless, because of the size of their economies, the United States and Japan consistently lead the ranking of bilateral aid donors.[15] In addition, the United States exerts further influence on international development through its appointment of president of the World Bank and an effective veto on major decisions in that institution.

All three nations dispense bilateral aid according to their interests. Table 5.9 lists the top fifteen recipients for each country from 2004 (the last year where comparative figures are available). As a global power, the United States spreads its aid widely but with a particular focus on countries of pressing strategic concern like Iraq, Egypt, Jordan, Afghanistan and Pakistan. In the case of the Democratic Republic of the Congo (DRC), as the US aid agency USAID notes, 'the DRC has the potential to attract vast US investment in mining, oil, gas, power and electricity'.[16]

In contrast, Japan has a more concentrated aid programme that is focused on Asia. China is the largest recipient of Japanese development assistance with India and the countries of Southeast Asia all figuring prominently in the ranking. Australia has a similarly focused programme which concentrates on the countries of the Southwest Pacific and maritime Southeast Asia.

Given the disparate foci of development assistance by the three countries, and their consensus on development goals, their aid programmes are largely complementary. Nonetheless, greater cooperation among the three could be worthwhile – especially where diplomatic sensitivities arise between specific donors and recipients. Alternatively, if any of the three wanted to achieve more from development

Table 5.8 Official bilateral development aid spending 2004

	Total (US$ billion)	% of GNI	% of DAC total
Australia	1,460	0.25	1.8
Japan	8,906	0.19	11.2
United States	19,705	0.17	24.8

Source: Organization for Economic Co-operation and Development, Development Co-operation Directorate. Donor Aid Charts. Available at: www.oecd.org/dac (accessed 18 September 2006).

Table 5.9 Official bilateral development aid recipients 2004

	Australia		Japan		United States	
	Recipient	*%*	*Recipient*	*%*	*Recipient*	*%*
1	Papua New Guinea	16.8	China	9.9	Iraq	11.8
2	Indonesia	7.2	Indonesia	6.0	Congo, Dem. Rep.	4.1
3	Solomon Islands	6.4	Philippines	5.5	Egypt	3.9
4	Viet Nam	3.3	Thailand	5.0	Jordan	3.4
5	Iraq	2.7	India	4.8	Afghanistan	3.3
6	China	2.6	Viet Nam	4.0	Pakistan	3.0
7	Philippines	2.5	Ghana	3.6	Colombia	2.8
8	Timor-Leste	2.4	Iraq	2.3	Ethiopia	2.6
9	Cambodia	1.7	Malaysia	2.1	Sudan	1.4
10	Bangladesh	1.4	Sri Lanka	2.0	Palestinian Adm.	1.2
11	Vanuatu	1.3	Bolivia	2.0	Peru	1.1
12	Afghanistan	1.1	Bangladesh	2.0	Bolivia	1.1
13	Nauru	1.1	Pakistan	1.4	Serbia & Montenegro	1.0
14	Fiji	1.1	Peru	1.2	Uganda	1.0
15	Sri Lanka	0.9	Afghanistan	1.1	Indonesia	1.0

Source: Organization for Economic Co-operation and Development, Development Co-operation Directorate, Statistical Annex of the 2005 Development Co-operation Report, Table 32, 2005. Available at: www.oecd.org/dac/stats/dac/dcrannex (accessed 16 September 2006).

assistance they could simply increase their spending to bring it in line with that of European countries.

It is important not to presume the impact that aid has. As a general rule, development assistance is only likely to have a significant impact when it makes up a substantial share of the recipient's GNI. Consequently, the extent to which aid makes a substantive difference, and therefore also has the potential to translate into real influence, varies greatly among recipient countries.

National security policy

In terms of security policy, Australia, Japan and the United States are countries in transition. The United States has undergone the clearest and most profound transformation.[17] To begin with, they have embraced a new doctrine of preventative war that transcends the bounds of traditional pre-emption. In addition, they no longer equate stability with favourable security; as further evidenced by their active promotion of regime change and democratization in the Middle East. Finally, they have moved from largely a reliance on fixed alliances and institutions towards ad hoc coalitions. However, with public opinion increasingly critical of the Bush administration's handling of Iraq, the durability of these shifts is unclear. That said, the United States will certainly not retreat into isolationism post-Iraq, and will therefore continue as the lynchpin in European and North Asian security.

Under Prime Minister Koizumi, Japan developed an increasingly forthright foreign and security policy. Not only did Japan sustain an assertive line with Russia over the disputed southern Kuril Islands, but it became increasingly strident with North Korea over missile tests and the issue of Japanese abductees. In addition, Koizumi paid annual visits to the controversial Yasukini Shrine – much to the consternation of China and South Korea. The 2005 joint declaration by Japan and the United States citing the peaceful resolution of the Taiwan issue as a 'common strategic objective' (which drew a predictable angry response from China) further attests to Japan's growing strategic purview and assertiveness. Koizumi also approved plans for an expansion of the capabilities of the Japanese Self-Defence Force (JSDF) while redefining their role to include non-combat deployments off-shore. This enabled the deployment of a six-hundred strong JSDF engineering detachment to Iraq in 2004. The extent to which this foreshadows the 'normalization' of Japan as a military power remains to be seen, especially with the new Prime Minister, Shinzo Abe, yet to show his hand and with North Korea's development of nuclear weapons capabilities.

Over the past seven years, Australian security policy has increasingly looked outwards. Beginning with the UN mandated intervention into East Timor in 1999, Australia's underwriting of stability in its immediate neighbourhood has expanded significantly. Further afield, Australia was quick to support US actions in both Afghanistan and Iraq – albeit with carefully circumscribed military contributions – and in 2004 the Howard government broke an election promise by deploying Australia troops in support of Japanese engineers in Iraq. Despite some domestic debate, Australia will almost certainly continue to divide its available resources between maintaining stability in its immediate neighbourhood and paying its due to the US alliance by contributing to coalition operations further afield where necessary.

All three nations are active in addressing 'non-traditional' security threats like terrorism, piracy, transnational crime and epidemic disease. Their responses include both domestic measures and international initiatives. On the vexed issue of WMD proliferation, all three are members of the Proliferation Security Initiative. And while Australia is only a minor player, both Japan and the United States play a key role in North Asian security diplomacy including in the Six Party Talks over North Korea's nuclear ambitions. These agendas may well constitute a key element in future TSD agendas.

The emergence of China as a major power is undoubtedly the key development in East Asian security, and each of the three countries have their own perspective on what this means. The United States declared policy[18] encourages China to play a constructive role in the Asia-Pacific while continuing to develop its own already formidable military capability as a hedge. Japan is more guarded in their posture but is nonetheless actively seized of the importance of China's rapid military modernization[19] – especially given Beijing's uncompromising public diplomacy towards them. Australia is clearly the most comfortable with China's rise and, arguably, the most accommodating of China's diplomatic overtures, as evidenced by the Australian foreign minister's comments in Beijing in 2004[20] that caused considerable consternation in the United States.[21]

Military capability

The United States spends more on defence than any other nation on earth. Five times more, in fact, than its nearest competitor China (calculated on a Purchasing Power Parity basis). In comparison, Japan spends less than one-tenth as much as the United States, and Australia one-thirtieth (Table 5.10).

However, it is important to recognize that Japan's defence spending is constrained by a self-imposed limit of 1 per cent of GDP and that its economy could feasibly support substantially higher levels of expenditure. For example, if Japan spent as much as the United States as a proportion of their economy, their defence budget would almost reach 40 per cent of the US figure (or more than twice China's current spending). In contrast, Australia is practically constrained by the size of its economy from being able to compete with the major powers. The situation with defence spending is reflected in the number of military personnel each of the countries can currently field (Table 5.10).

Table 5.11 compares the military equipment of the three countries along with that of various regional powers. It is important to recognize that, in many cases, the direct comparison of raw numbers conceals substantial disparities in the capability of platforms. For example, much of the inventory held by North Korea and China is effectively obsolete compared with modern Western equipment. The other factor that Table 5.11 fails to capture is the unparalleled capacity the United States has to project force. With 12 carrier battle groups, 7 marine expeditionary units and a substantial conventional long-range strike capability, the United States can bring more military force to bear more quickly than any other nation or existing alliance of nations.

But even with its impressive array of power projection assets, the United States has no choice but to rely on its allies for basing and local support. So it is, then, that

Table 5.10 Defence resources 2004

	Defence spending		Defence personnel	
	2004 $US (billion)	% GDP	Number (thousand)	% of population
Australia	14.3	2.4	53	0.26
Japan	45.2	1.0	260	0.20
United States	455.9	3.9	1,546	0.52
China	84.3	1.5	2,255	0.17
India	19.8	2.9	1,325	0.12
South Korea	16.4	2.4	688	1.44
Russia	61.5	4.4	1,027	1.67
Taiwan	7.5	2.5	290	0.34

Source: The International Institute for Strategic Studies (2006), *The Military Balance 2006*, London: Routledge, pp. 398–403.

Note
Defence spending for China and Russia have been estimated on the basis of Purchasing Power Parity.

Table 5.11 Comparative military capability 2005

	Land		Sea		Air	
	Tanks	Armoured vehicles	Major surface combatants	Submarines	Combat aircraft	Helicopters
Australia	101	1,039	13	6	156	156
Japan	980	900	53	18	380	640
United States	8,023	24,386	118	72	4,016	5,435
China	8,580	5,710	71	58	3,435	533
India	3,978	2,817	54	16	886	549
South Korea	2,390	2,622	43	20	556	497
North Korea	3,500	3,060	8	88	590	306
Russia	23,460	28,870	66	61	2,242	1,815
Taiwan	926	2,230	32	4	511	275

Source: R. Khosa, *Australian Defence Almanac 2006–2007*, Canberra: Australian Strategic Policy Institute, pp. 46–47.

Japan and Australia both figure prominently in the US global military posture. As the then US Defense Secretary William Perry remarked in 1996, Japan and Australia are the northern and southern anchors of US security arrangements in Asia.[22]

Almost 37,000 US military personnel are permanently based in Japan, and around 13,000 personnel crew US navy vessels operating out of Japanese ports.[23] In addition, there are more than 3,800 US civilian workers and around 45,000 accompanying family members resident in Japan. In comparison, the number of US personnel based on the Korean peninsula will have fallen to 25,000 by 2007.[24] Although there are no major US forces based in Australia, the several Joint Facilities maintained by the two nations on Australian soil play an important part in US intelligence gathering and ballistic missile early warning. These facilities would be hard to replace given Australia's fortuitous location in the southern hemisphere. Australia's willingness to support the United States is further reflected in plans for joint United States–Australia training facilities to be built in Australia.[25] It needs to be said, however, that the permanent basing of US forces in Australia is a very remote prospect given the likely Australian public response.

Beyond reliance on allied real estate, there are other limits to US military power. As Iraq shows, US ground forces can rapidly become overstretched in security and stabilization operations. There is little doubt that the United States would have liked something more than the symbolic military contributions it got from Japan and Australia in Iraq (but weak domestic support precluded that in both instances).

Even when it comes to air and maritime forces, there are increasingly limits to what the United States can hope to do. For example, if China continues on their path of increased defence spending and targeted equipment modernization – and there is no reason to think that they will do anything else – they will increasingly challenge US freedom of action in maritime North Asia, especially if they employ asymmetric tactics.

Finally, in judging US military capacity, it is worth remembering that as a global power the United States cannot afford to marshal all their forces in a single theatre. Thus, the seemingly limited military contributions available from Japan and Australia in the event of a conflagration are more valuable from a US perspective than they might first appear. Conversely, Australia and Japan benefit greatly from their military alliance with the United States whose presence in Asia insures against the emergence of Chinese hegemony.

Conclusion

The preceding survey of key facts and issues revealed many areas where Australia, Japan and the United States have shared interests and surprisingly few where there is real divergence. In most instances, however, the shared interests are far from unique. To some extent, all the nations of East Asia are concerned about the very same issues. So what is it that has drawn the three countries together?

Initially, it is important to recognize the high level of trust that has developed between the three nations in the five decades since World War II through economic and security ties. From a realist perspective, this might seem unimportant. But among the highly diverse and fractious region of East Asia, it is hard to find another three countries with a higher level of trust and willingness to cooperate. Add to this the reality that the multilateral forums of East Asia are unwieldy and ineffective, and there is good reason for the three to get together. Given their pooled resources, the three are well placed to address a diverse range of issues beyond what might be negotiated through the ponderous, consensus-driven multilateral diplomacy of East Asia.

Every bit as important is the fact that Australia and Japan are close allies of the United States. With the possible exception of South Korea, this sets the two apart from the rest of East Asia and, moreover, makes their grouping with the United States on security matters natural. Were it not for South Korea's antipathy towards Japan and adoption of a soft line over North Korea's strategic behaviour, we might have seen the development of a four-way dialogue.[26] But that is not the case, nor does it appear likely to change.

But while historical familiarity and overlapping alliances are sufficient to get the three countries to sit down at the same table to talk, that is only a beginning. How far the trilateral strategic relationship between Australia, Japan and the United States matures depends on at least three factors.

First is the extent to which the three countries can build mutual confidence through joint initiatives. Finding opportunities to do so should be easy. There are many areas where the three could work together, including transnational crime, counterterrorism and maritime security. While none of these areas are the exclusive purview of the three, they have the critical mass to make a difference while building greater trust in the process.

Second, the trilateral relationship will not deepen unless Australia and Japan can find further common ground on security issues. Here there can be cautious optimism. Japan assisted Australia by providing JSDF personnel to East Timor from 2000 to 2004, and Australia by providing security for JSDF engineers in Iraq's Al Muthanna province from 2004 to 2006. It is noteworthy that Australia's prime minister signed a Joint Security Declaration with his Japanese counterpart in March 2007.[27]

Finally, and critically, the future of a trilateral strategic partnership between Australia, Japan and the United States will hinge on finding common ground on China's rise. That is not to suggest that they will be looking for ways to 'contain' China – that would be both counterproductive and impractical. Rather, they will be looking for ways they can encourage the constructive rise of China while hedging against less palatable contingencies.

Given Sino-Japanese historical animosities, Australia's seemingly sanguine outlook on China's rise and American ambivalence over how to view China at all, finding common ground will not be easy. Each of the three countries is likely to perceive a different mix of accommodation and hedging to be in their individual interest. At very least, however, the TSD will allow the three to better understand each other's approach to the rise of China, and perhaps influence each other's approach. Even if nothing else is achieved by the TSD than this, it will have been worthwhile given that the rise of China is set to be the most important development in Asia-Pacific security in the coming decades.

Notes

1 *Joint Statement Australia–Japan–United States, Trilateral Strategic Dialogue*, Sydney, 18 March 2006, available at: www.foreignminister.gov.au/releases/2006/joint_statement-aus-japan_usa_180306.html (accessed 5 August 2006).
2 Organization for Economic Co-operation and Development (OECD) (2006), *OECD Factbook 2006*, Paris: OECD, pp. 12–15.
3 United Nations Department of Economic and Social Affairs, Population Division, *World Population Prospect: The 2004 Revision – Population Database*, available at: http://esa.un.org/unpp (accessed 15 September 2006).
4 Ibid.
5 OECD (2006), pp. 128–33.
6 OECD (2006), pp. 134–35.
7 World Bank, *Country Profiles*, available at: www.worldbank.org (accessed 7 September 2006).
8 OECD (2006), pp. 52–53.
9 World Trade Organization, *International Trade Statistics*, available at: www.wto.org/english/res_e/statis_e/statis_e.htm (accessed 23 August 2006).
10 Hamish McDonald (2004), 'China and Taiwan: flashpoint for a war', *Sydney Morning Herald*, 14 July; Hugh White (2005), 'Howard's Asian balancing act', *Age*, 13 April.
11 OECD (2006), pp. 252–53.
12 US Energy Information Administration, *International Energy Outlook 2006*, available at: www.eia.doe.gov/oiaf/ieo/index.html (accessed 12 October 2006).
13 Ibid.
14 US Energy Information Administration, *Persian Gulf Oil and Gas Exports Fact Sheet*, available at: www.eia.doe.gov/emeu/cabs/pgulf.html (accessed 7 September 2006).
15 OECD (2006), 'Aid rising sharply, according to latest OECD figures', available at: www.oecd.org/dataoecd/0/41/35842562.pdf (accessed 2 September 2006).
16 USAID, country summary for the *Democratic Republic of the Congo*, available at: www.usaid.gov/pubs/bj2001/afr/cd (accessed 3 September 2006).

17 Joseph S. Nye, Jr (2006), 'Transformational leadership and US grand strategy', *Foreign Affairs*, vol. 85, no. 4, pp. 141–48.

18 US Department of Defense (2006), *Quadrennial Defense Review Report*, Washington.

19 Government of Japan (2005), *Defense of Japan 2005* (White Paper), Tokyo.

20 Alexander Downer (2004), Media Conference Beijing, 17 August, available at: www.foreignminister.gov.au/transcripts/2004/040817_ds_beijing.html (accessed 18 August 2006).

21 Richard Baker (2006), 'US sent "please explain" to Downer over China comments', *Age*, 17 May.

22 Stephen Sherlock (1996–97), *Australia's Relations with China: What's the Problem?*, Canberra: Australian Parliamentary Library Current Issues Brief 23, available at: www.aph.gov.au/LIBRARY/pubs/cib/1996-97/97cib23.htm#TWO (accessed 15 July 2006).

23 US Department of Defense, *United States Force in Japan Fact Sheet*, available at: www.usfj.mil (accessed 20 August 2006).

24 Jim Garamone (2006), 'US set to leave 25,000 troops in Korea', *American Forces Information Service Press Release*, 8 August, available at: www.defenselink.mil/news/NewsArticle.aspx?ID=395 (accessed 14 October 2006).

25 Robert Hill (2004), 'Australia–US joint combined training centre', *Minister for Defence Media Release*, 8 July, available at: www.defence.gov.au/minister/Hilltpl.cfm?CurrentId=4016 (accessed 20 August 2006).

26 For a proposal along these lines see Robert D. Blackwill (2000), 'An action agenda to strengthen America's alliances in the Asia-Pacific region', in Robert D. Blackwill and Paul Dibb (eds), *America's Asian Alliances*, Cambridge, MA: MIT Press.

27 Paul Kelly (2006), 'Security pact to deepen Japan ties', *Australian*, 12 August and Australian Government, Department of Foreign Affairs and Trade, 'Australia–Japan Joint Declaration on Security Cooperation', 13 March 2007 at HYPERLINK 'http://www.dfat.gov.au/geo/japan/aus_jap_security_dec.html.%20Accessed%2025%20March%202007' http://www.dfat.gov.au/geo/japan/aus_jap_security_dec.html. Accessed 25 March 2007.
.

Part II
Regional dimensions

6 Triangularity and US–Japanese relations

Collaboration, collective hedging and identity politics

Yoshinobu Yamamoto

Introduction

To most Japanese observers of international relations, the recent triangular cooperation between the United States, Australia and Japan in the security arena is not well known. While many understand that the United States–Japan bilateral alliance has been the key to postwar Japanese security and economic development, triangular security relations with the Asia-Pacific's two other major maritime powers have only recently become visible.[1] Most evident is that Australian troops provided security for Japanese troops in Samawa, Iraq, until the Japanese contingent withdrew in June 2006. This development has underscored to Japan's electorate that triangular cooperation between Australia, Japan and the United States has become a more prominent feature in their own country's international security policy.

Prime Minster Junichiro Koizumi argued from 2002 that Australia should be a participant in the East Asia Summit.[2] Shinzo Abe, Koizumi's successor, had speculated prior to taking office in September 2006 about the possibility of security cooperation between the United States, Australia, India, Europe and Japan, on the basis of shared democratic values.[3] Most significantly, the foreign minister-level tripartite dialogue was held in March 2006, demonstrating an emergent saliency of trilateral security cooperation.

What are the roles, functions and meaning of trilateral security cooperation as embodied by the Trilateral Strategic Dialogue? The three country participants are the most advanced economies and democracies in the Asia-Pacific region. They comprise the heart of what is called the 'hub and spokes' alliance system in the Asia-Pacific that centres on the United States. As noted above, they are (perhaps along with India) the three key maritime powers in the Asia-Pacific. When one assesses triangular relations in a global context, it is usually done by focusing on some specific aspect of international relations. One such aspect is security. From this perspective, we consider triangular relations as state-centric trilateral cooperation vis-à-vis common threats or uncertainties of both a traditional and non-traditional mode. Another is economics. From this perspective, triangular cooperation is intended to promote economic prosperity and stability both within and beyond its three participants. A third aspect is related to 'identity'. Triangular cooperation in this vein is promoting such shared basic values as democracy and economic freedom. From this perspective, historical issues and nationalism, particularly those involving Japan's legacy and national identity relative to those of other Asian countries, are clearly important.[4]

The purpose of this chapter is to probe some of the possibilities of evolving triangular alliance relations between Australia, Japan and the United States, particularly from the Japanese perspective. It argues that if managed properly such relations can enhance Japan's sense of national identity in constructive ways without incurring excessive risk of destabilizing regional and international security in the process.

Sea changes in the global security environment

After the end of the Cold War, the global security environment changed radically. The traditional postwar geopolitics that was dominated by the rivalry between the two major superpowers – the USSR and the United States – disappeared from the global scene, even though bipolar (for instance, China and the United States) and multipolar (Europe's economy versus those of the United States and Japan) rivalries still existed. Weapons of mass destruction (WMD), international terrorism and the emergence of 'rogue states' all became concrete threats to the emerging, international order. In addition, domestic conflicts became a major international security issue. Their ability to 'spill over' to impose threats on neighbouring countries or their challenge to humanitarian norms that had been promoted strongly after the end of the Cold War were indisputable. Such norms had been embraced by successive post-Cold War Japanese governments which promptly raced to the assistance of victims of natural disasters. By the turn of the century, international security had become globalized and multifaceted, with many of the 'new threats' and crises situated in the developing world.

Even though international terrorism had already been recognized as a looming security threat in this new international security environment, the events surrounding 11 September 2001 underscored its centrality. The global community responded to the attacks in New York and Washington with a widespread consensus to check international terrorism. An impressive array of methods was proposed for application against the scourge of international terrorism, from actual military combat against terrorist elements to resolving political issues in ways that would de-legitimize the causes of terrorist movements. Such wide-ranging global cooperation entailed and linked numerous components of strategy, including controlling WMD proliferation, upgrading worldwide intelligence capabilities and working collectively to choke off financing to various terrorist networks.

September 11 galvanized America's anger and strengthened its national identity. The United States, with its coalition partners, attacked the ruling Taliban regime in Afghanistan because it refused to turn over al-Qaeda leaders. After the military victory of the American-led 'coalition of the willing', the international community (NATO and the United Nations, in particular) attempted to stabilize, and democratize, Afghanistan, even as US and allied forces were still waging war against Taliban there.

The United States also tried to get rid of Saddam Hussein's regime in Iraq on the grounds that it continued to develop and possess WMD and had developed connections with al-Qaeda, both of which turned out to be illusive. The United States, along with other countries such as Britain, attacked Iraq without an explicit authorization of the UN Security Council. Even though the multilateral coalition forces led by the United States won the initial conflict rather easily, the occupation of Iraq has largely failed and the war in that country continues unabated. The major task in Iraq has evolved into one directed as much towards nation-building as towards sustaining a military offensive within the global war on terror (although the latter mission continues incessantly within that country's boundaries). In May 2006, a formal government was formed in Iraq, but that country is anything but 'stabilized' and the ultimate outcome of the US-led intervention remains in doubt.

From alliance to security cooperation: changing Japanese security policies

The events of 9/11 and its aftermath constitute a watershed for Japanese security policies. Japan sent Maritime Self-Defence Forces (MSDF) to the Indian Ocean and engineering units of the SDF to Iraq. These actions are not strictly within the framework of the United States–Japan alliance since the Indian Ocean and Iraq are well beyond the area covered by its formal purview (that is, the Far East). Nor are they strictly within the framework of the United Nations since the United States made a unilateral decision to wage war in Afghanistan (in this case, one may argue that the United Nations authorized the American action for reasons of self-defence) and Iraq. These undertakings fall somewhere between the mandates of the United States–Japan alliance and of the United Nations. The Japanese government enacted the special laws that authorized sending SDF units to the Indian Ocean and Iraq. The fact that the Japanese government was compelled to enact such legislation indicates that these actions did not fall within the previously established legal framework of Japan. They also demonstrate close security cooperation between the United States and Japan, which goes beyond the traditional concept of bilateral alliance collaboration. The issue then is why Japan chose to endorse and support such actions and whether Japan will continue to do so should similar events occur in the future.

Japan decided to send MSDF units to the Indian Ocean to supply fuel to allied vessels involved with Operation *Enduring Freedom*. Japan demonstrated that it supported the American efforts to combat terrorism and that it wished to avoid a replay of the Gulf War in 1991 in which Japan faced strong American, and international, criticism for not sending actual troops to the Gulf area to defend its own oil supplies with the blood of its citizens – even though Japan contributed 130 billion dollars to that particular operation. The United States pressed Japan to make clear which side it would take ('show the flag' or 'with us or against us') in the case of Afghanistan, and Tokyo opted to side with the West. When the United

States invaded Iraq, Japan also supported the United States. The reasons included that Japanese security depends on the American commitment to maintain access to critical energy supplies and that Japan's own security is dependent upon maintaining credibility and trust in the eyes of Washington. The United States again generated substantial pressure on Japan to contribute to military operations ('boots on the ground') in Iraq. Japan responded by sending Ground Self-Defence Forces or GSDF (in addition to Air Self-Defence Forces or ASDF) to Iraq basically for humanitarian missions but also to take part in rear support functions (such as air transport missions). One of the important developments in Japan's staying in Iraq was that the security of Japanese Self-Defence Forces in Samawa was protected by Australian forces (after the Dutch and British troops had initially done so). Japan's dispatch of MSDF units to the Indian Ocean and GSDF elements to Iraq, therefore, contributed in quite tangible ways to the maintenance and enhancement of United States–Japan security cooperation and opened up security cooperation with countries other than the United States. Such an arrangement clearly illustrated the potential importance of trilateral security cooperation between the United States, Japan and Australia.

As previously intimated, approaches to neutralizing international terrorism are numerous and varied. To head off proliferation of WMD and particularly the link between international terrorism and WMD, however, is of particular importance. The Proliferation Security Initiative (PSI) is a highly appropriate case in point. PSI is a multilateral endeavour and, as far as Japan is concerned, not only the Coast Guard but also Marine SDF are the major participants in this specific regime. PSI represents a new and wide-ranging form of security cooperation between Japan on the one hand and other nations, including the United States and Australia, on the other, which goes well beyond the traditional purview of the bilateral United States–Japan security alliance.

In October 2002, North Korea disclosed that it was violating the Framework Agreement signed in 1994 that bans that country from developing nuclear weapons.[5] Since then, the North Korean nuclear issue has been a pressing security issue in Northeast Asia and particularly of Japan. Japan totally depends on the United States in terms of nuclear deterrence. Here, a traditional function of alliance politics is keenly alive, at least for Japan. Indeed, Japan has been strengthening its alliance relations with the United States since the middle of the 1990s when the first North Korean nuclear crisis erupted and when China test-fired missiles over Taiwan in order to influence the Presidential election there. The United States and Japan issued The Guidelines for Cooperation for Area Security in 1997 and Japan eventually enacted what is called the Surrounding Area Act in 1999 one year after North Korea test-fired a Taepodong missile over Japan. Japan subsequently moved to participate in the development of missile defence (MD) with the United States.[6]

The 'North Korea factor' has continued to spur Japan towards greater 'defence normalization'. In 2004, Japan passed several laws related to what is termed the 'armed attack on Japan' (also known collectively as 'the Emergency Act'). One such law spells out how Japan will cooperate with the United States if Japan actually is attacked. If the United States–Japan alliance in the Cold War era basically functioned as a deterrent against the Soviet Union, the United States–Japan alliance in the post-Cold War, particularly since the mid-1990s, has become more operational in the sense that a series of laws specify concrete Japanese actions under specified conditions.

Regarding the nuclear issue on the Korean peninsula, Six Party Talks have been held since 2003. Although these have produced some preliminary results – particularly the joint communiqué of the fourth meeting (September 2005) in which all the parties, including North Korea, agreed on a non-nuclear Korean peninsula – their overall momentum remains stalled. In July 2006, moreover, North Korea test launched seven missiles, six capable of carrying WMD warheads to South Korea and Japan and one designed to attack more distant targets (including the US homeland). In response to this action, the UN Security Council passed a resolution condemning the missile launchings and demanding that North Korea refrain from proceeding with further nuclear and missile developments.[7] As of this writing, however, the situation had deteriorated further. Despite ongoing international pressure on North Korea to refrain from provocative action, including Japan and Australia imposing financial sanctions in September 2006,[8] North Korea went ahead and detonated a nuclear device the following month.

Collective hedging towards China?

China has been strongly opposed to the United States–Japan alliance, at least publicly, particularly because bilateral alliance relations between Washington and Tokyo have recently been strengthened so overtly. For example, China has criticised Japan's enacting the Surrounding Area Act in 1999. It also has opposed US efforts to include Japan in its development of a Missile Defence system (see Chapter 14 of this volume).

Such concerns have intensified despite Sino-American relations becoming distinctly warmer after 9/11.[9] The United States has focused on the war on terror and tried to forge a grand coalition against terrorism. China has cooperated with the United States in this quest and did not openly criticize the American military intervention in Iraq. China has been arguing for a 'New Security Concept' since the late 1990s that emphasizes trust and cooperation in the process of building a new Asia-Pacific regional order, as opposed to accepting more traditional Cold War strategies such as deterrence and alliance politics.[10] China also promotes the concept of 'peaceful rise', which argues that China can rise without hampering the interests of neighbouring states.[11] Beijing has also been playing a key role in the Six Party Talks. China seems willing to coexist with American regional power and global hegemony rather than to directly challenge it. It is also beginning to contribute more tangibly to international peacekeeping activities under UN auspices (East Timor and Lebanon are cases-in-point).

With the United States preoccupied with the global war on terror, China has a 'breathing space' for concentrating on its own economic development – which is its number one priority – without too many US officials (US Secretary of Defense Donald Rumsfeld was one notable exception) worrying how growing Chinese economic prowess could transform China into a strategic rival of the United States. China's economic rise, moreover, provides vast economic opportunities to other nations (with Australia at the forefront of such beneficiaries). Accordingly, it makes sense for the United States, Japan and other countries to engage China and attempt to condition it into what has been termed a 'responsible stakeholder' in the Asia-Pacific region, or globally.[12]

However, the rise of China, particularly the rapid increases in its defence budget and modernization in armaments, still raises security concerns for other countries including the United States and Japan. Chinese resource exploitation around Japan has recently increased, as exemplified by Chinese petroleum exploration efforts around the Senkaku Islands.[13] As intimated above, moreover, there are American observers who ask if the rise of China is shifting the Asia-Pacific's balance of power more radically than the Bush administration admits publicly and who demand more transparency from Beijing about the meaning of rapidly increasing Chinese military capabilities. Chinese behaviour also at times seems to contradict basic American interests. China has been trying to check American influence through the Shanghai Cooperation Organization, to say nothing of the UN Security Council. In other words, China has been pursuing diplomatic or 'soft'-balancing vis-à-vis the United States.[14]

The United States therefore has adopted a double-edged strategy relative to China. On the one hand, it pursues engagement policies towards Beijing.[15] Simultaneously, it projects a very cautious hedging strategy towards the Chinese.[16] The United States and Japan share a basic understanding of how to employ this policy calibration to cope with China. In most instances Australia seems to share this position but it is not entirely identical. On the one hand, China is one of the most important trade partners of Australia and the two countries have been trying to develop closer economic relations. On the other hand, Australia is not so certain about future Chinese behaviour that it is willing to risk alienating its US ally or its long-standing Japanese economic partner to pursue closer relations with China at any cost. Therefore, trilateral cooperation between the United States, Japan and Australia can be perceived as both a policy instrument of collective engagement and collective hedging to be directed towards China. If the three countries opt too strongly for a collective hedging direction, China will perceive the TSD as nothing less than a mechanism for containing Chinese power by the region's three key maritime powers. This would clearly trigger an acute regional security dilemma. It is important for the three maritime allies to demonstrate that their main strategy concerning China is engagement. In this regard, it would be important for them to develop cooperative frameworks with China regarding such non-traditional security issues as epidemics, terrorism and natural disasters which do not divide these countries and which facilitate multilateral collaboration.

Open regionalism

In this regard, we have to pay closer attention to an evolving East Asian community. A few ideas and activities have been floating around that indicate the direction such a community would take. It would probably include the ten ASEAN states, China, Japan, and South Korea, collectively known as the 'ASEAN + 3'. Yet many 'regionalists' would like to see Australia and New Zealand – and even India – included as well. In December 2005, the inaugural East Asia Summit was held in Kuala Lumpur, and attended by all of these states – a triumph for those advocating an 'open regionalism' approach to future regional order-building. The ASEAN + 3 Summit was also held and this group declared that future East Asian community-building would be pursued mainly through the ASEAN + 3.[17] Even though the future is still largely uncertain, summit meetings have become a fixture in East Asia. They are economic and political in nature but dialogues on East Asian identity (or Asian identity) around which East Asian countries could come together to build closer politico-cultural and strategic cooperation have recently intensified. Since economic transactions among East Asian countries have become increasingly dense, it is natural for them to forge larger regional arrangements (for example, an East Asian free trade association). However, for the purposes of this volume, it would be constructive to examine any possible relationship between an East Asian community network and cooperative groupings such as the TSD. Can they be independently pursued? Is an East Asian community consistent with the United States–Japan security alliance or with the TSD?

On the one hand, it is desirable for East Asian countries to create their own framework to stabilize and promote political and economic relations. This would clearly be in the collective interest of the United States, Japan and Australia. On the other hand, an East Asian community could be designed to promote autonomy or 'exclusivism', as opposed to (or in addition to) more inclusive frameworks and arrangements vis-à-vis countries outside the core Asian area, particularly the United States (we may consider such moves as soft balancing of East Asia vis-à-vis the United States). Furthermore, if a sense of East Asian identity spearheaded by China, for example, prevails in East Asian community-building, the region might become highly exclusive and destabilized by those powers marginalized in the process.[18]

Japan has close relations with both the United States and its East Asian neighbours (for example, the United States and China are the two largest trading partners of Japan, with China recently surpassing the United States in terms of overall trade volume). Tokyo would thus not like to see an exclusive East Asian community. It has been very cautious about endorsing any exclusivist vision of an East Asian community. It was accordingly reluctant to participate in an East Asian Economic Caucus (EAEC), initially proposed by Malaysia more than a decade ago. When ASEAN requested Japan to join the Association of Southeast Asian Nations' Treaty of Amity and Cooperation or TAC, Japan was hesitant to do so lest it might jeopardize the United States–Japan security alliance (Japan finally signed the TAC in December 2003 after receiving assurances from the ASEAN Secretariat it would not force Japan to renounce existing security treaty obligations with the United States).[19] Japan will be trying to find ways to balance between its relations with the United States on the one hand and relations with East Asian countries on the other. One possibility is that Japan would pursue a free trade agreement or FTA with the United States even as it fully participates in an East Asian community. This Japanese balancing act could serve as a beneficial role model to other East Asian countries in the sense that they also need stable and balanced relations with the United States in both economic and security terms.

In order that an East Asian community does not become exclusive, Australian participation is important. Japan rightly supported Australian participation in the East Asia Summit in December 2005. Meanwhile, the United States has been generating its own efforts to make East Asian economies open and to gain entry into the East Asian market by trying to negotiate various FTAs with ASEAN countries and South Korea.

Japan: a security–identity nexus?

As described above, Japan has substantially changed its security policies in terms of sending the SDF overseas. It has enacted several laws to operationalize more 'normal' national defence postures. In addition, there have been arguments, both within and outside Japan, that the country should pursue collective self-defence strategies by changing how its constitution should be interpreted or even revising it.[20]

As a matter of fact, many uncertainties exist as to which direction Japan is moving in terms of security policies. Many problems also exist regarding collective self-defence and possible constitutional change. Collective self-defence and a modification of Japan's constitution may be no panacea for Japanese security problems or for United States–Japan security relations. For example, while collective self-defence is essential for Japan to develop a missile defence system in collaboration with the United States, it is hard to know whether United States–Japan security cooperation could be enhanced in general, if collective self-defence is allowed. Collective self-defence is the right to use force when an ally is militarily attacked, even though the country itself is not attacked. It is hard to believe that the United States will incur a direct external attack. The 9/11 episode was exceptional (and an attack by a non-state actor) and this was the first time NATO activated its collective self-defence mechanisms to help the United States (but the United States did not initially utilize NATO in military operations against al-Qaeda and the Taliban in Afghanistan). The Iraqi case has nothing to do with collective self-defence since it was the United States that launched the attack (but collective self-defence would be necessary if prospective SDF units sent overseas for peacekeeping operations were required to militarily help peacekeeping forces of other nations). There remains a question as to whether or not collective self-defence as it is envisioned within the bilateral United States–Japan alliance framework can be applied to US forces stationed overseas. That is, if American forces overseas are attacked, can Japan assist the American forces through collective defence? It is doubtful such is the case. If South Korea is attacked and if the United States comes to help South Korea, can Japan enter military engagements to support the United States (and South Korea) through collective self-defence? Since, in this instance, the United States is not attacked and since South Korea is not Japan's direct ally, collective self-defence does not apply. Given these problems surrounding collective self-defence, Shinzo Abe proposed, in his campaign for presidency of the LDP, to examine appropriate applications of collective defence on the case by case basis.[21]

While Japan's security 'normalization' has been supported by the United States, Japanese relations with neighbouring countries, particularly with South Korea and China, have deteriorated, particularly during the Koizumi administration. John Ikenberry has argued that normalization of Japan is desired and pushed by the United States – as envisioned by the 'Nye–Armitage Report' published in 2000[22] – while the normalization triggers deterioration in the relationship between Japan on the one hand and China and South Korea on the other. This is a trend unfavourable to US interests.[23]

There are two possible routes through which Japan's defence normalization may lead to deterioration in that country's regional relations. One is that it will lead to an intensified regional security dilemma. As Japan increases its security role and its defence capabilities, it will cause greater anxiety on the part of neighbouring countries, even though the Japanese intention may be merely 'defensive'. The other route is psychological and related to the aforementioned identity issue developing among Northeast Asian countries. Koizumi's annual visits to the Yasukuni Shrine since 2001 is a case in point. Even though there is little chance that Japan would go back to pre-war-like nationalism,[24] some Japanese nationalists argue, at least at the rhetorical level, that the Pacific War fought during the 1930s and 1940s was justifiable and that the Tokyo tribunal that convicted Japanese 'war criminals' after that conflict's termination was unjustifiable. These arguments within Japan trigger anti-Japanese feelings in China and in both Koreas and even generate anxiety within US policy-making circles.

Normalization will not inherently lead to deterioration in Japan's regional ties amidst fears of rising Japanese nationalism. However, it is important for Japan to proceed with 'normalization' without provoking its neighbours militarily and psychologically. In this regard, the Trilateral Strategic Dialogue may be important in the sense that the United States and Australia are two of the most important nations that created the original post-World War II 'San Francisco System' for managing regional security order in Asia. Furthermore, since the United States, Australia and Japan are the most advanced democracies in the region, such trilateral cooperation will demonstrate that Japanese identity is embedded firmly in democracy and freedom as opposed to atavistic pre-war nationalism.

Bilateral and trilateral security cooperation: recent developments

The United States became the sole superpower after the end of the Cold War. Thus, it must assume primary responsibility for maintaining global security. As a matter of fact, the United States now enjoys unparalleled global military superiority. The defence budget of the United States is far more than the sum total of the major powers and its R&D spending for the military is about 80 per cent of the world's total.[25] An American military transformation has been underway for some time both in Europe and Asia. This is designed for the United States to respond to emerging threats rapidly and flexibly and to narrow the gap between its overseas capabilities and international commitments (as well as America's own security).

Japan also recently revised its Defence Guidelines (*Boueikeikaku no Taiko*), in December 2004. The revisions are designed for Japan to better cope with the new international environment, such as a rising China, international terrorism and missile and nuclear issues related to North Korea. The Guidelines also argue for more active contributions to international peace.

The United States and Japan conducted a series of discussions and negotiations regarding the American military transformation. In February 2005, the two governments issued a joint statement that endeavoured to solicit common understanding of the basic security issues between the two countries. The statement notes, for example, that it is a common task for the two countries to promote liberal values such as democracy and human rights.[26] It also projects a common concern about China over such issues as a peaceful resolution of the Taiwan Strait. In October 2005, the two governments issued a joint statement that detailed the transformation of American bases and relocation in Japan. The statement declares, *inter alia*, that the two countries will enhance security cooperation such as joint use of military facilities, that eight thousand US marines will move from Okinawa to Guam, that the Japanese government will financially contribute to the transfer of these marines, and that the Futenama air base will be moved to Henoko, the northern part of Okinawa.[27] In May 2006, the two governments finalized the plan or 'roadmap' regarding the base and personnel re-arrangements in Japan.[28] In the negotiation process of American military transformation in Japan, the Japanese government pursued two objectives: lessening the burden on the people around the American bases; and maintaining deterrence extended to Japan by the United States.

In 'The Japan–US Alliance of the New Century' which was issued at the visit of Koizumi to President Bush on 29 June 2006, the two countries' common strategic identity on the basis of universal values was reiterated.[29] The statement insisted that: 'The United States and Japan stand together not only against mutual threats but also for the advancement of core universal values such as freedom, human dignity and human rights, democracy, market economy, and rule of law.' It also observed that: 'Asia's historic transformation is underway, creating a region that increasingly embraces the universal values of democracy, freedom, human rights, market economy, and rule of law.' Prime Minister Koizumi and President Bush 'reaffirmed the importance of advancing strategic dialogues with friends and allies in the region such as Australia'.

The joint statement of the Trilateral Strategic Dialogue between Australia, Japan and the United States on 18 March 2006 demonstrates that these three countries share a set of common agendas for cooperation.[30] The joint statement refers to greater cooperation in addressing contemporary security issues. It includes the following items for cooperation: supporting the emergence and consolidation of democracies and strengthening cooperative frameworks in the Asia-Pacific region; China's constructive engagement in the region; global partnership with

India; North Korean and Iranian nuclear issues; counterterrorism and weapons of mass destruction; non-traditional security issues such as pandemics; and so forth.

On the same day, Australian and Japanese foreign ministers issued a joint statement.[31] The bilateral joint statement by the foreign ministers overlaps the trilateral joint statements in content. The bilateral joint statement naturally focused more on Australia–Japan dyadic issues, including economic development and prosperity of the two countries and of the Asia-Pacific (APEC and East Asia Summit). It argued for 'the future based on open regionalism'. It also touched upon a possibility of free trade agreement between Australia and Japan. Finally, it also emphasized people to people relations between the two countries.[32]

Examination of the current status of bilateral and trilateral cooperation between Australia, Japan and the United States demonstrates that these three countries are developing cooperation in directions that have been reviewed in this chapter's previous sections. The interests of the three countries do not perfectly coincide (for example, Japan tries to protect its agricultural sector and thus it will be very difficult for Japan to form FTAs with Australia and the United States). However, wide-ranging common interests do exist in security, economic and normative areas. Moreover, bilateral and trilateral cooperation have been reinforcing each other.

Conclusion

As Japan assumes broader roles and responsibilities on the world stage, trilateral relations between the United States, Japan and Australia may well increase in importance and relevance to Japan. The SDF in Iraq had been protected by Australian troops. Consultation between Japan, Australia and the United States has become essential in regard to the Iraqi issue. Trilateral cooperation will have spillover effects beyond Iraq. East Timor and other areas in the South Pacific will become the issues for the three countries to cooperate more intensively (see Chapter 9). Australia and Japan, along with the United States, can develop mutual approaches, such as the PSI, to prevent proliferation of weapons of mass destruction. Coordinated policies towards North Korea are also illustrative. Regarding an East Asian Community, Australian participation in the East Asia Summit in 2005 was very important to preclude any East Asian community from becoming too exclusivist.

Security relations between Australia and Japan are the weakest link in the trilateral relations among the United States, Japan and Australia. Even though the so-called 'hub and spokes' system of the US-led bilateral security alliances in the region will continue for the time being, strengthening independent Australia–Japan security relations can contribute to stabilizing international politics in the Asia-Pacific. The March 2007 Australia–Japan Joint Security Declaration could be viewed as a first step in this process. However, in promoting trilateral cooperation, the Asia-Pacific region must not be bifurcated between a China-centric component on the one hand and a triangular group of the United States, Japan and Australia on the other (that is, China versus the hub and spokes alliance centring on the

United States, or maritime powers versus a great land power). In this respect, a close relationship between Australia and China is important. Australia and Japan as well as the United States should work to cooperate on non-traditional security issues and they need to invite China to become a part of such cooperation.

The emerging saliency of tripartite cooperation between the United States, Australia and Japan may be partly due to the fact that these three countries are among the major coalition partners in the war on terror and in Iraq. All three countries have also recently been led by conservative politicians (George W. Bush, John Howard and Junichiro Koizumi). This latter point is reflected in the seemingly excessive, at least to Japanese eyes, emphasis on expansion of universal values such as democracy, human rights and economic freedom. Therefore, if and when the nature of the leadership of the three countries changes, the content and emphasis in the trilateral cooperation might also be transformed. However, many of the common interests and agendas will not change over time and thus steady progress of tripartite cooperation is a strong prospect.

In this context, cooperation between the United States, Australia and Japan can open up a new space for Japan to think about what Japan can or should do in new security and economic environments in the region and the world.

Notes

All websites accessed 29 September 2006.

1 One Western observer, for example, has linked Japanese Prime Minister Koizumi's and Australian Prime Minister John Howard's strategic collaboration in Iraq as an effort to strengthen their respective political positions at home by being perceived as tough on national security issues. See Danile Widome (2005), *Natural Selection* (a blog hosted by The Watson Institute for International Studies at Brown University), 22 February, available at: www.watsonblogs.org/dwidome/archives/2005/02

2 See, for example, speech by Prime Minister Junichiro Koizumi (2002), 'Japan and ASEAN in East Asia – a sincere and open partnership', Singapore: Institute of Southeast Asian Studies.

3 Shinzo Abe (2006), 'Beautiful country, Japan'. This is a short pamphlet issued in September for his campaign for the presidency of the LDP, available (in Japanese) at: http://newleader.s-abe.or.jp/janews/653f6a2969cb60f3300c7f8e3057304456fd30016 5e5672c3002300d

4 These three perspectives roughly correspond to realism, liberalism and idealism (or constructivism or identity politics) in international relations theory. See Stephen Walt (1998), 'International relations: one world, many theories', *Foreign Policy*, no. 110, pp. 29–46; Jack Snyder (2004), 'One world, rival theories', *Foreign Policy*, no. 145, pp. 53–62; G. John Ikenberry and Michael Mastanduno (eds) (2003), *International Relations Theory and the Asia-Pacific*, New York: Columbia University Press; and Henry Nau (2006), *Perspectives on International Relations: Power, Institutions, and Ideas*, Washington, DC: CQ Press.

5 Prime Minister Koizumi visited North Korea in September 2002 and concluded what is called the 'Pyongyang Declaration' with Kim Jong-Il (September 17). At the same time, however, the abduction issue has become the most salient issue in Japan's relations with North Korea.

6 Australia is also developing an MD system with the United States.

7 United Nations Security Council, Resolution 1695 (15 July 2006).

8 Choe Sang-Hun (2006), 'Australia and Japan put penalties on North Korea', *International Herald Tribune*, 20 September, p.1 (Japanese edition).

9 For example, President Bush (2002) states in *The National Security Strategy of the United States of America*, Washington, DC: The White House, that 'Today, the international community has the best chance since the rise of the nation-state in the seventeenth century to build a world where great powers compete in peace instead of continually prepare for war. Today, the world's great powers find ourselves on the same side – united by common dangers of terrorist violence and chaos', p. 4, available at: www.whitehouse.gov/nsc/nss.pdf

10 'Comparing security concepts, Dec. 29, 1997', Document Source: Beijing China Radio International, 29 Dec 1997 \ FBIS-CHI-98-001, 01 Jan 1998, available at: www.shaps.hawaii.edu/security/china/comparing-security.html

11 Zheng Bijian (2005), 'China's "peaceful rise" to great-power status', *Foreign Affairs*, vol. 84, no. 5, pp. 18–24.

12 Regarding the concept of responsible stakeholder, see US Deputy Secretary of State Robert Zoellick, 'Whither China: from membership to responsibility?', remarks to National Committee on United States–China Relations, New York City, 21 September 2005, available at: www.ncuscr.org/articlesandspeeches/Zoellick.htm. In this speech, Zoellick is responding to the Chinese concept 'peaceful rise', which is argued in Zheng Bijian (see note 11, above).

13 The United States recognized that the Senkaku Islands are under Japanese administration and that the United States–Japan Security Treaty covers the area under Japanese administration. See Daily Press Briefing for 24 March 2004 by Deputy Press Spokesman, Department of State, Adam Ereli, available at: http://findarticles.com/p/articles/mi_ponn/is_200403/ai_2778152902/pg_1

14 Regarding soft balancing, see T.V. Paul *et al.* (eds) (2004), *Balance of Power*, Stanford, CA: Stanford University Press (particularly the Introduction).

15 For example, Thomas Christensen (2006), 'China's role in the world: is China a responsible stakeholder?', Deputy Assistant Secretary for East Asian and Pacific Affairs, Remarks before the United States–China Economic and Security Review Commission, 3 August, available at: www.state.gov/p/eap/rls/rm/69899.htm

16 The term 'hedge' is used in President George W. Bush (2006), *The National Security Strategy of the United States*, Washington, DC: The White House. It says: 'Our strategy seeks to encourage China to make the right strategic choices for its people, while we hedge against other possibilities.' Available at: www.whitehouse.gov/nsc/nss/2006/section VIII.html

17 See 'Kuala Lumpur Declaration on the ASEAN plus Three Summit, Kuala Lumpur, 12 December 2005', available at: www.mofa.go.jp/region/asia-paci/asean/conference/asean3/joint0512.html

18 'Identity' is a very elusive term and has diverse meanings. Identity can mean solidarity on the basis of specific values such as democracy and freedom or it may mean collective subscription to a particular set of norms about relationship among nations, such as non-interference into domestic matters or peaceful resolution of conflicts. East Asian identity, from the former meaning, may mean solidarity centring on 'being Asian' regardless of its content. If so, that type of identity may exclude non-Asians.

19 ASEAN requested Australia join the TAC in order for Australia to participate in the East Asia Summit and Australia joined the TAC in 2005.

20 Regarding the concept of normalization of Japan, see, for example, Bhubhindar Singh (2002), 'Japan's post-Cold War security policy: bringing back the normal state', *Contemporary Southeast Asia*, vol. 24, no. 1, pp. 82–105.

21 See, for example, 'Issues in the presidential election of the LDP, collective self defence' (in Japanese), Yomiuri Online, available at: www.yomiuri.co.jp/feature/fe6600/fe_ji_06090805_04.htm

22 Institute for National Strategic Studies (2000), *The United States and Japan: Toward a Mature Partnership*, Washington, DC: National Defense University, October, available at: www.ndu.edu/inss/strforum/SR_01/SR_Japan.htm

23 G. John Ikenberry (2006), 'Japan has a serious geopolitical problem – and increasingly it is an American problem as well', *Washington Post*, 17 August, p. A25.

24 Michael Green (2006), 'Understanding Japan's relations in Northeast Asia', testimony for the Hearing on 'Japan's Tense Relations with Her Neighbors: Back to the Future', House Committee on International Relations, 14 September, available at: wwwa.house.gov/international_relations/109/gre091406.pdf#search=%22Understanding%20Japan's%20relations%20in%20Northeast%20Asia%22

25 See, for example, G. John Ikenberry (ed.) (2002), *America Unrivaled: The Future of the Balance of Power*, Ithaca, NY: Cornell University Press (Introduction and Chapter 3).

26 Item 11 of the 'Joint Statement – US–Japan Security Consultative Committee' (19 February 2005) includes: 'Promote fundamental values such as basic human rights, democracy, and the rule of law in the international community'; available at: www.mofa.go.jp/region/n-america/us/security/scc/joint0502.html

27 'Security Consultative Committee Document, US–Japan Alliance: Transformation and Realignment for the Future', 29 October 2005, available at: www.mofa.go.jp/region/n-america/us/security/scc/doc0510.html

28 'United States–Japan Roadmap for Realignment Implementation', 1 May 2006, available at: www.mofa.go.jp/region/n-america/us/security/scc/doc0605.html

29 'Joint Statement: The Japan–US Alliance of the New Century', 29 June 2006, available at: www.whitehouse.gov/news/releases/2006/06/20060629-2.html

30 'Trilateral Strategic Dialogue Joint Statement Australia–Japan–United States 18 March 2006, Sydney', available at: www.mofa.go.jp/region/asia-paci/australia/joint0603-2.html

31 'Joint Statement: Building a Comprehensive Strategic Relationship' (Foreign Ministers' Talk between Japan and Australia), 18 March 2006, available at: www.mofa.go.jp/region/asia-paci/australia/joint0603.html

32 One of the interesting items commonly seen in joint statements between Australia, Japan and the United States is references to a Japanese bid for a permanent seat on the UN Security Council. The joint statement between the United States and Japan in February 2005 says, 'coordinate efforts to improve the effectiveness of the United Nations Security Council by making the best use of the current momentum to realize Japan's aspiration to become a permanent member'. The tripartite joint statement in March 2006 mentioned 'the support of our three Governments for Japan's bid for a permanent seat on the Security Council'. This shows that Japan has tried to utilize the bilateral and trilateral meetings to obtain support for its aspiration for permanent membership on the UN Security Council.

7 Trilateralism and Northeast Asia

Yoshihide Soeya

Introduction

The Trilateral Strategic Dialogue (TSD) between Australia, Japan and the United States, in theory, can substantially contribute to the stability of the Asia-Pacific region, including Northeast Asia. The benefits of the TSD for Northeast Asia are obvious and reflect those that could be applied to other sub-regions of the Asia-Pacific: it is a dialogue among three like-minded democracies in the Asia-Pacific, it is concerned with the stability and prosperity of the region, and it intends to improve the Northeast Asian sub-region's security environment through dialogue and cooperation. In practice, however, the potential sources of misperception and misconception are profound, and may only add to the complexity of the already difficult security problems in Northeast Asia. Rather than reiterating the merits of the TSD, this chapter will address several critical challenges and security issues in Northeast Asia that could undermine the process of the TSD despite its potential benefits.

The greatest challenge is a possible negative reaction by China. As noted in other chapters within this volume, China instinctively sees the development of the TSD directed against itself, and thus could work to minimize its impact, if not to confront the development outright. True, the TSD will concern itself about the future of China as well as the impact of its rise upon security landscapes in the region. The coping strategy by the trilateral countries, however, should not and cannot be to confront the inevitable trend of China's increasing influence, but to accommodate the rise of China and stabilize Northeast Asia's power balance over the long run. Naturally, the management of the Taiwan issue is critical in this respect.

The North Korean nuclear problem as well as the future of the Korean peninsula is also an issue of central importance for the TSD. The Six Party Talks process is currently the only viable multilateral mechanism dealing with these two issues through dialogue, and naturally the TSD should evolve in line with the overall direction taken by this existing process. Here, a somewhat hidden challenge for the trilateral countries is to create constructive relations with South Korea, which has tended to gravitate towards reconciliation with North Korea during the last several years.

In both of these critical domains, the role of Australia is crucial. This is because China, North Korea, and South Korea share similar concerns about a possible hardline coalition between the United States and Japan. A critical test case here should be whether South Korea, rather than China or North Korea, would accept the basic tenor of the TSD. This chapter will argue that in order for the TSD to evolve as an acceptable dialogue mechanism for South Korea, the central agenda and merits of the TSD should be promoted by 'middle powers', that is, Australia and Japan, whose strength should typically be exerted in advancing multilateral cooperation.

It is precisely in this context of middle power diplomacy that the importance of Australia–Japan cooperation in the TSD should be highlighted. It is often said that this bilateral tie is the weakest in the trilateralism in consideration here.[1] If the TSD turns out to be a set of the two bilateral alliances, it would simply contribute to the strategy of the United States and would reduce the incentive for the other regional countries to recognize the value-added of the TSD.

If the TSD evolves as a process led by Australia and Japan, rather than the United States, it would greatly enhance the possibility of modifying probable objections of China to trilateral security cooperation. This does not mean that the United States–China strategic relationship is not important. It is very important. Instead, this simply implies that the TSD has different, if not conflicting, merits than those provided by the US military presence, and that the chances of China accepting the process of the TSD should be greater in the domain of multilateral cooperation led by middle powers.

The same should apply to the situations in the Korean peninsula, including possible reaction by South Korea. As already noted, the Six Party Talks are the only viable multilateral framework for dialogue at the moment, which is founded upon strategic compromise between the United States and China. The Six Party Talks have actually become possible on the basis of United States–China strategic coexistence, but this does not mean that the substance of the dialogue should also be led by these powers. Particularly, Australia, Japan and South Korea can and should consult more between themselves, and conceptualize an alternative approach towards North Korea, within the framework of the Six Party Talks and without contradicting the logic of United States–China strategic coexistence.

Having established this, one would naturally be struck by the proposition of Japan as a middle power on a par with Australia and South Korea. True, Japan is often conceptualized as one of the 'four great powers' surrounding the Korean peninsula, but in reality Japan's diplomatic behaviours are of quite a different nature from those of the 'three great powers', that is, the United States, China and Russia. This perceptual distortion of Japan's security profile is often one of the critical sources of confusion, not only about Japan's security policies but of security situations in Northeast Asia.

The TSD has a great potential to provide a new perspective on an optimum security role for Japan in Northeast Asia. And, to the extent that this new conceptualization should take root, the contribution of the TSD to the stability of volatile security situations in Northeast Asia could also be enhanced. In the same vein, the role of Australia–Japan cooperation in providing middle power initiatives is of central importance.

Before examining concrete issues and developments in Northeast Asia from these perspectives, a quick overview of the Japanese middle power security profile is offered.

Japan's middle power diplomacy

The experiences of postwar Japanese diplomacy have been unique. Japan has become the number two world economy from the ashes of the devastation it experienced in World War II, but has not re-emerged as a typical traditional great power engaging in power politics. A critical fact to recognize in explaining the experiences of postwar Japan is that this country has become an economic power precisely by engaging in de facto middle power diplomacy in the domain of traditional security.[2]

This, however, did not evolve without cost. Arguably, Japanese security policies in the postwar years fell short even of those of a middle power, because Japan could not engage in the domain of international security, other than through the alliance with the United States. Moreover, contrary to a widely held perception, particularly held in Northeast Asia, Japan is still suffering from the legacies of minimalist security policies even today, which actually hinder the development of security cooperation with Australia.

Against this backdrop, amid and after the Gulf crisis in 1990 and 1991, a central concern of the Japanese government was how to overcome dominant postwar constraints on Japanese participation in international security. Most notably, enacting legislation in the Diet to authorize Japanese participation in UN Peacekeeping Operations (PKO) became paramount for the Japanese government. It was precisely in this context that Ichiro Ozawa raised the concept of Japan as a 'normal' country. These developments, emerging soon after the end of the Cold War, signalled that a new Japanese strategic aspiration was in essence premised on, and intended to modify, 'abnormality' in Japanese postwar security policies which had prohibited Japan from being part of the global community in the multilateral management of international peace and stability.

Japan's post-Cold War awakening to the mission of international security thus laid the groundwork for a series of changes in its security policies in the 1990s and in the overall context of responding to the challenges after the end of the Cold War.[3] It is important to note that the Japanese engagement in the TSD under consideration in this chapter has become possible only with these changes within Japanese parameters of defence policy and behaviour after the end of the Cold War.

The changes following those in the domain of UN PKO include the re-affirmation of the United States–Japan alliance in the 1990s, and eventually even more active Japanese participation in multinational coalition efforts to counter terrorism in Afghanistan and in Iraq in the aftermath of the 11 September 2001 terrorist attacks. Many observers have regarded the re-affirmation of the United

States–Japan alliance in the mid-1990s as a proactive move to counter the rise of China.[4] This, however, is a serious distortion of the central Japanese motive, which has had to do with a sense of crisis over the survivability of the alliance with the United States in the post-Cold War era unless postwar constraints on Japanese security policies could be addressed more directly.[5]

Moreover, this steady progress in Japanese security policies in a 'normal' direction has prepared the Japanese for facing traditional security issues squarely. This led to a rising awareness of traditional national defence among the Japanese public at large as well as opinion-makers and politicians. In this context, threat perceptions towards North Korea and China have had a significant role to play.

While awakening to traditional national defence is a natural phenomenon in itself, which should have happened in Japan a long time ago, it is important to recognize that traditional Japanese national defence cannot be fully accomplished without the US alliance, which still is, either consciously or unconsciously, a reasonably accepted assumption of Japanese policies. Also, quite contrary to the tenacious perception in China and South Korea, Japanese defence budgets have not increased during the last several years. In the constrictive budget system under the Koizumi administration, resource allocation and mission readjustment of the Ground Self-Defence Force, for instance, have progressed from the domain of traditional national defence to the area of multilateral security cooperation.

Equally important is that a new emphasis on traditional national defence does not mean that the significance of international security is to be diminished. Rather, it is the other way around. In the 'National Defense Program Guideline, FY 2005', approved by the Security Council and the Cabinet on 10 December 2004,[6] for instance, a premium is placed on more active Japanese promotion and participation in international security in the post-9/11 context than on traditional national defence. In essence, this signifies that Japan's postwar pacifism has been undergoing a transformation from 'one-country pacifism' to 'internationally relevant proactive pacifism'.

In sum, these apparent changes in Japanese security policies since the end of the Cold War, both in terms of international security and in regard to the United States–Japan alliance, have in fact consolidated the foundation of Japan's de facto middle power security policies. The United States–Japan alliance is the backbone of this, because refraining from adopting an independent strategy as a unilateralist great power is an important component of middle power diplomacy. Becoming a middle power has been made possible for Japan through it pursuing a revitalized alliance relationship with the United States in the post-Cold War timeframe. In other words, Japan's changes since the 1990s towards becoming a normal country are significant in transforming some of the 'abnormalities' apparent in postwar Japanese security policies, and its implications are significant regarding how and where Japan's actual strength is being exerted, that is, in the domain of middle power diplomacy.

Recent signs of change, which could be interpreted as indicating a more assertive Japan in the style of a traditional great power, are better categorized into two types. The first is a set of attempts to remedy exceedingly minimalist policies (often labelled as 'one-country pacifism'), which has opened up ways towards greater participation in UN PKO activities[7] as well as the re-affirmation of the United States–Japan alliance. As noted earlier, these changes, often seen as signs of Japan becoming a normal country, have in effect consolidated the foundations of Japan's security policies as a de facto middle power.

The second major change signalling Japan's 'return to normalcy' has been increasingly evident; postwar, sharp political divisions have been ameliorated. This has been particularly underscored by the demise of the so-called '1955 regime' (which caused the formation of the anti-Liberal Democratic Party coalition government under Prime Minister Morihiro Hosokawa in August 1993), and again with the collapse of the Japan Socialist Party (JSP) in the upper house elections in July 1995. These include the vocal protests by Japanese traditional nationalists against the postwar constitutional consensus, that is, the postwar state of Japanese defence and security policies. Occasional statements by various political actors against the Japanese postwar consensus, however, are by no means a true reflection of Japan's actual international role today and in the future, and therefore should not be exaggerated in the debate on Japan's changing security policies and attitudes.

The same applies to the debate about Article Nine of the Japanese postwar Constitution. Simply to say that the revision should be 'debated' used to sound hawkish. At present, however, various Japanese opinion-makers and politicians have begun to debate alternative revisions with respective future images of Japan and its role in the region and the world.[8] On balance, this is a sign of progress in the Japanese security debate.

Yet most countries, including Japan's Northeast Asian neighbours, view these changes warily. At the root of the scepticism is the persistent issue of history. In fact, some conservatives in Japan have begun making arguments, even if unconsciously, that appear to advocate a 'revolutionary' course of action that would contravene the postwar consensus and the peace formulated in San Francisco in 1951. Incidentally, newly elected Japanese Prime Minister, Shinzo Abe, is a primary advocate of such a thesis and has actually called for a departure from the postwar regime of Japan. I would stress, however, that this is nothing more than the venting of built-up frustrations and is not a part of an explicit strategy to turn back the clock.[9]

The irony here is that the Chinese and Korean obsession with, and vocal opposition against, the nationalist tone of these assertions only provides fuel for these conservative forces in Japanese domestic politics. To break the vicious cycle, one would have to look at the actual record of Japanese actions, and to appreciate their real potential for the stability of Northeast Asia. As implied at the outset, an examination of the role of the TSD should provide an important clue to this new approach to the security of Northeast Asia.

A brief overview of the strategic relationship between the United States and China is also in order and will be offered below. The highly strategic relationship between these two great powers is a major component against which the nature of middle power cooperation between Australia and Japan should be brought to light.

United States–China strategic coexistence

A common strategic reference point for Australia and Japan is the strategic relationship between the United States and China. The United States–China relationship is a typical but important case of strategic coexistence between great powers, which is in essence competitive, but will remain cooperative in the foreseeable future.[10]

The element of competition is embodied by the fact that their long-term strategies are divergent, with the United States fighting a long-term war against terrorism, wishing to create a more stable world for itself in terms of physical security and universal values, and China concentrating on its peaceful rise while occasionally showing signs of frustration with the US-centred global order. Precisely because their strategic preferences are firm, long-term and somewhat divergent, they cannot afford to engage in outright confrontation in the short term, thus accounting for the state of strategic coexistence.

Despite the fact that the Bush administration in principle conceptualizes China as a strategic competitor, it began efforts to create a relationship of strategic coexistence with China soon after its inauguration. The 9/11 incident created a new foundation for such a relationship. The same was true for China, as well. China, for instance, agreed to the UN Security Council resolution allowing the US-led multinational forces to engage in a war in Afghanistan, which became the first instance where China voted for the use of force by UN members against a sovereign state.[11]

Indeed, China had already stopped challenging US predominance in the late 1990s. This was basically the bottom-line of Chinese regional strategy since after the Taiwan crises in 1995 and 1996, when both Beijing and Washington sought to restore the relationship with mutual visits by Jiang Zemin and Bill Clinton in 1997 and 1998. In principle, Chinese regional and global strategy is founded upon its economy-centred orientation, making the most of its economic weight, both real and potential. As a consequence, the Chinese government has been keeping a low profile in recent years towards the US security presence in the region, including the Taiwan question and the United States–Japan alliance.

This gives rise to a favourable strategic environment in which Australia and Japan can initiate agendas somewhat autonomous from the strategic relationship between the United States and China. For Australia and Japan, the hedging function of the alliance with the United States – balancing its alliance affiliation against cultivating independent ties with Beijing – will remain important over the long term. In the short term, however, initiatives should not have to openly embrace hedging strategy. On the contrary, Australian and Japanese 'middle power agendas' vis-à-vis China should be promoted in such a way as to reduce both the probability and the cost of ultimate hedging.

In fact, the governments of Australia and Japan have sought to institutionalize security dialogues with China for some time, with a view to enhancing transparency of mutual security policies and intentions. This is particularly a middle power agenda, and there is no reason to limit these attempts to bilateral dealings. Naturally, the starting point for Australia and Japan is to engage in extensive dialogue about these China-related matters. Eventually, however, serious efforts should be made by Tokyo and Canberra jointly to inform China of the nature of this dialogue as a typical middle power cooperation independent of the United States–China strategic relationship.

New United States–Japan alliance and China

Precisely for the same purposes of engaging China, the role of the United States–Japan alliance should also be assigned a new context. Particularly, while the hedging function of the alliance should remain effective over the long run, Japan should make conscious efforts to advance functional security cooperation with China. While the discussion here is limited to the case of the United States–Japan alliance, the same should apply to Australia under the alliance with the United States, and eventually Australia and Japan should coordinate their mutual efforts within the TSD.

Under the present Bush administration, the role of alliances has undergone a significant transformation in line with its new global strategy. The Bush strategy basically defines US national interests as the core basis for global stability, with the assumption that promotion of US national interests would lead to a better world. The end of the Cold War, according to this outlook, has given the United States a unique opportunity to transform the world. The United States would carry out this mission by every available and effective means, including the unilateral use of its dominant military power. This conceptualization of global strategy has not fundamentally changed since Condoleezza Rice presented the argument in her seminal article (published in 2000 at the outset of the first George W. Bush campaign for the American presidency) in *Foreign Affairs*.[12] Allies are expected to go along with such a US global mission.

The initial attempt to conceptualize the United States–Japan alliance in these terms by key figures in the Washington policy community, many of whom later assumed important positions in the Bush foreign policy team, was the so-called 'Nye–Armitage Report'.[13] Although the reality fell far short of the American expectation, the message was explicit in calling for a United States–Japan alliance more closely modelled on the United States–UK relationship.

This conceptual clarity in the US strategy under the Bush administration is an important source of the currently strong condition of the United States–Japan alliance, often deemed the best since the end of World War II. Prime Minister Koizumi's performance with President Bush was quite effective under this new US definition of the alliance relationship. Koizumi in effect was a cheerleader for the Bush global strategy. This redefinition of the alliance for Bush global strategy, however, has changed the modality of the United States–Japan alliance, from a traditional tight alliance relationship to a more flexible coalition of the willing. Even though there would be no fundamental shift in the ultimate choice of the alliance relationship with the United States for Japan (as well as Australia), to the extent United States–Japan security relations move in the direction of a coalition of the willing, alliance management would become more political.

At the macro level, the Chinese 'new thinking' towards Japan may well be interpreted as a Chinese strategic response to this shifting nature of the alliance. China may indeed have given up, or postponed for the time being, its efforts to challenge the United States–Japan alliance. Instead, the new thinking towards Japan argues that China should not be preoccupied with historical and security problems with Japan, but should cultivate economic and political grounds for mutual cooperation.[14] In many of these arguments, the Chinese concern over US predominance, globally and regionally, constitutes the key background element.

In the end, therefore, just like the response to the United States–China strategic relationship, Australia and Japan need to develop a delicate balancing act between hedging against any long-term Chinese intention to drive a wedge between Australia, Japan and the United States, on the one hand, and accommodation to Chinese reconciliatory overtures in the short and medium term, on the other.

An interesting new reality is that, to the extent the alliance has become an explicit tool of US long-term global strategy, and United States–China strategic coexistence is likely to continue for some time to come, the function of the alliance as a China strategy has become implicit and less salient in the medium and short terms. This gives room for more active middle power initiatives for Australia and Japan to be generated within the TSD format.

Taiwan question

The Taiwan question has also increasingly been managed on the basis of United States–China strategic coexistence. Beijing has basically maintained a low-key posture against some of the initial provocative statements by President Bush regarding Taiwan, as well as sustained US arms sales to that island and a policy to allow stopovers in the United States by Taiwanese leaders, including Chen Sui-bien himself. In order not to exacerbate the Taiwan problem within the Sino-American relationship, however, the Bush administration also re-committed itself to the principle of 'one-China' and non-support of Taiwan 'independence'. This American position has been repeated on several occasions, including during bilateral China–United States summit meetings.[15]

In principle and over the long run, the Taiwan question will remain a wild card for United States–China relations. For now, however, the Chinese economy-centric strategy directed towards Taiwan appears to be working. Taiwan's economic dependence on China is ever deepening, which in turn gives confidence to Beijing advancing its 'united front' policy towards 'comrades' in Taiwan. The framework of United States–China strategic coexistence is clearly providing a favourable environment for the Chinese peace offensive directed towards Taipei.

This state of strategic coexistence between the United States and China provides a great opportunity for Japan and Australia to develop more flexible regional engagement strategies. After all, if Australia and Japan should currently face the ultimate situation of having to 'choose' between the United States and China (over the worst-case scenario of military confrontation over Taiwan, for instance), their choice to back Washington would, under the current circumstances, be obvious.

The natural intermediate goal for Australia and Japan, therefore, should be to reduce the probability and the risk of such an ultimate scenario, which could be pursued independent of the logic of the alliance with the United States in the military domain. This type of initiative would include cultivating independent channels and dialogues with both Beijing and Taipei, with a view to stabilizing the status quo across the Taiwan Strait. The difficulty associated with Australia and Japan adopting this fairly self-evident strategy however, is typically embodied in the misconception, dominant among the Chinese, that Japan, rather than the United States, has been leading a hardline strategy vis-à-vis China.

Actually, the truth is the other way around. In promoting United States–Japan security cooperation in the hard security area, US policy-makers, not to mention the so-called 'neo-conservatives' that have been so influential in the Bush administration, used to be frustrated with their Japanese counterparts over the latter's reluctance to talk about China and Taiwan in the strategic dialogue.

In recent years, there have been two important developments in the Japanese government's approaches towards the China and Taiwan problems. One is a reference to concerns about Chinese military modernization and operations in the new National Defense Program Guideline[16] adopted in December 2004, and the second is a reference to China and Taiwan in a joint statement issued after the 'two-plus-two' meeting of ministers in charge of foreign and defence affairs on 19 February 2005 in Washington.[17]

The former, the new National Defense Program Guideline, was widely reported as designating China as a 'threat'. After mentioning Russian military power in the Far East, unpredictability and uncertainty on the Korean peninsula and the Taiwan Strait, and North Korea as a major destabilizing factor, the relevant part on China states:

> China, which has a strong influence on the security in this region, has been modernizing its nuclear and missile capabilities as well as naval and air forces, and expanding its area of operations at sea. We have to remain attentive to its future course.[18]

The fact that an important Japanese government document has made an explicit reference to concerns about Chinese military tendencies is new, and thus is an important change. The substance of the statement itself, however, is not new at all, and the important and primary reference point of the Japanese response still remains the United States–Japan alliance rather than the development of Japan's own autonomous defence capability.

The same would apply to the 'two-plus-two' joint statement. There are three relevant points regarding China and Taiwan, which are stated under the heading of the 'common strategic objectives in the region'. Namely, Japan and the United States (1) welcome Chinese constructive roles in the region and the world, and wish to develop cooperative relations with China; (2) wish to encourage peaceful resolution of problems over the Taiwan Strait through dialogue; and (3) encourage China to increase transparency in the military domain.[19]

Again, the fact that they are openly stated in an official document is novel, but the substance of the statements is not news to anyone, including the Chinese. Moreover, according to my conversations with several Japanese officials involved in the process, it was the Japanese government that insisted on toning down the extent of implied criticism towards China, which was more explicit in the original US proposal.

The cliché arguments that Japanese approaches towards China are getting ever tougher and the relationship is on a collision course, therefore, are overstatements to say the least, and highly misleading. They contribute to unnecessary confusion over the already complex security situation involving the Taiwan issue.

In reality, it is not easy to make a clear distinction between long-term strategic constants which could antagonize China, on the one hand, and short- to medium-term opportunities to enhance cooperation, on the other. As has been previously asserted, however, unless the distinction is made explicitly, it would be extremely difficult for Australia and Japan to engage in a delicate balancing act between expanding cooperation with China by middle power initiatives and premising these initiatives on the ultimate choice of alliance with the United States.

North Korean problem

The state of United States–China strategic coexistence provides a general background for the evolution of the North Korean problem as well. First and foremost, the policy of the Bush administration continues to set the baseline. Initially, the Bush policy towards North Korea may well have frightened Pyongyang. In particular, denying the legitimacy of the North Korean leadership regime with missionary zeal – a process often instigated by Bush himself – must have convinced Pyongyang that the Bush administration was aiming at regime change. In fact, President Bush has often expressed his sympathy and the need to assist the people of North Korea. This aspect of the Bush policy towards North Korea, compounded by the rhetoric of the 'axis of evil',[20] would have naturally aroused a strong sense of crisis for the leadership in Pyongyang.

This perceived deep crisis for regime survival was a central factor motivating Kim Jong-il, the supreme leader of North Korea, to launch a surprising move to host Japanese Prime Minister Junichiro Koizumi in Pyongyang during September 2002. The determination on the part of Kim to seek a helping hand from Japan was unmistakable in Kim himself confessing and apologizing for the abduction of Japanese citizens.[21]

When the gamble to normalize diplomatic relations with Japan stalled, however, Kim Jong-il once again faced, or did not have any other choice but to face, the United States squarely and to employ unusually provocative measures, climbing up step by step the ladder of nuclear escalation. Against these escalation tactics of Pyongyang, the Bush administration, pushed by ever mounting domestic pressures from the Congress, seriously considered the option of going to the United Nations for sanctions in early 2003. Perhaps this move alarmed China, which would account for the timing of the Chinese diplomatic shift from advocating bilateral talks between Washington and Pyongyang to taking the initiative to convince Pyongyang it must participate in multilateral talks.

As is often the case with its diplomacy, China initially moved very cautiously, but engineered de facto three-party talks in Beijing on 23 April 2003. At the time, China refused to label this process 'three-party talks', due to the felt necessity of dealing with Pyongyang with care, as well as because of its own previous insistence on bilateral dealings between Pyongyang and Washington. But the Chinese shift in diplomacy was obvious. China then upgraded its efforts to persuade Pyongyang, and hosted the first Six Party Talks in August 2003, followed by the second round of talks in February 2004.

Differences between Washington and Pyongyang, however, remained deep, and the third round of Six Party Talks held in June 2004 did not bear much fruit. In the meantime, the impasse between the United States and North Korea simply widened, giving rise to a serious sense of crisis among the participating countries, including North Korea and the United States, about the utility and the survivability of the Six Party Talks framework.

The major policy dilemma here is that, while a compromise between North Korea and the United States has remained elusive, there is no other realistic alternative for all the parties concerned to the ongoing Six Party Talks. Against this backdrop and in light of the negotiation breakthrough achieved in mid-February 2007, it appears that it has become almost an end in itself for all the parties not to terminate the talks.

When the six parties met in Beijing for the fourth round of talks, from 26 July to 7 August and from 13 to 19 September 2005, they could not afford to break up without some form of agreement for keeping the Six Party Talks' momentum alive. Key agreed items in the joint statement, the first of the kind in the Six Party Talks, included the following:[22]

> The DPRK committed to abandoning all nuclear weapons and existing nuclear programs and returning, at an early date, to the Treaty on the Non-Proliferation of Nuclear Weapons and to IAEA safeguards.
>
> The United States affirmed that it has no nuclear weapons on the Korean Peninsula and has no intention to attack or invade the DPRK with nuclear or conventional weapons.
>
> . . .
>
> The DPRK stated that it has the right to peaceful uses of nuclear energy. The other parties expressed their respect and agreed to discuss, at an appropriate time, the subject of the provision of light water reactor to the DPRK.

The basic disagreement between the United States and North Korea, however, will still be hard to overcome: the United States asserts that North Korea should abandon nuclear weapons and programmes before the provision of a light water nuclear reactor can be discussed, while North Korea insists that both negotiations should proceed side by side. Washington in fact upgraded its hardline stance when the deals in the fourth Six Party Talks were being negotiated, by freezing North

Korean bank accounts in Macao in September. Pyongyang responded by refusing to return to the Six Party Talks, citing the lifting of financial sanctions a pre-condition.

In early July 2006, in the absence of serious responses from the Bush adminis-tration to North Korean grievances, Pyongyang escalated its brinkmanship tactics against Washington by launching seven missiles, including a Taepodong, into the Sea of Japan. The reaction by the Japanese government was exceptionally quick and assertive, initiating a UN Security Council resolution denouncing the North Korean action and calling for North Korea's return to the Six Party Talks. It also hastened to prepare and implement its own sanctions against North Korea under the strong leadership of the cabinet secretary Shinzo Abe, who succeeded Koizumi as prime minister in September 2006. The situation became even more acute following the detonation of a nuclear device by North Korea in October 2006.

But following international condemnation to the North Korean nuclear test, including a strong reaction from China, Pyongyang returned to the Six Party Talks in December 2006. An advertised 'breakthrough' was announced in February 2007 whereby North Korea promised to dismantle its nuclear weapons production capability in return for the United States offer extensive economic and significant diplomatic incentives. The North Korean nuclear problem, however, has followed a cyclical pattern in past years between hope and despair. Given that no party can afford to risk a war on the Korean peninsula, while there is a consensus that a nuclear North Korea is not acceptable the cycle is likely to continue for some time to come.

As in other issues in Northeast Asia, strategic coexistence between China and the United States is at the core of these cyclical patterns. It appears the United States has decided to assign a leadership role to China in the Six Party Talks for the time being, and will deal with North Korea without discrediting that framework. True, the Bush administration does not have much trust in the multilateral framework as an effective means of settling the North Korean nuclear problem. It does not, however, have any viable alternative.

At least in theory, this situation provides much room to manoeuvre for Australia and Japan on their own initiative. Any measures to build upon the recent Six Party Talks breakthrough should be welcome for China, and equally for South Korea. Even North Korea would welcome them, if only for survival purposes, just as it once responded to the scenario of diplomatic normalization with Japan very positively. Perhaps, the issue of Japan–North Korea diplomatic normalization is a critical one to be re-examined at the TSD, rather than leaving it simply as a matter for Japan to resolve. After all, Japan–North Korea diplomatic normalization has the potential to change the entire regional context of the North Korean problem, and is therefore a significant issue for all the countries concerned.

Conclusion: the South Korean factor

In the overall context discussed above, the relationship between Japan and South Korea has the potential to cause what might be viewed as a paradigm change in Northeast Asian politics. To put it concisely, the basis of Japan–South Korea relations is rooted in the geopolitical reality that Japan and Korea are surrounded by the three unilateralist powers, that is, the United States, China and Russia.

The conventional wisdom of the Korean peninsula being surrounded by the four great powers including Japan does not provide a realistic perspective to the understanding of the security policy of postwar Japan in Northeast Asia, and has even been an important source of confusion in the evolution of a regional order. This, for instance, is a breeding ground for the myth of Japan–China geopolitical rivalry. The South Korean self-appointed role as a balancer between Japan and China also appears to be a product of this 'conventional wisdom'.

Rather, this particular geopolitical perspective is a reminder that an equal partnership between Japan and South Korea is not a mere political symbol but can be a substantive foundation for the two countries' bilateral relationship. It is against the backdrop of this geopolitical reality that democracy in Japan and South Korea, and civil society exchanges between the two peoples, have impacted the bilateral relationship in a fundamental way.

It certainly takes political leadership to fill the emotional gap between the two nations emanating from history and territorial issues. Currently, the leadership in both countries is playing an entirely different role, aggravating the gap rather than easing it. The emotional vicious cycle, however, is clearly based on entirely misplaced assumptions about each other. For instance, the Korean accusation of Japan's 're-militarization' and 'aggressive' diplomacy towards Takeshima (Dok-to) is clearly a misconception of the nature of the changes occurring in Japan, as explained at the outset. Likewise, a dominant Japanese perception that South Korean leaders often use the history card for domestic political purposes is too simplistic. Exactly the same vicious cycle exists between Japan and China, occasionally providing an incentive for South Korea and China to join together in fighting against a misconceived Japan problem.

If it were not for the prejudice creating these emotional gaps, South Korea and Japan, like Australia and Japan, would be natural partners who could cooperate on an equal basis for the stability and prosperity of the region and the world. The merits of Australia–Japan cooperation as middle powers could actually be doubled if South Korea became involved in their initiatives and shaped a 'strategic triangle' that could effectively supplement that between Australia, Japan and the United States. By the same token, if the existing TSD can propose new ideas to stabilize the process of the historic transformation of Northeast Asian security landscapes, based on this conceptual foundation of Australia–Japan cooperation explicitly, its role may eventually become acceptable to China's long-term strategy of peaceful rise without contradicting the ultimate hedging function of the alliances with the United States.

Notes

All websites accessed 28 September 2006.

1 See, for example, the observation of Andrew Shearer, a Minister at the Australian Embassy in Washington, DC at an American Enterprise Institute (AEI) forum convened in April 2005 that 'The least developed leg of this kind of strategic triangle that I have set

out is the Australia–Japan defense relationship and there are various reasons for that'. A transcript of these remarks is available at: www.aei.org/events/filter.,eventID.1045/transcript.asp

2 Yoshihide Soeya (2005), *Nihon-no Middle Power Gaiko* [Japan's Middle Power Diplomacy], Tokyo: Chikuma-shobo.

3 Yoshihide Soeya (2005), 'Japanese security policy in transition: the rise of international and human security', *Asia-Pacific Review*, vol. 12, no. 1, pp. 103–16.

4 This may have been an important consideration on the part of Washington, with which Tokyo has gradually come to agree in later years. See Thomas Christensen (2006), 'Fostering stability or creating a monster? The rise of China and US policy toward East Asia', *International Security*, vol. 31, no. 1, pp. 81–126. While generally favouring US engagement towards China, Christensen's preferred 'moderate mixed strategy' model also recognizes the tightening of the United States–Japan alliance as part of a zero-sum process of geopolitics. 'A healthy degree of Japanese wariness about the rise of China may indeed be good for the United States, especially as Washington hopes to encourage Tokyo to adopt a more active regional and global role in the alliance', p. 125.

5 Yoshihide Soeya (2002), 'The China factor in the US–Japan alliance: the myth of a China threat', *Journal of East Asian Studies*, vol. 2, no. 2, pp. 37–66.

6 Available at: www.kantei.go.jp/foreign/policy/2004/1210taikou_e.html

7 L. Williams Heinrich, Akiho Shibata and Yoshihide Soeya (1999), *United Nations Peace-Keeping Operations: A Guide to Japanese Policies*, Tokyo: United Nations University Press.

8 The trigger was the proposed revision by the *Yomiuri Shinbun* announced in November 1994, while most recently the Institute for International Policy Studies, where former Prime Minister Yasuhiro Nakasone serves as chairman, issued its revision proposal in January 2005. The former stressed the importance of self-defence and participation in UN PKO, while the latter placed more emphasis on the right of collective self-defence.

9 Yoshihide Soeya (2006), 'The misconstrued shift in Japan's foreign policy', *Japan Echo*, vol. 33, no. 3, pp. 16–19.

10 See Christensen (2006), 'Fostering stability or creating a monster'.

11 David Shambaugh (2002), 'Sino-American relations since September 11: can the new stability last?', *Current History*, September, pp. 243–44.

12 Condoleezza Rice (2000), 'Promoting the national interest', *Foreign Affairs*, vol. 79, no. 1, pp. 45–63.

13 Institute for National Strategic Studies (2000), *The United States and Japan: Toward a Mature Partnership*, Washington, DC: National Defense University, October, available at: www.ndu.edu/inss/strforum/SR_01/SR_Japan.htm

14 For instance, Ma Licheng, a *People's Daily* senior commentator, published an article to this effect in an influential journal, *Strategy and Management*, in December 2002, right after the 16th CCP Congress.

15 For instance, 'President Bush, Chinese President Jiang Zemin discuss Iraq, N. Korea', October 2002, available at: www.whitehouse.gov/news/releases/2002/10/20021025.html

16 'National Defense Program Guideline, FY 2005-', 10 December 2004, available at: www.kantei.go.jp/foreign/policy/2004/1210taikou_e.html

17 Available, in Japanese, at: www.mofa.go.jp/mofaj/area/usa/hosho/2+2_05_02.html

18 Available at: www.kantei.go.jp/foreign/policy/2004/1210taikou_e.html

19 Available, in Japanese, at: www.mofa.go.jp/mofaj/area/usa/hosho/2+2_05_02.html

20 'The President's State of the Union Address', 29 January 2002, available at: www.whitehouse.gov/news/releases/2002/01/20020129-11.html

21 Yoshihide Soeya (2003), 'Japanese diplomacy and the North Korean problem', *Japan Review of International Affairs*, vol. 17, no. 1, pp. 53–61.

22 'Joint Statement of the Fourth Round of the Six-Party Talks', 19 September 2005, available at: www.mofa.go.jp/region/asia-paci/n_korea/6party/joint0509.html

8 Trilateralism and Australia

Australia and the Trilateral Strategic Dialogue with America and Japan

Hugh White

At first glance, it seemed an impressive diplomatic coup. The foreign ministers of the world's two richest countries, one Australia's major ally, the other its biggest trade partner, travelled all the way to Sydney just to discuss regional and global strategic developments with Australia's foreign minister. This is the stuff that the dreams of middle powers are made of: to be sought out to join the conclaves of the powerful, and help shape their policies on great issues. The smaller and more elevated the group, the greater the honour, and for Australia there could be no more select gathering than this.

And yet things were not as rosy as they seemed. Like one of those uneasy dreams in which a perfect setting seems subtly but pervasively awry, the 2006 Trilateral Strategic Dialogue (TSD) was an ambiguous event which demonstrated the tensions and difficulties of Australia's diplomatic position more than its strengths. Nor was it especially satisfactory for Mr Downer's great and powerful guests. Their presence in Sydney together reflected, more than anything else, their countries' concerns about China's growing influence, and their hopes that Australia could be brought to share those concerns more strongly and more vocally. In this they were disappointed, and their failure only went to show how serious a problem they both have with China: if a country as close and dependent on each of them as Australia is not prepared to join them in taking a frostier approach to China, what hope do they have of building support among others in Asia? It says much for the complexity of Australia's place in the strategic dynamics of Asia today that the Howard government, with its strong record of support for the United States and a reputation among some for being too compliant to Washington, should find itself standing up to pressure from its two most powerful friends on the key issue that brought the three countries together in March 2006.

This chapter, exploring an Australian perspective on the TSD, seeks to locate this unusual and significant event in the evolution of Australia's post-Cold War strategic diplomacy in Asia, and to assess its importance for Australia's future relations with Asia's great powers. Its approach is to look behind the public words of national leaders and spokesmen and try to discern the deeper evolving patterns of interest and alignment that have shaped the attitudes of the three parties to the TSD and brought them to the Sydney meeting. In doing so it reaches a somewhat sceptical view of the TSD as an instrument of trilateral diplomacy. It suggests that there is little to bring the three partners together in this kind of forum except to discuss how best to respond to the rise of China. On this issue, Japan's and America's interests and policies may be converging, but Australia's are heading in a different direction, and so far the TSD has done nothing to bring Australia into line with its interlocutors. It argues that from America's and Japan's point of view the first meeting must therefore be considered a failure, and from Australia's an uneasy and uncomfortable experience. It concludes that the TSD is unlikely to become a durable and substantive new forum for regional diplomacy, unless all three countries choose to use it creatively and substantively to address the genuine and important strategic issues that arise from the need to adapt regional power structures to the rise of China. None of the three partners so far show signs of wanting to do that; until they do, the TSD will be at best an awkward and embarrassing lost opportunity, and perhaps no more than a historical curiosity.

An old idea

Australia has long displayed the enthusiasm for multipolar diplomacy characteristic of middle powers, including in its approach to promoting its strategic interests in Asia. Before World War II, Joseph Lyons proposed a regional security pact covering Asia and the Pacific, and after the war Percy Spender wanted to create a regional multilateral alliance in Asia – an Asian NATO – until he was compelled to settle for the more modest trilateral arrangement enshrined in the ANZUS treaty.[1] But the idea did not die, and it has resurfaced again, in different but still recognizable forms, ever since. It is worth asking why the original idea was not taken up, and why subsequent proposals have not prospered. The short answer is that, with the unhappy exception of the Southeast Asia Treaty Organization (SEATO), the United States has never, at least until now, favoured a multilateral alliance structure over the 'hub and spokes' structure of bilateral alliances it has built and maintained under the San Francisco System. There are many possible explanations for that, but the most compelling is that the United States simply did not need a multilateral alliance structure in Asia to achieve its strategic objectives, compared to Europe where it did. America built a multilateral alliance in Europe, not for political but for operational reasons. Politically, a series of bilateral alliances between the United States and its West European allies would have been sufficient to provide the confidence they needed to stand up to Soviet intimidation. But operationally, the defence of Europe from a Soviet attack could hardly be managed through a series of bilateral treaties and relationships. To contain the Soviet Union in Europe, the United States had to prepare to fight and win at short notice a continental campaign that would have to be waged simultaneously across the territories of a large number of West European allies, and would have to rely on their forces for victory. To organize this immensely complex operation required mutual sharing of plans, information and resources among all the allies, full operational freedom of movement through one another's territory, and firm commitments, long in advance, about their military operations in war. All this could not have been achieved nearly so effectively through a hub and spokes structure of bilateral alliances. In Asia, the situation was completely different. American strategy in the western Pacific was basically maritime, and it relied much more on American forces than on allies. For that it needed bases on its allies' territory, but not much more. The complexities and intimacies of continental coalition warfare were absent, so a multilateral structure was unnecessary. That being so, the United States naturally opted for the much simpler hub and spokes model that has lasted until now.

For their own reasons, America's allies were fairly happy to go along. Japan's restrictive postwar attitudes to strategic affairs made multilateral cooperation politically difficult, as did, at first, Australian attitudes towards Japan after the war. But in the late 1960s, as US commitments in Asia seemed to be sapped by Vietnam, interest in multilateral structures revived. Australia scholars like Hedley Bull and Coral Bell started to explore the implications for Australia of a more multipolar strategic structure in Asia,[2] and proposals were floated for new security arrangements including closer strategic cooperation between Australia and Japan, and trilateral security cooperation between them and the United States.[3] In the event, these predictions of a more multipolar Asia turned out to be a little premature, and by the mid-1970s Asia had settled into the stable strategic structure that it would retain until the end of the Cold War. The United States returned to direct containment of the Soviet Union, supported in different ways by Australia, Japan, ASEAN states and China; with SEATO's final interment, this loose network of bilateral relationships and alliances served it well for this purpose. For Australia in this period the strategic affairs of Northeast Asia receded from the forefront of its strategic concerns to a degree unmatched at any time before or since: the 1976 White Paper going so far as to say that:

> No more than the former great powers of Europe can we expect these powers [India, China and Japan] individually to play a large military role in strategic developments directly affecting Australia's security in the foreseeable future.[4]

A new beginning

Australia remained largely disengaged from the strategic affairs of the wider Asia-Pacific until the end of the Cold War, when it quickly became apparent that a new strategic era was opening in Northeast Asia with uncertain implications for Australia's future security. America's future role in Asia was unclear, Japan had an opportunity to redefine its strategic posture, and China's economic growth constituted a major new factor in regional strategic affairs. The 1994 Defence White Paper saw the future this way:

> the strategic affairs of the region will be increasingly determined by the countries of Asia themselves ... Much will depend on the policies of the major Asian powers themselves – Japan, China and India – and on their relationships with one another and with other countries in the region.[5]

While noting some hopeful signs, the paper identified a number of trends that 'could produce an unstable and potentially dangerous strategic situation in Asia and the Pacific over the next fifteen years'.[6] It was against this background that Canberra started to pay new attention to its strategic relationships in Northeast Asia. With Japan especially, concerted efforts were made to add a stronger political and strategic dimension to a relationship that had remained, from both sides, narrowly focused on trade. The first visit to Australia by a Japanese defence minister took place in 1990, and a program of official and semi-official dialogues and exchanges on regional strategic affairs developed. These exchanges soon highlighted a close alignment of interests between the two countries in the evolution of Asia's strategic system. They were accompanied by growing practical cooperation on security-related diplomatic initiatives including the establishment of Asia Pacific Economic Cooperation (APEC) and the ASEAN Regional Forum (ARF), and the Cambodian peace process. Australia played a modest but useful role in encouraging Japan to send troops to help with peacekeeping in Cambodia – their first postwar deployment. Australia became, over the 1990s, the country in the western Pacific that consistently expressed strongest support for Japan to play a more active role in regional security and did most to encourage it to become more involved in peacekeeping operations.

One of the major motives for Australia's energetic security diplomacy with Japan in the 1990s was a growing recognition of the importance of the United States– Japan alliance to the stability of post-Cold War Asia, and hence to Australia's security. America's strategic commitment to Japan prevented what might otherwise become overt and destabilizing strategic competition between Japan and China. This came to be seen as the most important contribution that the United States made to Australia's security, and Australia's alliance with the United States came to be seen increasingly as a way Australia could support continuing US engagement in the western Pacific.[7] Canberra recognized the stresses in the United States– Japan relationship in the mid-1990s, and understood that a more active Japanese strategic posture would help consolidate Washington's commitment to their Japanese ally. Canberra therefore vocally supported measures such as the 'Revised Defense Guidelines' introduced in the mid-1990s to enhance Japan's capacity to support the United States in Asia. The result was that by the late 1990s Australia had already developed a robust strategic dialogue with Japan, including a strong interest in the trajectory of the United States–Japan relationship. Two limits should be mentioned, however. First, Australian officials remained a little frustrated that the strategic relationship with Japan could not develop faster and further. Political sensitivity to activities outside Japan's self-imposed limits, bureaucratic inertia, and a certain lack of interest in the strategic perceptions of other countries all contributed to a certain sluggishness from the Japanese side. Second, US officials showed little interest in the development of the Australia–Japan security relationship: true to Washington's bilateralist traditions, they saw dialogue between the spokes as harmless but insignificant.

At the same time, Australia's relationship with China was growing strongly too, especially in the late 1990s. This was driven, of course, by fast-growing trade relations, but it had a political and even strategic dimension. In the early 1990s bilateral strategic dialogues with China at the semi-official and official levels had developed in parallel, though slightly behind, the dialogues with Japan. Then in March 1996, within a few weeks of the Howard government taking office, China and the United States came to a stand-off over Chinese attempts to influence Taiwan's presidential election by firing missile 'tests' towards the island. The Howard government, reflecting an instinct to support the United States as fully as possible, strongly supported Washington's decision to deploy aircraft carriers to the waters around Taiwan, going further even than Tokyo in doing so. China reacted sharply to that, and to other signs that under Howard Australia was drawing closer to the United States at China's expense: ministerial-level contacts were frozen for much of 1996, and only lifted after Howard met Jiang Zemin at the APEC Summit late in the year. Howard learned his lesson, and since then has been careful to steer a careful course on any issues on which China might be sensitive. He has been handsomely rewarded, as Australia's exports to China have grown strongly. By the late 1990s, the scope for tension between the high priority that Australia gave to its increasingly warm relationship with China and its close relationship with the United States was becoming evident. Around this time concerns became more explicit that China's phenomenal growth might shift the strategic balance in Asia to America's disadvantage. In 1999, Richard Armitage informed an unofficial meeting of influential Australians and Americans that the United States would expect Australian military support if conflict with China occurred over Taiwan, and some Australians informed him in return that Australian support should not be taken for granted.

   This then was the environment in which the idea of a trilateral strategic dialogue between the United States, Japan and Australia began to emerge.

Thinking trilaterally

As bilateral strategic dialogue between Tokyo and Canberra developed over the 1990s, and the convergence of Australian and Japanese strategic interests in Asia became clearer, the idea of a trilateral exchange of strategic ideas with the United States almost inevitably emerged in Australia.[8] By the mid-1990s the issue had obtained a foothold of sorts in Australia's strategic policy agenda. In part this was driven by the simple fact that their US alliances were central to the strategic policy of each country, and meeting trilaterally seemed to Australians a natural way to push the bilateral relationship with Japan a little further. In part it was driven by a desire to help support the United States in pressing Japan on the bilateral agenda between them. Some saw scope for Australia to contribute to Japan's missile defence plans. Thought was given to providing Japan with missile early-warning data collected by the Australian ground stations from US satellites. Others saw scope for Japan and Australia to combine their influence on US policy by speaking to Washington together on issues that mattered. For example, in the late 1990s there was a sense in Canberra that both Australia and Japan agreed that the United States might need to be more artful in its response to the rise of China, and that this might be a useful issue for the two countries to discuss jointly with the United

States. However the idea of trilateral discussion met with little enthusiasm from either the United States or Japan: both apparently felt that Australian intrusion into sensitive and complex issues like missile-defence cooperation would only complicate things further, and that in the end there was little of real weight to discuss trilaterally which could not be better and more frankly discussed bilaterally. And both worried about how China might react.

However, at the same time some new ideas were stirring in Washington. In the late 1990s some American policy thinkers turned their minds to ways that America's strategic position in Asia could be strengthened in the new century. The most active were Republicans, then out of office and exploring policy options for a possible Republican administration after 2000. They started to consider whether America should erect a new regional multilateral security architecture, based on and linking its existing set of bilateral relationships, and eventually spreading to draw in a wider group of hitherto non-aligned but pro-US countries, for example in Southeast Asia. The idea was floated, for example, by Robert Blackwill, later a senior Bush administration official, in a book jointly edited with Paul Dibb.[9] Blackwill's idea was for an Asian NATO. The same idea was promoted by members of a group called the 'Project for a New American Century', which was formed in the late 1990s to promote what we would now call a neo-conservative strategic policy agenda.[10] Naturally, as America's two closest allies in Asia, Japan and Australia would be the key foundations of any multilateral alliance architecture.

The key purpose to be served by a strengthened US-led multilateral security structure in Asia was to respond to the growing power of China. On this point, US and Australian views tended to diverge. Paul Dibb, in his contribution to the volume jointly edited with Blackwill, sharply criticized the idea of building an Asian NATO to contain China,[11] and in this he was clearly supported by the majority of Australian policy-makers. The Howard government was by then strongly committed to its policy of building strong trade relations with China, and was keen to avoid any moves that might revive Chinese concerns about 'encirclement' by US allies that had caused such problems for Canberra in 1996. The divergence in strategic perceptions between the United States and Australia over China was therefore becoming more obvious, especially because, as it happened, the initial discussions to plan the Dibb–Blackwill volume were held in Sydney on the margins of the meeting at which Armitage issued his warning to Australia about US expectations over Taiwan, and received such a cautious response.

So by the time President Bush was elected in 2000, bringing with him into office many of those who had been engaged in these debates from the American side, Washington had become more interested in multilateral networking between the US alliances in Asia, and Canberra had become more cautious. Washington, becoming more wary of China's growing power and influence, wanted to build structures that would consolidate America's influence and counteract China's. Canberra, becoming more wary of offending China, wanted to avoid anything that might look to Beijing like containment. All of this made the issue a rather complex and delicate one between the two governments.

Accidental diplomacy

All that complexity and delicacy was fully on display when the issue came up at the joint press conference following the AUSMIN talks of July 2001 – the first round of these annual talks held with the new Bush administration – at which the Trilateral Strategic Dialogue process was initially launched.[12] The proposal was aired in a strange and awkward way that carries a distinct whiff of accidental diplomacy. The suggestion that the three countries might meet to discuss strategic affairs was not announced as an outcome of the meeting. It grew out of comments by Secretary of State Colin Powell in reply to a broader question from a journalist who was evidently aware of the divergent views on proposals for an 'Asian NATO'. Significantly, the question came at the end of a lengthy press conference in which US policy on China, and especially whether China was seen as a threat, had been the dominant subject. Powell in his reply did not mention a Japan–Australia–United States meeting specifically, but he did say that ideas for a forum between US allies in Asia had been discussed earlier in the day. Downer then spoke:

> ... so as not to allow a hare to rush away here, we obviously – I think it must be obvious – wouldn't want sort of new architecture in East Asia which would be an attempt to kind of replicate NATO or something like that. We are talking here just about an informal dialogue, and the question of whether we could do it at a more numerous level than two – that is, we obviously have a dialogue with the Japanese; the Japanese with the United States, the United States with us – would there be a formulation where we, the United States and Japanese, for example, might be able to sit down together, not necessarily, by the way, at ministerial level, but perhaps at a lower level, to engage in some sort of dialogue. That is something that we've been talking about.[13]

Downer's words here are telling. So as not to alarm China, he was evidently anxious to avoid the impression that anything like the 'Asian NATO' idea was under discussion, and instead redirected attention towards the trilateral dialogue concept that Australia had earlier favoured. However, it is clear that this is not something he had intended to raise, let alone announce. The idea would not have been aired at all had Powell not responded as he did to the question, and anecdotal evidence at the time suggested that the issue had not in fact been discussed at the AUSMIN meeting; Powell's comment that it had been discussed earlier may have referred to US briefing sessions before the meeting proper. In short, the whole initiative seems to have been inadvertent. Once the idea had been aired, however, it suited all sides to make it happen. In line with Downer's post-AUSMIN ad-lib, it was established at senior official's level, and such talks took place several times between 2002 and 2004. The personalities involved – especially Rich Armitage as US Deputy Secretary of State and Ashton Calvert as Australian Secretary of Foreign Affairs – would have ensured that the discussions were substantive, and no doubt created a useful opportunity to exchange views. However, there is no evidence that the talks significantly affected the policies of any of the three countries, nor that they changed significantly the level or nature of strategic interaction between them. In short, the Trilateral Strategic Dialogue quickly became simply a routine fixture in the annual diplomatic schedules of the three countries.

The trilaterals go ministerial

Then, in early 2005, the new US Secretary of State, Condoleezza Rice, announced at a press conference with Mr Downer in Washington that the Trilateral Security Dialogue would be elevated to ministerial level.[14] There was nothing accidental about this step. The circumstances of the announcement strongly suggested that this was a US initiative, and this was supported by anecdotal evidence at the time. The question, of course, was why? Some explanations have focused on personalities, especially the replacement of Rich Armitage as Deputy Secretary of State by Robert Zoellick,[15] and this is no doubt part of the story. But there is important evidence of deeper imperatives driven by perceptions in Washington and Tokyo of a drift in Australia's policies towards China that both countries found worrying. Concerns in Washington about China's growing power had been a major element of the Bush administration's strategic policy when it took office, but became muted after 11 September 2001. However, by 2003 they were starting to revive, as signs accumulated that Chinese power and influence were growing faster than Washington had perhaps appreciated. At the same time, Japan's concerns about China were also growing, as the tone of that bilateral relationship deteriorated. Superficially this chill was caused by issues like Prime Minister Koizumi's visits to the Yasakuni shrine, but the more significant reasons related to the deepening sense of strategic competition between Beijing and Tokyo as China's power and influence in Asia grew. The result was a clear convergence of strategic perceptions between the United States and Japan on this key issue, which probably did more than anything else to create the impression of a closer strategic relationship between them over this period.

Both of them therefore had cause to worry about mounting evidence that Australia was moving in the opposite direction. The first wake-up call that, notwithstanding close support for the United States in the war on terror, Australia was taking its own course in relation to China came in October 2003. That month, as both returned home from the APEC summit, George Bush and Hu Jintao visited Canberra on consecutive days, and were accorded scrupulously equal treatment, including an invitation to Hu to address the Australian Parliament, an honour previously extended only to US presidents. United States observers were quietly disconcerted by this display of symbolic parity in Australia's treatment of the two relationships. Then in August 2004 Alexander Downer, visiting Beijing, answered a media question by saying that Australia did not consider itself bound to support the United States in any conflict with China over Taiwan. In February 2005, Australia pointedly declined to join the United States and Japan in pressing the European Union not to lift limits on arms sales to China. This worried not only the United States, but Japan: senior Japanese figures expressed their disappointment at Australia's approach quite plainly at a bilateral leadership dialogue meeting held in Melbourne at that time.

Against this background, the most natural and compelling reason for Washington and Tokyo to have agreed to send their foreign ministers all the way to Sydney to talk to their Australian counterpart was to air their shared concerns about Australia's growing accommodation with China, and from the comments that both Dr Rice and Mr Aso made before arriving in Sydney, it seemed that this was indeed uppermost in their minds. Dr Rice, for example, speaking about the purposes of the Trilateral Strategic Dialogue before leaving for Sydney, said:

> This is a region that's in tremendous flux and change and on a number of different perspectives. It's in flux and change, first and foremost, because of a rising China. And I think all of us in the region, particularly those who are long-standing allies, have a joint responsibility and obligation to try and produce conditions in which the rise of China will be a positive force in international politics, not a negative force.[16]

And so it turned out. At the press conference after the meeting – interestingly, not a joint press conference with either of his two guests – Mr Downer cited a long list of issues discussed, but it was clear that China was the big issue. However, there is no evidence that the United States and Japan succeeded in pressing Australia to take a tougher line on China. Important differences of view between the ministers glinted through Mr Downer's reply to the first question he received: 'Look, I think we all pretty much agree, even if we use different language, that we want to have a constructive relationship with China.'[17] And all the Joint Statement issued after the meeting had to say on the subject was 'We welcomed China's constructive engage-ment in the region.'[18] As an exercise in tactical diplomacy Downer's performance at the time of the TSD meeting was quite impressive; he avoided any blatant display of divergence between Australia and its two most powerful friends. But the substantive difference remains, and remains to be addressed.

A useful future?

For those who worry that Australia is often too compliant to the wishes of larger powers, the sight of Alexander Downer defying pressure from the United States and Japan on this vital issue might seems rather heartening. But the growing gap between Canberra's views of China and those of Tokyo and Washington poses a major foreign policy problem that has yet to be fully acknowledged, let alone substantively addressed. John Howard has tended to sweep the issue aside by arguing, rather optimistically, that escalating strategic competition between the United States and China is 'not inevitable',[19] but in reality it is already occurring, and it raises fundamental questions about the way Asia's strategic system will adapt to the tectonic changes in the distribution of power that the rise of China, and India, represent. That in turn raises fundamental questions about Australia's interests in the future alignment of strategic power and influence in Asia. In essence,

Australia seems already to have accepted that China should be accorded some kind of leadership role in Asia as its power grows, while the United States and Japan have not. For America, conceding a larger role in Asia would mean accepting a dilution of its own influence in favour of a power that represents different values and poses a long-term threat as a future peer competitor. For Japan, China's rise threatens to squeeze Japan's already cramped scope for regional leadership, and poses the threat of subordination to China over the long term. Australia apparently shares neither of these concerns. This magnitude of differences, especially with the United States, is unprecedented in the history of Australia's foreign policy. They constitute the deepest divergence of view on core strategic interests between the United States and Australia since the alliance was established in World War II.[20]

There is no evidence that the discussion of China among the three ministers in Sydney in March 2006 touched on these deep questions. Instead, we may surmise that they focused on how best to finesse the differences that had emerged between their public positions in the days leading up to the meeting. Unless the TSD can do better in future, and evolve to address these really major issues, there is no reason to expect that it will have a very useful, or a very long, future as a diplomatic forum at ministerial level. There is no evidence that important conclusions or decisions were reached on any of the other issues cited by Mr Downer as being discussed at the March 2006 meeting,[21] and no reason to expect that there would be. There is nothing inherent in the composition of the TSD that makes it a promising forum for addressing wider regional or global security issues, because the three parties have few if any interests or concerns in common that they do not share with many others as well. If so, Australia faces a choice: either let the TSD die, or take its courage in both hands and use the TSD to open real discussions with its most important friends in Asia about how best to respond to the most important strategic development of our time – the rise of China. On that issue, a more multilateral and inclusive approach is almost certainly the way forward, but persuading Tokyo and Washington – and Beijing – of that would place demands on Australian diplomacy of a quite unprecedented order.

Notes

1 J. G. Starke (1965), *The ANZUS Treaty Alliance*, Melbourne: Melbourne University Press, chapter 1.

2 Hedley Bull (1974), 'Australia and the great powers in Asia', *Australia in World Affairs – 1966–1970*, Melbourne: AIIA/Cheshire, pp. 225–350; Coral Bell (1968), *A New Balance of Power in Asia*, Adelphi Paper 44, London: IISS.

3 Makoto Momoi (1970), 'Australia and Japan', in H. G. Gelber (ed.), *Problems in Australian Defence*, Melbourne: Oxford University Press, pp. 53–61.

4 Commonwealth of Australia (1976), *Australian Defence*, Canberra: Australian Government Publishing Service, p. 5.

5 Commonwealth of Australia (1994), *Defending Australia*, Canberra: Department of Defence, p. 8, para. 2.7.

6 Ibid., p. 8, para. 2.8.

7 Commonwealth of Australia (1997), *Australia's Strategic Policy*, Canberra: Department of Defence, pp. 19, 24.

8 Material in this paragraph is drawn from the author's personal recollection: in the late 1990s he was an Australian official engaged on these issues.

9 Robert D. Blackwill and Paul Dibb (eds) (2000), *America's Asian Alliances*, Cambridge, MA: MIT Press.

10 See for example Ellen Bork (2002), 'An axis of Asian democracies', *Asian Wall Street Journal*, 25 March, available at: www.newamericancentury.org/taiwan-20020325.htm (accessed 18 October 2006).

11 Robert Blackwill (2000), 'An action agenda to strengthen America's alliances in the Asia-Pacific region', pp. 111–34, and following comments from Paul Dibb, pp. 135–36, in Blackwill and Dibb (eds) (2000), *America's Asian Alliances*.

12 'Australian Minister for Foreign Affairs Alexander Downer, US Secretary of State Colin Powell and US Secretary of Defense Donald Rumsfeld Discuss the Australia–US Ministerial Consultation with Australian and American Press', transcript of press conference, 30 July 2001, available at: www.dfat.gov.au/media/transcripts/2001/010730_fa_ausmin.html (accessed 5 October 2006).

13 Ibid.

14 'Joint Press Conference with Secretary of State Condoleezza Rice – Washington', 5 May 2005, available at: www.foreignminister.gov.au/transcripts/2005/050505_rice.html (accessed 6 October 2006).

15 See Chapter 4 by Michael Wesley in this volume.

16 Secretary of State Condoleezza Rice (2006), *Roundtable with Australian, Indonesian and Latin American Journalists*, Washington, DC, 9 March, available at: www.state.gov/secretary/rm/2006/62968.htm (accessed 6 October 2006).

17 Alexander Downer (2006), *Doorstop Interview Trilateral Strategic Dialogue, Sydney*, 18 March, available at: www.foreignminister.gov.au/transcripts/2006/060318_ds-3lat.html (accessed 6 October 2006).

18 *Joint Statement Australia–Japan–United States, Trilateral Strategic Dialogue*, Sydney, 18 March 2006, available at: www.foreignminister.gov.au/releases/2006/joint_statement-aus-japan_usa_180306.html (accessed 6 October 2006).

19 John Howard (2005), *Australia in the World*, address to the Lowy Institute for International Policy, Sydney, 31 March, available at: www.pm.gov.au/news/speeches/speech1290.html (accessed 6 October 2006).

20 For a fuller treatment of this topic see Hugh White (2005), 'The limits to optimism: Australia and the rise of China', *Australian Journal of International Affairs*, vol. 59, no. 4, pp. 469–80; White (2005), 'Australian strategic policy', in Ashley J. Tellis and Michael Wills (eds), *Strategic Asia 2005–06: Military Modernization in an Era of Uncertainty*, Seattle, WA: National Bureau of Asian Research, pp. 305–41.

21 Downer (2006), *Doorstop Interview Trilateral Strategic Dialogue, Sydney*.

9   Trilateralism and the South Pacific

Susan Windybank

The South Pacific is a microcosm of global concern over failed states. During the past decade, the region has gone from a relatively peaceful backwater to an 'arc of instability'. Military coups in Fiji, ethnic conflict in the Solomon Islands, violence and bloodshed in East Timor, and the breakdown of law and order in Papua New Guinea have shattered images of an idyllic tropical paradise. Several states are at risk of failure. They are unable to control effectively their territory, let alone defend and monitor their borders. This makes them easy prey for international criminals and other malign elements seeking a staging post into Australasia or a backdoor into Southeast Asia.

Each of these countries alone presents serious challenges for Australia now that the 'arc of instability' has become an 'arc of responsibility'. Together they pose a daunting set of complex and deep-seated problems that is going to preoccupy Canberra for a long time to come. The security crises that led to the deployment of Australian military and/or police – to East Timor in 1999 and again in 2006; to the Solomon Islands in 2003 and again in 2006; and to Papua New Guinea (briefly) in 2004 (and possibly again ahead of the 2007 elections) – are symptoms of a deep and chronic malaise: weak and dysfunctional government, systemic and systematic corruption, and the failure of economic development.

Into this fragile area, external powers previously inactive in the South Pacific are moving to establish influence. Over the past decade, China has been building a strong diplomatic presence, with embassies in six Pacific states and more diplomats in the region than any other country. It has also emerged as a major aid donor. Its immediate aim is to sideline Taiwan – Beijing currently has eight Pacific governments on its side to Taipei's six – but its activism is also part of a longer-term investment in the outer contours of a possible Chinese sphere of influence in the greater Asia-Pacific. While Australia (and New Zealand) still dominate the South Pacific, Asian interests can no longer be taken for granted.

Although less prominent in the region than is Australia, Japan and the United States share a common interest in a stable region free from conflict and competition generated by external rivalries. Yet specific trilateral security cooperation is absent. East Timor provides a precedent for greater security collaboration and coordination of trilateral diplomacy with regional and international organizations, but such responses have been conceived largely in defence and military terms. This absorbs the lion's share of bureaucratic and financial resources. Rising crime and corruption, state weakness and stagnant economies, however, demand non-military solutions, including greater regional cooperation on illegality of all kinds and coordinated aid policies that promote growth not dependency.

This chapter explores the problems of the South Pacific and the overlapping interests of Australia, Japan and the United States in the region. It begins by surveying the geopolitical dynamics of the South Pacific before focusing on the increasingly acute problems of corruption and instability. It then looks at the responses of Australia, Japan and the United States to these problems and asks where the three might work more closely together to effect solutions. The chapter concludes with specific recommendations on trilateral cooperation in the South Pacific.

Geopolitical dynamics

The importance of the South Pacific has waxed and waned. Australia and New Zealand have traditionally seen the island region as the first line of defence against invasion through the Pacific Ocean, an assessment borne out by World War II. Its isolation and vast expanses provided a site for British, American and French nuclear testing in the 1950s and early 1960s when the region was still separated into colonies. By 1975 French tests had been forced underground but did not end for another twenty years.[1] Independence came to most Pacific islands in the 1970s and early 1980s, but there was no real progress in economic development despite large aid transfers.[2] The islands remained of interest only to the former colonial powers, Japan (which had major fishing interests in the region) and France (which retained colonies in New Caledonia, French Polynesia and Wallis and Futuna). They were remote, peaceful and uncontested.

The Cold War barely touched the South Pacific, except for a brief but intense interlude in the mid to late 1980s when Russian fishing fleets were seen as the harbinger of a Soviet naval presence.[3] The United States and Australia – with the cooperation of Japan – responded with a Pacific-wide policy of 'strategic denial' aimed at preventing the Soviet Union from gaining a foothold in the region. In the end, this foothold amounted to a short-lived Soviet embassy in Papua New Guinea and a fishing agreement negotiated by Moscow with Kiribati.

China and Taiwan have made greater diplomatic and economic inroads into the region but lack the immense military power of the unlamented Soviet Union. China does not yet have a blue water navy. An element of strategic denial nonetheless lingers in Australian government concerns over intensifying Chinese–Taiwanese competition for the diplomatic allegiance of Pacific states. This has led to a bidding war involving non-transparent financial transfers not reported by Pacific governments. Unlike Australia, the two Chinas do not insist on 'good governance' as a condition of receiving such 'aid'.[4] Another problem is that they mostly fund prestige projects aimed at softening up the political elite (such as parliament house in Vanuatu), or bankroll crowd-pleasers (such as a new sports stadium in Fiji) that do not lead to economic development.[5]

Changing partners

The increasing presence of China and Taiwan reflects a long-term shift away from the Western-dominated postcolonial order towards a more fluid and complex state of regional affairs in which Asian powers play a greater role. Aside from Chinese–Taiwanese competition for diplomatic recognition, Asian interest is mainly in the region's resources (timber, fish and minerals), with Japan, South Korea, China, Taiwan and Malaysia all active in the region. The flag is following trade. For instance, Malaysian Prime Minister Mohamad Mahathir chose Papua New Guinea for his last overseas trip before standing down after more than twenty years in office in 2003. An entourage of some 200 people in four jets accompanied him, including five cabinet ministers and high-powered businessmen. The Malaysian timber company Rimbunan Hijau ('forever green') dominates Papua New Guinea's logging industry.[6]

Apart from resources, the region's other main attraction is as a voting bloc at international forums. The islands may be small, but they are also numerous and in some forums numbers count – particularly the UN General Assembly with its one-country one-vote system. The South Pacific also provides an arena for emerging powers seeking status and prestige. Indonesia recently opened a mission in Fiji and is likely to play a bigger role in regional affairs. Some Solomon Island politicians even considered approaching Jakarta as they waited for Canberra to respond to their (second) request for help in 2003.[7]

But only China has a real potential to reshape South Pacific geopolitics. China's overtures to the region mirror its diplomatic charm offensive in Southeast Asia, where it has become clear that Beijing is trying to build a regional constituency for a possible Chinese version of the Monroe Doctrine. Such a sphere of influence would not resemble an exclusive zone of total domination like the Soviet Union had in Eastern Europe. It is more likely to be an area in which smaller and weaker states defer to the interests, views and anticipated reactions of Beijing. The South Pacific may well become a low-risk (and low-cost) testing ground for China's ability to establish footholds of influence, recruit new allies and command allegiance in a region hitherto dominated by Western powers.[8]

Trilateral interests

While Australia, Japan and the United States share an overall interest in the security of the South Pacific and its freedom from external hegemony, they also have separate and distinct interests in the region that will determine their degree of involvement.

The United States maintains a policy of strategic denial in the North Pacific as a 'hedge' against uncertainty. Compacts of Free Association with Micronesia, the Marshall Islands and Palau give the United States control over defence – including the right to establish military bases, exclude other powers and veto elements of foreign policy – in return for billions in American aid. But technology has reduced their strategic utility. Improved long-distance air and sea capabilities make plane refuelling and ship resupply on the islands unnecessary. The US missile defence testing facility on Kwajalein Atoll in the Marshall Islands has the main claim to strategic significance.[9]

The United States has little interest in the Melanesian and Polynesian islands of the South Pacific. Washington expects Canberra (and Wellington) to take care of these areas. Historically, they have been on the 'ANZAC' side of the postwar Radford–Collins maritime patrolling zone in the wider Pacific region.[10]

Japan also defers to Australia in the South Pacific. Its main interest is in the oceans surrounding the islands. As the largest fishing nation in the region and biggest market for its fresh tuna, it is concerned to keep access fees low. Japanese interest in potential seabed minerals in the islands' extensive Exclusive Economic Zones (EEZs) resulted in a 2000 agreement for deep ocean mineral exploration with the Cook Islands, Fiji and the Marshall Islands. Japan also wants free and secure access to sea lanes to ship radioactive waste for reprocessing in France and Britain.

Japan's diplomatic interest in the islands themselves boils down to international votes. Japan's bid for a permanent seat on the UN Security Council (which China opposes) has thus led to a flow of yen to the Pacific island states that hold twelve votes at the world body. Japan's 'marine aid' to influence the whaling vote of Pacific countries continues to give Tokyo bad press in Australia, where the government holds a strong contrary position. At the June 2006 International Whaling Conference all six Pacific members – the Solomon Islands, Kiribati, Tuvalu, the Marshall Islands, Palau and Nauru – called for the 1986 moratorium on commercial whaling to be lifted.[11]

Australia is clearly the regional hegemon and leading aid donor. Canberra views the South Pacific as an Australian sphere of influence. 'This is our patch', explained the Australian Prime Minister John Howard after the watershed 2003 Australian-led police and military intervention in the Solomon Islands. 'We have a special responsibility in this part of the world.'[12] Australia does not want a band of failed states on its doorstep that invites criminals, terrorists or foreign powers potentially hostile to its interests. Further Australian interventions are on the cards if the region disintegrates.

Pacific corruption and instability

From the end of World War II to the mid-1980s the 'Pacific' more or less lived up to its name. But two important factors have changed: the region has become increasingly unstable and corruption has become endemic. These problems are most acute in the largest and resource-rich countries of Melanesia (Papua New Guinea, the Solomon Islands, Fiji and Vanuatu), which are also the most conflict-prone states. The smaller Polynesian countries (Tonga, Samoa, the Cook Islands, Tuvalu and Niue) have traditionally been more tranquil, but also face increasing political instability and internal discord.

The scale of corruption in the region has been of increasing concern ever since the end of the Cold War meant that Western donors could attach conditions to their aid without fearing they would drive the recipient country into the arms of Moscow. It has also allowed new external players to use the economic vulnerability of South Pacific countries to vie for diplomatic advantage.

As intimated above, China and Taiwan are competing sharply for greater influence in the region. Pacific politicians view their rivalry as an opportunity to be milked for cash, but jobless youth with no hope for the future are sick of watching their leaders' conspicuous corruption and consumption. This tension erupted into the April 2006 riots in the Solomon Islands. Angry mobs scapegoated Chinese migrants by burning down Chinatown. The violence was sparked by allegations that Taiwanese slush funds were used to rig national elections, the first since Australia led the Regional Assistance Mission to the Solomon Islands (RAMSI) in 2003. As a result, the newly elected Prime Minister resigned after less than a week in office.

The Australian Prime Minister John Howard referred to 'countries that are [not] geographically part of the region ... involving themselves and gathering allies and partners ... not necessarily with the longer-term interest of the region at heart'.[13] This was a pointed reference to China's and Taiwan's 'chequebook diplomacy' that is undermining Australian efforts to improve governance in the South Pacific by funding – if not fostering – corruption and further destabilizing already weak and unstable governments.

The Solomon Islands marked the fourth time that competition between the two Chinas has been the catalyst for a change of government in the region. In October 2004, Vanuatu Prime Minister Serge Vohor made a secret trip to Taipei to establish diplomatic ties in exchange for aid dollars. At the time the Australian government was threatening to cut aid if Vanuatu did not crack down on corruption. Vohor fell from office after a vote of no confidence and his successor Ham Lini stayed with China. In 1998, the Prime Minister of Papua New Guinea, the late Sir Bill Skate, tried to strike an under-the-table cash deal with Taiwan in return for diplomatic recognition. Skate resigned to avoid a no-confidence motion and Australia convinced his successor to stay with China.

The other casualty was Kiribati, where more than usual was at stake. This collection of coral atolls that some 100,000 people call home lies close to the equator, the ideal position for launching rockets and parking satellites in orbit. For six years the Chinese government operated a satellite tracking station on Tarawa Atoll. The station played a role in sending China's first astronaut into space in October 2003. Beijing denied that the station also played a role in the development of its space warfare capability and that it was used to spy on a US testing facility for its missile defence program (that China opposes) on Kwajalein Atoll in the nearby Marshall Islands. The secrecy surrounding the base became a major election issue, but it is now closed because Kiribati suddenly recognized Taiwan following bitterly contested November 2003 elections. Both China and Taiwan were accused of bribing their preferred presidential candidates. Taiwan reportedly paid $11 million in aid for the switch but there was much speculation that the United States provoked the change and paid the bill. China still maintains a 'care-taking' mission in Kiribati, suggesting that Beijing may be biding its time until a more 'China-friendly' government comes to power again.

Growing illegality

But it is the unofficial Chinese presence that is potentially the most worrisome issue. Pacific countries have resorted to selling their sovereignty through sales of passports, citizenship and resident permits to Chinese crime networks.[14] Degraded immigration procedures and corrupt officials facilitate scams. In late 2003 the immigration database and passport-making machinery was stolen from the Papua New Guinean immigration department. Not long after streams of Chinese migrants began arriving.[15] The Papua New Guinean police minister has since admitted that corruption is rampant. Chinese triads are colluding with police, operating illegal businesses and buying off officials throughout the system. A former Papua New Guinean deputy prime minister even provided a character reference for the citizenship application of a notorious 'snakehead' or people-smuggler.[16]

The illegal entry and practices of many recently arrived migrants are fuelling local resentment. Some do not pay taxes while others bribe customs officials. This, combined with envy over the commercial success of Chinese small business compared to the tiny indigenous sector, is producing Solomons-style tensions in Tonga, Papua New Guinea and Fiji. These tensions are likely to worsen as more mainland Chinese arrive in the Pacific, both legally or illegally. Concern for their welfare could provide a pretext for intervention. Beijing organized a special flight to rescue Chinese escaping from the April 2006 torching of Honiara's Chinatown. As China grows in power and confidence, its interest in the protection of the diaspora will increase.

Questions have recently been raised about the connection between the official Chinese presence in the region and the growth of Chinese criminal networks.[17] The sheer scale of criminal infiltration suggests an unpalatable degree of collusion. Chinese diplomats are thought to cultivate criminals to spy on countries and to corrupt politicians and bureaucrats. Chinese cooperation on crime syndicates was sought by the Australian government following the first Australia–China talks in April 2005. The extent to which China is willing to collaborate with Australia by modifying such tendencies will become a more significant factor in Sino-Australian relations in the years ahead.

Trilateral responses

Australia, Japan and the United States have a common interest in preventing the emergence of a comparative advantage for illegality in the Pacific.

In the early 1990s the threat of transnational crime in the region was considered more apparent than real.[18] Law enforcement and cross-jurisdictional cooperation ranked low on the regional security agenda. By the early 2000s, however, there was clear evidence that criminal infiltration had progressed further and faster than anticipated.[19] Fiji, for instance, has moved from being a drug-trafficking transit point to a production site. Even the smallest microstates have become a breeding ground for international corruption. Tiny Nauru earned the dubious reputation of 'safest haven for money-laundering in the South Pacific'. At its peak, the island atoll hosted around 400 offshore banks. Vanuatu, the Cook Islands, Fiji, Samoa and Niue were other Pacific havens favoured by the Russian mafia.[20]

Criminal networks target countries where the rule of law is weakest and social mores are most tolerant of illegal economic activities. Of these two conditions, the former is more amenable to cooperative regional solutions.

Regional cooperation

Japan and Australia are top financial supporters of the peak sub-regional multilateral body, the Pacific Islands Forum. Both have demonstrated a strong interest in a multilateral approach to Pacific policy as a way of managing security across the island states. Since 2004 Australia has reinvigorated the Forum to address regional security, governance and infrastructure. Japan and the United States have supported this move by providing technical and other assistance.

The Forum's principal task should be to pursue a common stance on illegality of all kinds. Pressure from the US State Department and the Financial Action Task Force on money laundering from Nauru and Niue to Vanuatu and the Cook Islands revealed that adherence to the Forum's Declarations on such issues was poor, if not non-existent. While there are no longer any Pacific states on the Task Force's blacklist, it may only be a matter of time before anti-money-laundering legislation, now in place, is watered down. Reporting of transactions remains weak.

The checkerboard of jurisdictions and legal systems that criminals exploit must be harmonized to reduce 'arbitrage' opportunities. Police waited over a year before closing in on a major crystal methamphetamine or 'ice' lab on the outskirts of Suva in 2004 because Fijian law banned only the finished product, not its ingredients. A new bill increasing the maximum penalty for drug trafficking in Fiji from eight years to life – in line with Australia – went before parliament on the day of the raid.[21] This legislation was based on a 2002 Illicit Drugs Control Bill that would enable a common and consistent regional approach to offences, penalties, and investigation and enforcement. But legislation is not keeping up with advances in technology.[22]

Such regional cooperation has already borne fruit, but regional integration is a dead end. The Forum's energies are best directed at regional cooperation on transport (airlines and shipping) and communications rather than economic and political integration. The European Union has increased its aid in an attempt to create its mirror image in a Pacific Community, but the Pacific is not Europe. Intra-regional trade is negligible. Moreover, integration will not solve the problems of stagnation and aid dependency that have hobbled growth in the region for thirty years. Economic development can only be tackled island by island. The reforms that would create jobs, improve education and health, and raise living standards are well known.[23] What is needed is the political will to act.

State failure

The Pacific Islands Forum provides multilateral legitimacy to regional interventions within member-states. Its support was essential for the Solomon Islands 2003

'Helpem Fren' intervention. Australia could not have taken this to the United Nations. China would have vetoed it in the Security Council because the Solomons recognizes Taiwan. The Forum thus played the legitimating role that the United Nations played in the 1999 East Timor intervention.

East Timor was an example of major collaboration between Australia and Japan (as well as other participants). The United States provided vital logistical and diplomatic support but Australia and, later, Japan sent the largest numbers of military personnel. Under the UN banner, some 1,600 Australian combat troops were deployed to restore and maintain law and order in the bloody aftermath of the 1999 independence referendum. Once the situation stabilized, Japan sent nearly 700 Ground Self-Defence Force (SDF) personnel to assist with reconstruction in areas close to the Indonesian border. Hailed by the Japanese government as an 'epoch-making initiative', the deployment followed a 2001 amendment that widened the scope of SDF participation in UN missions. Despite the fanfare, however, they were a non-combatant engineering battalion, mostly unarmed and reliant on other personnel for security.

But just as the United Nations was claiming its biggest success ever in East Timor and just as Australia was congratulating itself on the Solomon Islands, law and order broke down again. In early April 2006 rioting and looting returned to Honiara nearly three years after Australian-led forces intervened to restore law and order. Less than two months later, a political power struggle, police–military rivalry and simmering popular discontent erupted on the streets of Dili.

What lessons can be drawn from this? While the proximate causes of the upheaval were political – a disputed election in the Solomons, internal feuds in East Timor – the root causes lie in the failure of economic development. Nothing has been done to provide jobs and income to young and growing populations. Massive unemployment has led to gangs of youths prowling the streets of Dili and Honiara. Jobless young men with no future prospects are like tinder waiting to be ignited by a small spark. In the Solomons that spark was Taiwanese corruption of politicians. In East Timor it quickly became apparent that the gangs that rampaged through Dili were linked to political factions. The use of criminal gangs for political ends is a time-honoured tactic in Papua New Guinea. Election candidates routinely distribute high-powered weapons to criminals and tribal groups to impress or intimidate rivals and voters. Most of these weapons come from police and military armouries.[24]

Australia should lead in providing long-term guarantees of external security to East Timor. The creation of a standing army was a mistake. It should be downsized, if not disbanded. Credible guarantees would save East Timor the costs of external defence and enable it to de-militarize. The Timorese government could then focus on internal security by strengthening the police force to protect life and property.

Suggestions that Australia should consider stationing troops in semi-permanent garrisons in East Timor, the Solomon Islands and across the troubled Pacific region to pre-empt rather than respond to crises recognize that military forces can protect, reassure and build confidence as well as threaten or deter.[25] But this is a band-aid solution. Unless Australia wants to lead interventions every other year, underlying economic problems must be tackled.

Aid

The trilateral countries must work together on aid and development to ensure economic growth and hence stability. The new US Millennium Challenge Corporation's recent selection of Vanuatu for a $65 million grant came just as Australia was threatening to withdraw its aid if Vanuatu did not address corruption, thus throwing the government a lifeline.[26] Japan, Australia and New Zealand recently issued a Joint Statement on Enhanced Donor Cooperation for a More Robust and Prosperous Pacific Region.[27] This can be seen as a warning to regional governments not to try playing them off against each other.

A proposal that Australia should consider joint Australia–China aid ventures in an attempt to persuade China to cooperate on development rather than compete with Taiwan is unlikely to get off the ground.[28] Beijing's hardline stance towards the 'rebellious province' will take precedence. Recent signs that a third Sino-Japanese front is emerging in this longstanding Chinese–Taiwanese regional competition do not augur well. China's first summit with Pacific leaders (from the eight countries that recognize Beijing) in Fiji in April 2006 saw a pledge of $494 million in aid over the next three years. Not to be outdone, the following month Japan increased its aid to $528 million over three years at its triennial Pacific Islands Leaders' Meeting (PALM) in Okinawa.[29] But Japan's aid has traditionally been designed to complement Australian initiatives.

Maritime security

Australia, Japan and the United States should also stress practical cooperation on maritime security issues such as illegal fishing and migration. The aptly named 'Oceania' is an area roughly the size of Africa (including US and French territories but excluding Australia and New Zealand). Scope exists for greater trilateral cooperation on constabulary operations at sea. This could involve a mix of coast-guard, naval and other government officers. The Japanese concept of 'ocean peacekeeping' – that is, multinational naval patrols of international and national waters – could apply in the South Pacific as Japan 'normalizes' its maritime forces. Such patrols could also lead to greater cooperation on protection of the ocean environment as well as contributing to the general security of sea lanes.

Specifically, Australia should take the lead on fisheries monitoring and enforcement on the open seas as a party to the Convention on the Conservation and Management of Highly Migratory Fish Stocks in the Western and Central Pacific Ocean. Island governments are already struggling to enforce their Exclusive Economic Zones. Kiribati, for instance, has the second largest EEZ within the region (excluding Australia). Existing aerial surveillance with France and New Zealand could be expanded to include the United States and Japan in cooperative sea patrols. Pacific island police observers and fisheries inspectors could be carried on board.[30]

Pacific pieces in the global puzzle

Japan is clearly trying to become a more visible regional and global player.[31] The Pacific is a stage on which Japan can demonstrate its diplomatic skills and test its influence. This has involved moving beyond the role of distant financier to getting more diplomatic bang for its aid buck, most notably votes for a permanent seat on the UN Security Council. Japan has also discovered that multilateralism can be a useful device for managing regional concerns and safeguarding Japanese interests. For instance, Tokyo inaugurated the PALM summit in 1997 not long after Japan's controversial trans-shipment of nuclear waste began. Generous financial contributions to the Pacific Islands Forum demonstrate Japan's commitment to fostering institutions and regional cooperation. A focus on peacekeeping operations, maritime security and so-called human security is intended to portray Japanese security 'normalization' as positive. By normalizing its Self-Defence Force within the US alliance, Japan hopes to reassure countries that it is not re-militarizing but pulling its weight in helping to underpin global and regional order. Regional initiatives deepen and broaden ties with Australia and the United States while giving Japan more Pacific clout.

Australia's assertive and interventionist approach to Pacific state failure and regional instability demonstrates a growing confidence about its regional and global role. In the South Pacific, Canberra accepts that as the biggest and wealthiest country in the region it has a responsibility to underwrite regional security. This responsibility will grow, not diminish. At the same time, Australia's niche contributions to the Long War led by the United States can be seen as a reinvented form of forward defence for the age of transnational threats. A bedrock of Australian strategic policy is that it is better to counter threats before they reach its shores and preferable to do so in the company of like-minded allies. Since 11 September 2001 Australia has thus broadened and deepened ties to the United States. Similarly, Australia–Japan relations are now undergoing a 'complete transformation'.[32] Indeed, the Australian Foreign Minister envisages a formal security agreement that would see Japanese and Australian defence forces building upon cooperation in East Timor and Iraq by undertaking joint exercises and peacekeeping training, including on Australian soil. Working together the two could achieve more than as individual nations.

Closer Australia–Japan security cooperation fits into emerging American regional and global strategy. Historically, the United States has preferred to manage regional security in the Asia-Pacific on a strictly bilateral 'hub and spokes' basis. But now the 'hub' is actively encouraging greater initiative from the 'spokes'. Since 9/11, Washington has insisted that allies do more to share the burden of security by taking on more active regional and international roles. The United States is a global power and views regional security through a global lens. The alliances provide a framework for American military dominance in the Asia-Pacific and enable the forward projection of force, both operationally and politically. But they also play a crucial role in America's broader global security strategy.

The United States is beefing up its military assets in Guam, the forward bastion of American power in the northwest Pacific and, crucially, US territory. Upgrading of Andersen Air Force Base and naval facilities indicates a less ambiguous 'hedging' strategy than in the Compact territories discussed earlier. The aim is to be able to prevail in limited regional conflicts (such as the Korean peninsula and the Taiwan Strait) and to project smaller and nimbler forces faster to counter terrorism and respond better to regional crises. The May 2006 United States–Japan 'roadmap' agreement fits this strategy as does Australia's out-of-area niche contributions. Washington wants force structure changes for the global war on terrorism and regional contingencies to complement each other. Counterterrorism cooperation with Southeast Asia, for instance, may double as a 'soft' containment policy aimed at offsetting China's growing power. The trick will be to anticipate problems rather than precipitating them.

Conclusion

If the problems in the Pacific are not addressed more systematically, they could intensify to become major security concerns. The United States and Japan will continue to defer to Canberra's geopolitical leadership in the South Pacific, but they are unlikely to give military support or extensive economic assistance to an area they deem marginal to the Asia-Pacific and global power balances. The Trilateral Strategic Dialogue may be one venue, however, where these qualified American and Japanese interests could be coordinated with Australian concerns about the region that are understandably more central to that country's foreign policy and security postures.

This chapter has discussed the potential for modest trilateral cooperation in three main areas – maritime security, transnational crime and state failure/lack of development, but more could be done. Specifically:

1   a Japanese component down the Radford–Collins patrolling line could be added to existing arrangements to enhance freedom of the seas and maritime security, especially as demand increases for constabulary operations to counter illegal fishing and migration;
2   a greater focus on regional cooperation to counter transnational crime – and less attention to the mirage of regional integration – could draw on both Japan's past experience of fighting organized crime in Australia and other Pacific locales; and
3   joint aid ventures could be initiated that combine Australian knowledge of the region with Japanese technical expertise and resources so that aid leads to economic growth, rising incomes and improved living standards – and hence stability.

Working together to solve underlying economic – and hence governance – problems in the region is the most effective way to address the counterproductive engagement of China and Taiwan. But an aid race should be avoided at all costs.

If the 'arc of instability' is not to become a self-fulfilling prophecy, Australia, Japan and the United States need to find ways to help the region develop and stand on its own feet. Ultimately the biggest threat that failing states represent is to themselves. The South Pacific is a rare example of where humanitarian and strategic interests converge.

Notes

All websites accessed 4 October 2006.

1 See Greg Fry (1999), *South Pacific Security and Global Change: The New Agenda*, Working Paper no. 1999/1, Canberra: Australian National University, Research School of Pacific and Asian Studies, Department of International Relations, pp. 5–7.
2 The South Pacific demonstrates the inverse relationship between aid and growth. It holds the world record for the highest aid per capita yet ranks among the world's worst performing regions. Over the past thirty years per capita income has barely risen. Population has grown faster than the economy so that living standards have stagnated. See Helen Hughes (2003), *Aid Has Failed the Pacific*, Issue Analysis 33, Sydney: The Centre for Independent Studies, available at: www.cis.org.au/IssueAnalysis/ia33/ia33.htm
3 Owen Harries (1989), *Strategy and the Southwest Pacific*, Sydney: Pacific Security Research Institute.
4 Jane Perlez (2006), 'China competes with West in aid to its neighbours', *International Herald Tribune*, 19 September.
5 Susan Windybank (2005), 'The China Syndrome', *Policy*, vol. 21, no. 2, pp. 28–33, available at: www.policymagazine.com; see also John Henderson and Benjamin Reilly (2003), 'Dragon in paradise: China's rising star in Oceania', *The National Interest*, Summer, pp. 94–104.
6 See 'Mahathir's Pacific Solution', *Dateline*, Sydney: Special Broadcasting Service, 29 October 2003. Several recent reports have documented how forests are ripped out without appropriate licences, without benefit to landowners and without due payment of royalties to the government. To limit exposure of its depredations, Rimbunan Hijau owns one of Papua New Guinea's daily newspapers, *The National*. It is thought to have political protection at the highest levels. See Greg Roberts (2006), 'The rape of PNG forests', *Weekend Australian*, 24–25 June.
7 'Solomons riddle', *Dateline*, Sydney: Special Broadcasting Service, 27 August 2003.
8 See Henderson and Reilly (2003), 'Dragon in paradise', p. 94.
9 See the United States General Accounting Office Report to Congressional Requesters (2002), *Foreign Relations: Kwajalein Atoll is the Key US Defense Interest in Two Micronesian Nations*, Washington, DC: GAO, available at: www.gao.gov/new.items/d02119.pdf
10 Thomas-Durell Young (1992), *Australian, New Zealand, and United States Security Relations, 1951–1986*, Boulder, CO: Westview Press.
11 David McNeill (2006), 'Scale of Japan's aid to pro-whaling nations revealed', *New Zealand Herald*, 24 June.
12 Mark Forbes (2004), 'Pacific leaders back Australian role', *Age*, 9 August, available at: www.theage.com.au/articles/2004/08/08/1091903444430.html?from = storylhs#
13 John Howard (2006), 'Address to the Queensland Division of the Liberal Party of Australia, Sofitel Hotel, Brisbane', 19 April, available at: www.pm.gov.au/News/speeches/speech1889.html
14 Andreas Schloenhardt (2003), 'Transnational crime and island state security in the South Pacific', in Eric Shibuya and Jim Rolfe (eds), *Security in Oceania in the 21st Century*, Honolulu, HI: Asia Pacific Center for Security Studies, p. 176.

15 James Laki (2006), *Non-Traditional Security Issues: Securitisation of Transnational Crime in Asia*, Working Paper no. 98, Singapore: Institute of Defence and Strategic Studies.

16 Mark Forbes (2005), 'Danger on our doorstep: organised crime takes hold in Papua New Guinea', *Defender*, Autumn, pp. 22–24.

17 Anna Powles and Brendan Taylor (2005), 'Double-headed dragon', *The Diplomat*, July, pp. 32–33.

18 Rod McCusker (2006), 'Transnational crime in the Pacific Islands: real or apparent danger?', *Trends and Issues in Crime and Criminal Justice*, no. 308, Canberra: Australian Institute of Criminology.

19 As acknowledged by the Pacific Islands Forum. See *Thirty-Second Pacific Islands Forum*, Republic of Nauru, 16–18 August 2001, *Forum Communique*, para 38.

20 Schloenhardt (2003), 'Transnational crime and island state security in the South Pacific', pp. 178–83.

21 Elizabeth Feizkhah (2004), 'Ice: from gang to bust', *Time Magazine Asia*, 15 June, available at: www.time.com/time/asia/magazine/article/0,13673,501040628-655460,00.html

22 For more detail on regional and country policy responses, see Madonna Devaney, Gary Reid and Simon Baldwin (2006), *Situational Analysis of Illicit Drug Issues and Responses in the Asia-Pacific Region*, ANCD Research Paper 12, Canberra: Australian National Council on Drugs, pp. 84–89, 308–12.

23 Helen Hughes (2004), *The Pacific is Viable!*, Issue Analysis 53, Sydney: The Centre for Independent Studies, available at: www.cis.org.au/IssueAnalysis/ia53/IA53.pdf

24 Philip Alpers (2005), *Gun Running in Papua New Guinea: From Arrows to Assault Weapons in the Southern Highlands*, Special Report no. 5, Geneva: Small Arms Survey.

25 Greg Sheridan (2006), 'Throw troops at Pacific failures', *Australian*, 3 June.

26 Helen Hughes and Gaurav Sodhi (2006), *Annals of Aid: Vanuatu and the Millennium Challenge Corporation*, Issue Analysis 69, Sydney: The Centre for Independent Studies, available at: www.cis.org.au/IssueAnalysis/ia69/IA69.pdf

27 Peter Alford (2006), 'Canberra pledges co-operation on Pacific aid', *Australian*, 29 May.

28 Peter Jennings (2005), *Getting China Right: Australia's Policy Options for Dealing with China*, Strategic Insights no. 19, Canberra: Australian Strategic Policy Institute, p. 9.

29 Malcolm Farr (2006), 'Island forum a test of Costello's skills', *Daily Telegraph*, 3 July.

30 For further details, see Chris Rahman (2005), Submission 4 *Inquiry Into Australia's Regional Strategic Defence Requirements*, Canberra: Joint Standing Committee on Foreign Affairs, Defence and Trade – Defence Sub Committee, p. 11, available at: www.aph.gov.au/house/committee/jfadt/esstrends/subs/sub4.pdf

31 See Alan Dupont (2005), 'The schizophrenic superpower', *The National Interest*, Spring.

32 Australian Foreign Minister Alexander Downer quoted in Paul Kelly (2006), 'Warming up to Tokyo', *Australian*, 12 August.

10 Trilateralism, Southeast Asia and multilateralism

Taizo Watanabe and William T. Tow

The Australia–Japan–United States Trilateral Strategic Dialogue (TSD) should be a consensus-building instrument, facilitating security cooperation among the three countries to meet the current security challenges in East Asia in both the 'traditional' and 'non-traditional' security policy sectors. 'Facilitation' of regional stability, however, is not synonymous with 'replacement' of already established regional multilateral security forums such as the ASEAN Regional Forum (ARF) or the Asia Pacific Economic Cooperation (APEC) annual heads of state summits. These instrumentalities have already established positive track records in such policy areas as confidence-building, maritime security and other components that are particularly critical to Southeast Asia.

Trilateralism cannot stand alone as an approach to either alliance politics or regional security community-building. If the TSD is to be effective in the ASEAN sub-region, it must complement those existing multilateral organizations in East and Southeast Asia by addressing emerging security challenges such as terrorism, the forced movements of displaced peoples, a widening drug trade problem, pandemics and other 'human security' problems. It can do so, in part, by combining aspects of ongoing Japanese Overseas Development Assistance (ODA) programmes with commensurate Australian and US development aid initiatives. However, the TSD cannot be restricted to merely non-traditional security politics. It will also need to confront traditional, 'state-centric' threats to regional stability such as the proliferation of weapons of mass destruction (WMD), maritime security threats, territorial disputes and regional arms build-ups. If left unchecked, these could lead to an intensification of security dilemmas throughout Asia. In the current Southeast Asian environment, such traditional security issues include stabilizing the South China Sea, interdicting WMD contraband from traversing key straits and littorals, and stopping the resumption of the arms build-ups that were a major feature of ASEAN defence postures prior to the Asian financial crisis.

This chapter argues that the TSD can play a constructive and enduring role in complementing existing multilateral efforts to pursue preventative diplomacy and comprehensive security in Southeast Asia. In the process, Japan can use the diplomatic and strategic 'cushion' provided by an evolving trilateral mechanism to better establish its own contemporary security identity and to transform into a 'normal power' that assumes greater security responsibilities. But it must do so in ways that are not viewed as threatening or destabilizing by its regional neighbours. With the assent of ASEAN, and the help of Australia and the United States in a TSD context, a 'normalized' Japan can become a positive regional security actor if it is seen as acting to defuse lingering historical tensions in the region and is therefore perceived as legitimate in that role. If Japan's security evolution is not managed properly, however, its rising military and strategic influence may well be interpreted as a dangerous mechanism of misguided containment strategy that could intensify rather than alleviate regional tensions. Japanese policy-makers must work assiduously and sensitively to overcome a deep rooted 'anti-Japan' psychology that until now may have been fostered by China and both Koreas. By using the TSD to help establish its strategic legitimacy in the region, Japan may well enhance its prospects to establish an accepted regional security status in ASEAN politics.

Initially, an assessment of major contending perspectives regarding Japan as a security actor in the early twenty-first century will be presented. How Japan might utilize its growing diplomatic, strategic and 'soft power' relationships with ASEAN member-states will then be set out. The chapter will then conclude by appraising how the TSD could be employed to cultivate greater legitimacy and support for a future Japanese regional security role, within ASEAN and throughout the Asia-Pacific region.

Japan's role as an international and regional security actor

In the post-9/11 timeframe, the average Japanese citizen has developed a perspective on international relations very much at odds with that which prevailed ten years before when the United States and other Western allies fought the first Gulf War against Saddam Hussein's Iraq. There was previously a powerful psychological resistance against the dispatch of self-defence forces overseas. When hostilities commenced in Iraq in early 1991, Japan declined to contribute military forces to the UN coalition, citing constitutional restraints. This position was castigated by US and coalition critics as a Japanese failure to accept strategic responsibility and defence burden-sharing, notwithstanding its enormous dependence on Persian Gulf oil supplies. The US$13 billion Japan contributed to help defray Desert Storm's operational costs was accepted with contempt by a number of alliance critics.[1]

This humiliating lesson led to the Japanese Diet passing the UN Peacekeeping Cooperation Bill in 1992. The framework created, however, still imposed strict conditions for Japanese participation in UN peacekeeping operations, limiting Japanese Self-Defence Forces (SDF) activities to logistical support operations at most and prohibiting actual combat missions. The law was strengthened in 1998 and, again, in 1999. Following the events of 11 September 2001, the Diet passed an Anti-Terrorism Special Measures law (ATSML) in October 2001 (revised in 2002 and, again, in 2004) and a Law Concerning Special Measures on Humanitarian and Reconstruction Assistance (LCSMHRA) in July 2003 authorizing the deployment of small elements of Ground Self-Defence Force and Air Self-Defence Force units in support of the US-led Operation Iraqi Freedom.

Some analysts, such as Christopher Hughes, conclude that:

> there is still no consensus among [Japanese] policy-makers and commentators with regard to exactly what type of precedent the ATSML and LCSMHRA set for the overall future trajectory of Japan's security policy ... [they] may not lead to any fundamental deviation from the traditional pattern of the incremental expansion of Japan's security role, both independently and in conjunction with the US, which still leaves in place the constitutional and other prohibitions on the use of Japanese military power.[2]

We disagree. Japanese public opinion has been galvanized into supporting Japan's development as a 'normal power' in an increasingly uncertain world. North Korea's missile test conducted over the Sea of Japan in August 1998 and the sense of vulnerability it created in Japan, were especially shocking for a Japanese populace that had become accustomed to the protection afforded by the US extended deterrence guarantees that were forged under the 'Yoshida Doctrine' at the outset of the Cold War. Increasingly fragile oil lifelines, the rise of a truly international terrorist threat and 'China's rise' competing with Japan's economic dominance throughout Asia were further catalysts for changing the fundamental mindset of the Japanese electorate. When the United States decided to attack the Taliban in Afghanistan on 7 October 2001, and asked Japan for its support, Prime Minister Koizumi overcame what political opposition to dispatching SDF units abroad remained in Japan, dispatching a Maritime Self-Defence Force flotilla to the Indian Ocean in support of US and other coalition forces. A year later, the Japanese government sent additional naval firepower (including an Aegis vessel) to those waters. The aforementioned Japanese deployments to Iraq in 2003 signalled the Koizumi government's acceptance of the Bush administration's premise that a new 'Long War' threatening US and allied economies and societies was under way and that Iraq was a fundamental part of this geopolitical equation. The murder of two Japanese diplomats in Iraq during November 2003 only reinforced Japan's resolve to contribute more directly to international security peace-building. Japan has thus become more proactive in authorizing SDF participation in numerous military operations around the world, as well as bolstering its military and defence capabilities and technologies at home.[3]

Japan's shift towards strategic normality has perhaps been somewhat underplayed relative to the economic and military rise of China but it is no less significant. How Japan applies its growing military power will become increasingly important in Asia-Pacific security politics and to the future of the entire international order. It will also affect how effective the United States can be in dealing with China and North Korea.[4] Central to these outcomes is Japan's future security image in the Asia-Pacific. Will ASEAN states and Japan's Northeast Asian neighbours ever be able to accept a more 'normal' Japan that demonstrates the will and capacity to engage in international security operations? Various perspectives of a 'normalizing' Japan are currently being debated. Among the most significant are: (1) Japan as an intensified 'spoke' within the US-led regional bilateral and international security networks; (2) Japan as a 'fortress state', trying to neutralize North Korean and Chinese power with or without American help; and (3) Japan as an increasingly committed 'multilateralist' employing comprehensive security and other strategies to 'socialize' its security identity within processes of regionalization. Other models (including Japan as an instigator of 'middle power regional diplomacy') exist but these three variants are prominent in the contemporary literature and will be evaluated here.

Japan as an intensified spoke

Japan has been an integral part of the US 'hub and spokes' strategy which has predominated in East Asia over the past half century. This concept features the United States as the 'hub' extending its power into the region via bilateral alliances with its formal bilateral treaty allies: Japan, Korea, Thailand, the Philippines and Australia. It was formed to contain Soviet and Chinese power during the Cold War and to compensate for the lack of a common history, culture and geography among US Asian allies commensurate to that in the North Atlantic Treaty Organization (NATO). Various American and Japanese security analysts insist that hub and spokes is still the best means for ensuring Asia-Pacific regional stability in the early twenty-first century, sustaining a strategically predictable security order within which Asian states can develop politically and economically without risking regional instability. In Japan's case, it may mean that the United States would be better able to constrain an unwarranted 'breakout' of Japanese military power that would intensify apprehensions about Japan by its regional neighbours while still encouraging Japan to engage in constructive defence burden-sharing.[5]

To be sure, constraints on the 'intensified spoke' approach still exist. Many residents of Okinawa, where the core of US military deployments in Japan is still located, view these American contingents as nothing less than occupation forces. There are major differences between the sentiments of Okinawans who constantly live with the spectre and inconvenience of US military operations on their doorstep and those of mainland Japanese who not only have not suffered such an inconvenience but who have actively resisted shifts of American forces to their own parts of the country.[6] While the roadmap agreement reached in early 2006 (see below) modified these concerns to some extent, the reality of American policy-makers needing to take into account 'several Japans' with different perceptions on the US military presence in their vicinity will continue to challenge their quest to ensure future alliance support.

Embodiments of the hub and spokes dynamic in United States–Japan security relations include the recent willingness of the so-called 'two-plus-two' summit of Japanese and US foreign and defence ministers to address regional issues (such as the Taiwan Strait) more candidly, and global issues more comprehensively. The Trilateral Strategic Dialogue's elevation to the ministerial level of discussions in early 2006 expands this pattern. The culmination of the so-called 'roadmap' agreement in May 2006 more closely integrating US and Japanese defence command and control networks, and growing cooperation on missile defence research and development constitute other significant milestones in United States–Japan bilateral ties.[7]

Notwithstanding these developments, however, the era of 'tight bilateralism', underscored by the exclusivist dyadic orientation of separate US alliances with each of its security partners in Asia, appears to be disappearing. No less an authority than US Secretary of Defense Donald Rumsfeld observed this at the 2006 Shangri-La Dialogue by noting that:

> for much of my adult lifetime, security and stability in the Pacific was maintained essentially by a network of bilateral defence relationships between the United States and our allies and partners. This was notably unlike the situation in Europe, where we had a relatively large and more formal alliance – the North Atlantic Treaty Organization. But now we see an expanding network of security cooperation in this region, both bilaterally between nations and multilaterally among nations – with the United States as a partner. We see this as a welcome shift.[8]

For its part, Japan appears to have embarked on a 'multi-tiered' approach to replace its complete adherence to hubs and spokes. As early as 1991, Japanese Foreign Minister Nakayama proposed a multilateral security forum that ultimately proved to be a model for the evolution of the ASEAN Regional Forum. It has also been an integral player in such multilateral organizations as the Trilateral Coordination and Oversight Group (with the United States and South Korea), the Korean Peninsula Energy Development Organization (KEDO), and the ASEAN + 3 initiative that led to the inaugural convening of the East Asia Summit at Kuala Lumpur in December 2005. As argued by Kuniko Ashizawa, the multi-tier approach still preserves Japan's bilateral alliance with the United States but simultaneously lifts the 'psychological bar long entrenched in the thinking of [Japanese] policy-makers that excluded the exploration of multilateral options for regional security management'.[9] As will be discussed in more detail below, this trend has been increasingly accepted by the ASEAN states due to their increased economic interdependence with Japan, to generational change softening historical animosities, and to their perception of Japan as a possible balancing power against a rising China.[10] The multi-tiered system reflects the same design for stability and continuity as its hub and spokes predecessor: '[i]t is incrementalist because … [it] … does not completely discard the previous approach – hub-and-spoke bilateralism – but rather evolves from it by maintaining the United States–Japan bilateral alliance as one of the core functions'.[11]

Japan as a multilateralist?

Although hub and spokes is acknowledged by many observers as a critical part of Japan's transition as a regional and international strategic actor, others insist that Japan is already a full-fledged multilateralist. John Ikenberry is one of the most prominent advocates of the 'multilateral' school of thought, asserting that as Japan gradually diversifies its security contacts a future regional order is emerging 'that goes well beyond the logic of hub and spokes'. He posits that a neo-imperial logic would anticipate that Japan would be an important component in a 'global hub and spoke' system built around the American cultivation of 'bilateralism, "special relationships", client states, and patronage-oriented foreign policy' as a foundation for a 'new world order'.[12] Certainly Japan has been a primary spearhead in the development of the ARF and has also been a proponent for 'functional' approaches to defence communications that would enhance regional cooperative security. It has frequently hosted such conclaves as the Forum for Defence Authorities in the Asia-Pacific Region, the Western Pacific Naval Symposium and the annual Asia-Pacific Security Seminar (convened by Japan's National Institute of Defence Studies or NIDS).

Its support for comprehensive security initiatives is couched, however, in the knowledge that multilateral security dialogue bodies can only supplement rather than replace its existing bilateral defence relationship with Washington.[13] In fact, most of Japan's ongoing security links with ASEAN states are bilateral: exchange visits with defence ministers since the late 1980s, bilateral coordination with ASEAN maritime states via anti-piracy cooperation, and bilateral mechanisms contained within the December 2003 Japan–ASEAN Plan of Action operational-izing counterterrorism cooperation.[14] Only during a brief time (during the socialist Murayama government in 1994 to 1995) did Japan seriously contemplate priori-tizing multilateralism to promote regional security but this initiative was opposed by the Clinton administration and dropped in 1996.[15] Yet, a 'soft power' multilateral strategy can be pursued by Tokyo without compromising its traditional defence arrangement with the Americans. Unlike collective defence and collective security, cooperative security arrangements do not entail formal commitments to protect other member-states. They are more conducive to pursuing 'comprehensive security' approaches that integrate economic-orientated security concerns (that is, energy security, financial stability) with military security. Eric Heginbotham and Richard Samuels have termed this Japanese approach as a 'double hedging' doctrine – using the United States as a hedge against military threats while culti-vating different partners, including some clearly anathematic or potentially threatening to the United States such as Iran and China, to safeguard against economic isolation. But this strategy is expendable during times of acute regional and global crisis when the US alliance is again elevated to predominance as the 'ultimate insurance policy' against Japanese subservience to hostile forces.[16]

Another facet of the multilateralism occupying Japan's attention is the treatment given to its campaign to secure permanent voting status in the UN Security Council (UNSC). Given recent events in the Middle East, one could plausibly argue that the United Nations has ceased to function as the main instrument of world security. But the fact that Japan, the second largest contributor of funds to that body, is excluded from becoming a UNSC permanent member may well render to the majority of the Japanese people a feeling of resignation that the international society is not ready to accept Japan as a normal member-state after all.[17]

Until this and related 'global' issues are resolved in ways that render Japan at least a minimal status as an international power, it appears unlikely that successive Japanese governments will depart significantly from the judicious combination of regional bilateral and multilateral security politics they are now pursuing in favour of becoming a truly 'globalist' actor and/or an unmitigated 'good international citizen'.

Japan's security 'identity'

Apart from the realist embrace of the hub and spokes model and the institutionalists' endorsement of Japanese multilateralism, a third school of thought has materialized to explain Japan's security character: the 'analytical eclecticism' approach to understanding and reconciling countervailing forces of Japanese nationalism versus pacifism, the foreign policy approaches of bilateralism versus 'incipient' multilateralism and the ideational factors of an Asia-Pacific 'collective identity'.[18] Security policy interests and security institutions, that approach argues, can only be assessed properly if the norms and identities underwriting them are clearly understood and are incorporated into a coherent body of 'social knowledge'. Japanese policy problems can be best evaluated by discerning 'tight causal linkages' among 'subsystems' of factors shaped by both structure (the regional security environment and the structures or arrangements comprising it) and agency (who is successfully pushing for what policy or posture at a given time?).

The abstract reasoning and lexicon underlying many such theoretical approaches may, at times, inhibit the broader policy community, consumed with time-urgent deadlines and imperatives, from embracing them to the extent that it might other-wise do so to enrich its thinking about various policy areas. A more fundamental problem exists, however, with the application of 'social knowledge' as a dominant component of Japanese security politics. Such analysis usually (if not invariably) overrates the influence of pacifism and models of interdependence in Japanese foreign policy and invariably concludes that the anti-militarist strands in that policy will prevail over alternatives such as geopolitics, power balancing or other structural explanations.[19]

Japan's pacifism in the early Cold War years was certainly, in part, the product of American occupation and the price of economic reconstruction following war-time defeat. So, too, did it flow from the legacy of Hiroshima and Nagasaki where untold thousands of Japanese died at the hands of the world's only two nuclear attacks that have been launched. However, Japanese pacifism was also precipitated by Soviet and Chinese efforts to cultivate and to fund the propagation of such sentiments. Recent studies reveal that such funding played a key role in the spread of early Japanese postwar pacifism and that the declining influence of communism in Japan as the Cold War drew to a close can be attributed to the drying up of such financial support.[20] Yet the pacifist movement in Japan was decisively modified as early as the 1970s, when the United States requested greater alliance burden-sharing across the board in response to rising Soviet military power. At the time, Japanese leaders exhibited courage and foresight in overcoming the nearly univer-sal denial of a need for strategic thinking predicated on that country's unprecedented wartime experience as a victim of nuclear attacks. Japanese pacifism has more recently been transformed again (to increased levels of 'normal state' behaviour in a security context) by structural change: 'rogue state' missile threats to its sovereign territory, intensifying energy crises and the convergence of regional and global security dynamics. The constant element of Japanese behaviour in this process was alliance affiliation with the United States. As Jennifer Lind has concluded:

> A grand strategy based on antimilitarist norms would have led Japan to grad- ually distance itself from the United States and increasingly favor neutrality in the superpower standoff. Japan would have built a truly defensive military – one organized to protect the home islands from invasion, rather than equipped to fight air and naval battles across East Asia. And Tokyo would have urged the United States to reduce its military presence and activism in the region. Instead, Japan worried when the US military presence decreased; it responded to US force reductions by substantially increasing its own military power. A truly antimilitarist foreign policy was possible – and was advocated by the Japanese Left throughout the Cold War – but was not pursued.[21]

In concluding this brief survey of leading explanations for Japanese security policy and behaviour, we agree with Lind's observation that 'international relations scholars do not have well-developed theories of foreign policy'.[22] More certain is that both traditional and non-traditional security politics in East Asia are under- going a historical and comprehensive transformation that will require new Japanese and allied policy approaches to confront and overcome the very difficult challenges that are part of that transformation process. The two 'flashpoints' of the Korean peninsula and Taiwan (that are assessed in other chapters in this volume) are accom- panied by non-traditional security problems of terrorism and human security disasters (such as pandemics, natural disasters and resource disparities) that require new instrumentalities for consultation and coordination such as those promised within the TSD framework. Prior to addressing TSD directly, however, it may be useful to address Japan's evolving security relations with the ASEAN sub-region, where many 'non-traditional' security tests are bound to emerge for the remainder of this decade and beyond.

Evolving Japan–ASEAN politico-security relations

Japan commenced its post-Cold War relations with ASEAN positively by assuming an active role on the Cambodia issue (including the hosting of the June 1990 Tokyo Conference and with substantial financial support for the UN Transitional Auth- ority in Cambodia, UNTAC), and by advancing the 'Miyazawa Doctrine' in January 1993 that explicitly stipulated Japan's willingness to help underwrite ASEAN-based multilateral security dialogues.[23] This approach was reinforced by the 'Hashimoto Doctrine', enunciated in January 1997, that expanded Japanese– ASEAN security dialogues to cover global as well as regional issues. Japan's basic approach to ASEAN is to strengthen its image as a reliable politico-security and economic partner for ASEAN (and its individual member-states) and to generate responses to sub-regional crises in the form of economic assistance and political support whenever appropriate. This posture underwrote the 'Koizumi Doctrine' (first articulated in Singapore by the Japanese Prime Minister in January 2002) that offered a vision of 'East Asian community-building' through a Japan–ASEAN Comprehensive Economic Partnership and through prioritizing and strengthening ASEAN + 3 mechanisms (significantly the Japanese government's Basic Strategies report released a few months before the Koizumi speech in Singapore made no mention of APEC or the ARF as tools for community-building).[24] Yet Japan remains aware that ASEAN + 3 and the East Asia Summit (EAS) process that has emanated from it have their limitations regarding its own national security strategy. As evidenced by Japan's resistance to China's 'exclusivist' policies, Tokyo remains highly concerned that any effective ASEAN community-building process cannot proceed without the endorsement and participation of the United States.[25]

The need for Japan to be viewed as a regional security actor largely compatible with US objectives and policies in the region has constrained its propensity to shape its own regional security identity, and those security ties it has cultivated with ASEAN are proving to be no exception. Japan's highly homogeneous society contrasts noticeably with most ASEAN countries' struggles to cope with, and overcome, widespread racial, social and cultural diversities and tensions. Accordingly, recent Japanese forays into the Southeast Asian security arena have tended to be low-key or 'functional' (directed towards specific policing or order-building tasks that will generate widespread consensus) and usually (but not always) coordinated with Washington beforehand. Australia has a deep familiarity with these issues and challenges and could also advise Japan constructively on how to better adjust and become more sensitive to the heterogeneity of ASEAN cultures and societies as they collectively struggle towards transforming an 'imagined community' into reality.[26] It must also be noted that Japan continues to incur an 'image problem' with Southeast Asia over unresolved historical issues and relative to its worsening tensions with China.[27]

Recent Japanese security initiatives directed towards ASEAN have been particularly focused towards the counterterrorism and maritime security areas. Counterterrorism cooperation appears to be an especially relevant and urgent area of ASEAN policy coordination. A number of terrorist incidents have already taken place in Indonesia, the Philippines and Thailand. Those activities have been instigated by extreme religious or ideological activists with support from outside elements, but they tend to gain support from people at the grassroots level when there are also seriously deteriorating social and economic conditions in the countries concerned. A visible gap is widening between the rapidly growing rich and the remaining poor in Southeast Asia, and increased public transportation costs resulting from skyrocketing oil prices, together with rumours of corruption and collusion involving high government officials are testing ASEAN governments' political legitimacy and affecting region-wide stability. In order to cope with this kind of situation, it is not enough to solicit the citizens' power to strengthen their own society and governments. More coordinated efforts on the part of nations like

Australia and Japan can materially assist the citizens of the countries concerned. If regional terrorist activities increase the need for internationally coordinated measures to contain terrorist activities and if necessary, disarm the terrorist groups, Japan can play a key role in shaping and implementing such measures.

While the benefits of closer counterterrorism coordination may seem obvious, those initiatives involving Japan to date have been only partially successful due to ASEAN's still strong apprehensions over dealing with Tokyo in a security context. The November 2004 Joint Declaration on Counterterrorism Cooperation, for example, set the framework for upgraded collaboration on this issue by emphasizing upgraded cooperation on checking transnational crime. Progress in actually operationalizing the objectives designated in that proclamation, however, has been decidedly mixed due to differences among ASEAN states on how to implement common measures responding to the key problems it identified.[28] Despite slow progress in counterterrorism coordination, an annual counterterrorism dialogue was instituted in late June 2006 when ASEAN officials pledged closer cooperation with their Japanese counterparts in implementing joint measures for cooperating in combating terrorism in the sectors of transport security, border control/immigration, law enforcement, maritime security and public involvement in countering terrorism.[29]

Efforts to coordinate maritime security issues have been similarly hindered by intra-ASEAN rivalries. The respected think tank, the International Institute for Strategic Studies, recently observed that the interest of Japan and other great powers in helping to safeguard peninsular Southeast Asia's major straits and littorals has intensified because of the ongoing war on terrorism, increased threats of piracy, and concerns about emerging threats to energy supplies transiting the region en route to Northeast Asia.[30] Yet Japan's recent proposal to supplement trilateral Indonesia–Malaysia–Singapore coordinated patrolling (begun in July 2004) with an 'Ocean Peacekeeping Concept', envisioning a multinational naval force to patrol both international and national waters, has been rebuffed by the Malay ASEAN states as encroaching upon their sovereignty. This response is consistent with ASEAN's rejection of a similar proposal (the Regional Security Maritime Initiative) forwarded by the US Pacific Command. Since 2000, however, Japan's coastguard has conducted joint training exercises with separate ASEAN-state navies.[31]

One means by which closer Japanese cooperation with Southeast Asia can develop in the broader context of 'regional security' is through human security-related interaction and assistance. The monumental tsunami disaster exploding on the scene on Boxing Day 2004 prompted Japan, the United States, Australia, European Union states and others to undertake remarkably effective coordination for rescuing victims and reconstructing afflicted infrastructure in the damaged areas. This not only created greater impetus for engaging in cooperative security but presaged a more enduring framework of cooperation to hedge against future natural disasters, pandemics or other non-traditional security contingencies. Timely humanitarian operations on the part of Japan's SDF forces, working in conjunction with their Australian and American counterparts, greatly enhanced the images of these industrialized states because they demonstrated a willingness to employ military capabilities to carry out humanitarian missions. In spite of some unfounded speculation that Japan might intend to exploit the tsunami disaster for political purposes, Japan's action has been accepted by most of its beneficiaries at face value.[32] Future joint security operations for non-combat purposes, coordinated by a TSD-style mechanism, could provide a 'human face' for trilateral alliance cooperation.

Conclusion: the Trilateral Security Dialogue as a multilateral security instrument

Given the rapidly changing context of Japan's regional security politics in both Northeast Asia (covered by Chapters 6 and 7 in this volume) and Southeast Asia, the Trilateral Security Dialogue (TSD) is surfacing as a highly appropriate consultative forum for allied consensus-building. Moreover, the issues it must address to achieve and sustain policy relevance cut across these two sub-regions. Responding to Chinese power, whether by initiating a mutual engagement strategy with Beijing or, more intermittently, posing a collective united front against Chinese geopolitical assertiveness, can be most effectively achieved by Washington, Tokyo and Canberra working together in a TSD. Australia's extensive trade ties with Northeast Asia, combined with its formal diplomatic ties with North Korea and its missile defence collaboration with the United States and Japan, justify its systematic entrée into United States–Japan strategic deliberations on Northeast Asian problems. Similarly, Japan's substantial commercial and maritime interests merge with its intensifying human security agenda to make it a natural partner with Australia and the United States in shaping the Southeast Asian security environment. In that context, however, all three countries must take pains not to give an impression that the TSD is exclusively concerned with 'containing' China, North Korea or any other third country.

It is important, therefore, that the three allies develop a joint perspective on regional security. The TSD provides one mechanism for realizing their common security objectives. In this context, it is essential that Japan, while maintaining its fundamental security framework with the United States, should nevertheless play a greater ASEAN security role by supporting and undertaking well-defined collective security responsibilities in the region, including those that may involve selected SDF applications to conflict prevention or to peace-building. This may imply further careful review of constitutional prerogatives and revisions.

Australia, the United States and Japan share fundamental democratic values and an enduring respect for freedom. The three countries enjoy sustained prosperity by adhering to and applying market economy principles. However, they live in a region where security challenges are becoming increasingly complex. Japan's and Australia's regional neighbours reflect widely diverse cultures and different levels of living standards. The TSD partners must cooperate closely and effectively if they are to realize their common vision of regional and international peace and prosperity and facilitate institutional approaches to achieving that end.

Notes

1 See, for example, T. R. Reid and John Burgess (1990), 'US critics not satisfied with Japan's $4 billion contribution', *Washington Post*, 6 October, p. A24.
2 Christopher W. Hughes (2004), 'Japan's security, the US–Japan alliance and the "war on terror"', *Australian Journal of International Affairs*, vol. 58, no. 4, p. 429.
3 Comprehensive accounts of Japan's path to becoming a more proactive military power from the early 1990s onward include Christopher W. Hughes (2005), *Japan's Re-emergence as a 'Normal' Military Power*, Adelphi Paper 368, London: International Institute of Strategic Studies; Hughes (2004), 'Japan's security', pp. 427–45; and Alan Dupont (2004), *Unsheathing The Samurai Sword: Japan's Changing Security Policy*, Lowy Institute Paper 3, Sydney: Lowy Institute for International Policy.
4 These points are underscored by Hughes (2005), *Japan's Re-emergence as a 'Normal' Military Power*, pp. 15–16.
5 For a recent and typical official US rationalization of this alliance system, see Ambassador Marie T. Huhtala, Deputy Assistant Secretary for East Asian and Pacific Affairs (2005), 'US–Asia relations: the next four years', remarks to the Asia Society/Texas Annual Ambassadors Forum, Houston, Texas, 11 February, available at: www.state.gov/p/eap/rls/rm/2005/42792.htm (accessed 20 September 2006). Recent, favourable academic appraisals of the hub and spokes arrangement include David Shambaugh (2005), 'The evolving Asian system: implications for regional security architecture', delivered at a conference sponsored by the German Institute for International and Security Affairs and the Stiftung Wissenschaft und Politik, Berlin, 14/15 December; Kent E. Calder (2004), 'Securing security through prosperity: the San Francisco System in comparative perspective,' *Pacific Review*, vol. 17, no. 1, 135–57; Michael Mastanduno (2005), 'US foreign policy and the pragmatic use of international relations', *Australian Journal of International Affairs*, vol. 59, no. 3, especially pp. 322–23.
6 See, for example, Robert D. Eldridge (2000), 'Okinawa and the Nago heliport problem in the US–Japan relationship', *Asia Pacific Review*, vol. 7, no. 1, pp. 137–56.
7 See US Department of State, 'United States–Japan Roadmap for Realignment Implementation Issued Following May 1, 2006 Meeting of the United States–Japan Security Consultative Committee involving Secretary of State Condoleezza Rice, Secretary of Defense Donald Rumsfeld, Japanese Minister of Foreign Affairs Taro Aso, Japanese Minister of State for Defence Fukushiro Nukaga', available at: www.state.gov/r/pa/prs/ps/2006/65517.htm (accessed 20 September 2006).
8 US Department of State, Office of International Information Programs (2006), 'International cooperation vital to fight extremists, Rumsfeld says. Defense secretary outlines views on Pacific region, world affairs at Singapore meeting', *Washington File*, 3 June, available at: http://usinfo.state.gov (accessed 20 September 2006).
9 Kuniko Ashizawa (2002), 'Japan's approach toward Asian regional security: from "hub-and-spoke" multilateralism to "multi-tiered"', *Pacific Review*, vol. 16, no. 3, pp. 363, 366 and 378.
10 Bhubhindar Singh (2002), 'ASEAN's perceptions of Japan', *Asian Survey*, vol. 42, no. 2, pp. 277–78.
11 Ashizawa (2002), 'Japan's approach toward Asian regional security', p. 377.
12 John Ikenberry (2004), 'American hegemony and East Asian order', *Australian Journal of International Affairs*, vol. 58, no. 3, p. 353; and Ikenberry (2005), 'Power and liberal order: America's postwar world order in transition', *International Relations of the Asia Pacific*, vol. 5, no. 2, p. 134.
13 Glenn D. Hook *et al.* (2005), *Japan's International Relations: Politics, Economics and Security*, 2nd edn, London: Routledge, p. 263.
14 Ibid., pp. 258–59.
15 Ibid., pp. 159, 263.

16 Eric Heginbotham and Richard Samuels (2002), 'Japan's dual hedge', *Foreign Affairs*, vol. 81, no. 5, pp. 110–21.

17 Comprehensive background on the UN issue is offered by Ronald Dore (1997), *Japan, Internationalism and the UN*, London: Routledge.

18 Exemplifying the 'analytical eclectic' approach are Peter J. Katzenstein and Naburo Okawara (2001/2002), 'Japan, Asian-Pacific security and the case for analytical eclecticism', *International Security*, vol. 26, no. 3, pp. 153–85; Nobuo Okawara and Peter J. Katzenstein (2001), 'Japan and Asian-Pacific security: regionalization, entrenched bilateralism and incipient multilateralism', *Pacific Review*, vol. 14, no. 2, pp. 165–94; and various sections of Richard J. Samuels (1994), *Rich Nation, Strong Army: National Security and the Technological Transformation of Japan*, Ithaca, NY: Cornell University Press. A robust realist rejoinder to the points developed in much of the above literature is offered by Jennifer Lind (2004), 'Pacificism or passing the buck? Testing theories of Japanese security policy', *International Security*, vol. 29, no. 1, pp. 92–121.

19 Lind (2004), 'Pacificism or passing the buck', p. 101.

20 These are assessed by Ivan Ivanovich Kovalenko, former deputy director of the International Department of the Soviet Union's Communist Party, in his book published in Japanese, Tai-nichi Kosaku-no Kaiso, 'Reflections on the Soviet Union's operation towards Japan', published by Bungei Shunju in 1996, pp. 222–26. Stanislav A. Levchenko (1988), *On the Wrong Side: My Life in the KGB*, Washington, DC: Pergamon-Brassey's International Defense Publications, also asserts similar points. He was an intelligence officer of the Soviet Union betrayed to the West in the late 1980s. Both Levchenko and Kovalenko assert that the financial aid to the Japan Communist Party from foreign communist sources amounted to US$500,000 during the period from 1945 to 1964. The Japanese Socialist Party (JSP) requested financial aid from the Soviet Union but refused to accept any direct transfer of such funds. Accordingly, various Japanese companies with JSP connections received assistance from Moscow disguised in the form of 'friendly trade'. Also see Akihiko Tanaka, Professor of the Tokyo University who quotes those documentations from Soviet sources in his book, *Atarashii Chuusei [The New Middle Ages]*, Tokyo: Nihon Keizaishinbun, 2003, p. 31 which refers to financial aid directed to the Japan Communist party as well as the Japanese Socialist Party. This study compares such funding to the financial assistance from the United States' Central Intelligence Agency (CIA) to the Liberal Democratic Party (LDP) and other conservative Japanese political elements. One of this chapter's authors (Watanabe) served as a private secretary to Chief Cabinet Secretary Susumu Nikadio (from 1971 until 1973) and recalls such assistance, particularly from Beijing, as generating serious concern within Japanese government circles.

21 Lind (2004), 'Pacificism or passing the buck', pp. 119–20.

22 Ibid., p. 120.

23 Hook *et al.* (2005), *Japan's International Relations*, p. 223.

24 Mike Mochizuki (2003), 'Strategic thinking under Bush and Koizumi: implications for the US–Japan alliance', *Asia-Pacific Review*, vol. 10, no. 1, pp. 92–93.

25 An objective account of the EAS inaugural session is provided by Mohan Malik (2005), 'The East Asian summit: more discord than accord', *Yale Global Online*, 20 December, available at: http://yaleglobal.yale.edu/display.article?id = 6645 (accessed 20 September 2006). Most ASEAN + 3 members share the Japanese approach. For background, see Markus Hund (2003), 'ASEAN Plus Three: towards a new age of pan-East Asian regionalism? A skeptic's appraisal', *Pacific Review*, vol. 16, no. 3, pp. 383–417.

26 For a worthwhile account on how to approach the problem of socially and culturally diverse polities with the intent of achieving greater consensus and unification see Benedict Anderson (1983), *Imagined Communities: Reflections on the Origins and Spread of Nationalism*, London: Verso.

27 See Eric Teo Chu Cheow (2005), 'Aftershocks in Southeast Asia', *Asia Times Online*, 24 May, available at: www.atimes.com/atimes/Southeast_Asia/GE24Ae02.html; and Barry Desker (2006), 'Southeast Asia casts wide net for cooperation', *Yale Global Online*, 30 May, available at: http://yaleglobal.yale.edu/display.article?id=7484 (both sites accessed 20 September 2006).

28 See David Fouse and Yoichiro Sato (2006), 'Japan's comprehensive counterterrorism assistance to Southeast Asia', Asia-Pacific Center for Security Studies, February, available at: www.apcss.org/Publications/APSSS/JapanCTCooperation.pdf (accessed 20 September 2006).

29 See Japan Ministry of Foreign Affairs (2006), 'Co-chair's summary of discussions and recommendations, ASEAN–Japan Counterterrorism Dialogue', 29–30 June, Tokyo, Japan, available at: www.infojapan.org/region/asia-paci/asean/dialogue/summary 0606.html (accessed 20 September 2006).

30 International Institute for Strategic Studies (2006), *The Military Balance 2006*, London: Taylor & Francis, p. 254.

31 Lieutenant John F. Bradford, US Navy (2005), 'The growing prospects of maritime security cooperation in Southeast Asia', *Naval War College Review*, vol. 58, no. 3, pp. 76–77; and Bradford (2004), 'Japanese anti-piracy initiatives in Southeast Asia: policy formulation and the coastal state responses', *Contemporary Southeast Asia*, vol. 26, no. 3, pp. 488–93.

32 The Spanish think tank Real Elcano Institute of International and Strategic Studies (based in Madrid) observed that the SDF deployment to Aceh may have been part of what could be termed Japan's 'disaster diplomacy' to trump Chinese influence that had been growing in Southeast Asia since the Asian financial crisis. See Soeren Kern (2005), 'The geopolitics of tsunami relief', US-Transatlantic Dialogue Report No. 8, January.

11 Trilateralism and the United States

Satu P. Limaye

US strategy for the Asia-Pacific and the Trilateral Strategic Dialogue

Though the inaugural ministerial-level meeting of the United States–Japan–Australia Trilateral Strategic Dialogue (TSD) occurred in March 2006, trilateral meetings at the senior officials' level have taken place since 2002. It is important to understand the developments in United States–Japan–Australia cooperation in the context of the Bush administration's approach towards the Asia-Pacific region, including continuities and changes over the past half decade. Several aspects of the Bush administration's approach to security and foreign policy in general, and to the Asia-Pacific in particular, have favoured more coordinated ties between the United States, Japan and Australia.

The first has been the emphasis placed on relations with 'allies and friends'. The first of four goals identified in the 2001 Quadrennial Defense Review (QDR) – much of which was written prior to the terrorist attacks on the United States in September 2001 and released just two weeks after – was assuring allies and friends of the United States' steadiness of purpose and its capacity to fulfil its security commitments.[1] This emphasis on revitalizing alliances was calculated to signal a divergence from the Clinton administration, which some in the Bush administration perceived as having neglected America's key partnerships. Hence, the Bush administration initially sought to focus on the Republic of Korea (ROK or South Korea) over the Democratic People's Republic of Korea (DPRK or North Korea), Taiwan over China, and most importantly Japan.[2] Australia, too, received considerable administration attention. With slightly less emphasis, the Bush administration revived consideration to a number of Southeast Asian friends, including Singapore,[3] Thailand and the Philippines, and sought restored but limited security links with Indonesia – this latter objective now achieved. Indeed, the concept of an 'East Asian littoral' articulated in the 2001 QDR gave importance to Asian friends beyond traditional allies Japan and ROK.

Other than to distinguish itself from the preceding administration, the early emphasis on 'allies and friends' also was designed to reinforce ideological components of US foreign policy (that is, democracies, open markets), American primacy in the region based on politico-military relationships with welcoming partners rather than engagement through weak multilateral organizations, a revised regional threat assessment (that is, a rising China), and a distinction between those countries the United States considered like-minded, cooperative and non-threatening, and those it did not.

Since 2001, the Bush administration's emphasis on alliances has not abated. Indeed, two of the most recent policy documents, the 2006 Quadrennial Defense Review and the 2006 National Security Strategy (NSS), place a premium on alliances. Of the NSS's eight 'substantive' chapters (ten if one includes the introduction and conclusion) three explicitly or implicitly speak to the importance of alliances for US strategy. The specific chapters are entitled: *Strengthen Alliances to Defeat Global Terrorism and Work to Prevent Attacks against Us or Our Friends*; *Work with Others to Defuse Regional Conflicts*; and *Prevent Enemies from Threatening Us, Our Allies, and Our Friends with Weapons of Mass Destruction*. As these chapter headings make clear, the purposes of alliances are focused on three objectives: defeat terrorism, defuse regional conflicts, and prevent WMD threats. As these objectives suggest, the purpose of alliances, partnerships and friendships are not only to protect a particular state from traditional Cold War era threats such as invasion – which today are extraordinarily unlikely – but a much more proactive, geographically unconstrained and non-traditional threat-based function.[4] The 2006 QDR articulates the US view of the evolution of alliances in the following way:

> Long-standing alliance relationships will continue to underpin unified efforts to address 21st century security challenges. These established relationships continue to evolve, ensuring their relevance even as new challenges emerge. The ability of the United States and its allies to work together to influence the global environment is fundamental to defeating terrorist networks. Wherever possible, the United States works with or through others: enabling allied and partner capabilities, building their capacity and developing mechanisms to share the risks and responsibilities of today's complex challenges.[5]

Official US documents and the comments of senior officials also identify other evolutions for long-standing alliances. One element is the need to link long-standing alliances with new, emerging partnerships. For example, in the 2006 QDR, immediately following a comment about the utility of alliances with Japan, Australia and Korea, the document notes that:

> India is also emerging as a great power and a key strategic partner. Close cooperation with these partners in the long war on terrorism, as well as in efforts to counter WMD proliferation and other non-traditional threats, *ensures the continuing need for these alliances and for improving their capabilities* [emphasis added].[6]

Implicit is the desire to 'knit' long-standing alliances together and potentially include new partners (for example, India). As Secretary of Defense Donald Rumsfeld told an audience at the 2006 Shangri-la Dialogue organized by the International Institute for Strategic Studies in Singapore, 'an important and constructive trend

... [is] an *expanding network of security cooperation* [emphasis added] in this region, both bilaterally between nations and multilaterally among nations – with the United States as a partner. We see this as a welcome shift.'[7]

Related to thinking and action about alliances, another aspect of the context of United States–Japan–Australia trilateral relations has been the views of the administration regarding multilateralism. It will be recalled that the Bush administration's scepticism about regimes, treaties and multilateral organizations was a feature of the early approach towards Asia – and elsewhere. The Bush administration's objective was a US foreign and security policy built on self-reliance – itself based on unrivalled (and not to be rivalled) power, assured self-defence (for example, through missile defence), flexibility (fewer regime and treaty commitments), and key bilateral relationships around the globe. The Director of Policy Planning at the State Department, Richard Haass, famously spoke of 'a la carte multilateralism' – a formulation apparently designed to suggest that multilateralism was not rejected out of hand, but would be engaged only as and when the United States chooses to participate. The favoured phrase in President Bush's White House for more than one country working with the United States was 'coalition of the willing'. It must be said that administration thinking about the utility of multilateralism has shifted to a more accommodative stance, but concerns about such multilateralism in the Asia-Pacific now centre on developments that seek to exclude the United States. Secretary of Defense Rumsfeld, speaking at the Shangri-La meeting, argued that 'Inclusive, multinational institutions and activities such as this conference, as well as the ASEAN Regional Forum, and the Asia-Pacific Economic Cooperation (APEC), are leading the way.'[8] It is noteworthy that the Secretary did not mention other on-going efforts such as the ASEAN + 3 (APT) or last year's East Asia Summit (EAS) – both of which exclude the United States. In such a context, trilateral relations between the United States, Japan and Australia are not meant to replace multilateralism that is inclusive, but have the effect of reinforcing relationships so that prospects for the development of exclusionary groupings will be less attractive. The 2006 QDR alludes to this effect in saying that 'alliances with Japan, Australia, Korea and others *promote bilateral and multi-lateral engagement in the region* [emphasis added] and cooperative actions to address common security threats'.[9]

In the context of multilateralism, the economic aspect is especially important, and related to the efforts at trilateralism. Given that one of America's core interests in the Asia-Pacific, as elsewhere, is continued access to commercial engagement, the United States will remain wary of multilateral efforts that seek to create a closed economic community. There are many ways for the United States to prevent being closed out. One way is through the negotiation of free trade agreements (FTAs) as it has concluded with Australia and Singapore and is in the process of doing with Thailand, Malaysia and South Korea. A second way is of course to help ensure that world trade talks succeed. A more indirect way is to continue to buttress ties with major trading partners who are also allies in order for there to be little attraction for them to a closed economic community in the Asia-Pacific.

A third element of the context for trilateral relations relates to the military and defence realm of involvement in the Asia-Pacific. It will be recalled that in the 2001

QDR, of the five 'critical areas' described in the QDR, three encompassed Asia (Northeast Asia, the East Asian littoral – 'stretching from south of Japan through Australia and into the Bay of Bengal' – and Southwest Asia).[10] The administration initiated numerous studies as part of a planned process to re-allocate US resources, personnel and attention to the region. The 2001 QDR also articulated plans to re-deploy military assets to East Asia and to increase 'access' for US forces in the region. Specifically:

> The QDR ... call[ed] for an increase in aircraft carrier presence in the region ... increased contingency stationing for the US Air Force ... and the possibility that three or four more surface combatants ... and a yet to be converted Trident-class SSGN (with capability for 'stealthy' cruise missile strikes), could be forward stationed in East Asia.[11]

Moreover, 'theater engagement' was replaced by 'theater security cooperation', indicating an emphasis on access, interoperability and intelligence cooperation. Both the proposed re-deployments and the move from military-to-military engagement to security cooperation suggested a more military-oriented approach to regional security based on repeated administration warnings that war in Asia was more probable than in Europe. Under the earlier 2001 QDR there was to be a continued commitment to forward-stationed forces – though these forces were to be adjusted in scale and location to meet a range of missions and respond to technological innovations. Finally, the commitment to missile defences was in part aimed at 'undermining China's growing strategic capability'[12] as well as threats from rogue countries with weapons of mass destruction.

In the latest 2006 QDR, the commitment to enhanced and increased forces is retained. Specific references are made to air force rotations in Guam, the operational availability of six carriers, and basing 60 per cent of the US submarine fleet in the region. A second element of the military aspect of the continuing US role relates to adjustments in the US military 'footprint' in regional countries. Again, the motivations of the force posture adjustments have been to meet new non-traditional security challenges such as terrorism and 'update and modernize' Cold War alliances so as to gain flexibility for the use of forces. An additional compelling motivation has been to work with host governments and communities to reduce the burdens on local populations. In this context, enhanced as well as adjusted military and security ties with both Japan and Australia contribute to the overall positive realignment of US regional forces. In Japan, the Defense Policy Review Initiative (DPRI) talks between Washington and Tokyo have led to important adjustments including the planned relocation of several thousand marines and their families to Guam and the movement of marine facilities to the northern part of Okinawa to reduce the irritations that have built up over their presence in the southern, more populous areas. Other changes also work to reduce the burdens on Okinawa while working towards more closely coordinated activities.

Similarly, there have been significant increases in United States–Australia military cooperation, and in bilateral discussions of the overall global posture review that the United States has been conducting over the last few years. For example, given that the global posture review (GPR) focuses on increasing flexibility, mobility and lethality, the Joint Combined Training Center (JCTC) contributes to these GPR priorities. In fact, the JCTC must be seen as a capability rather than a stand-alone facility. Some time ago a US official explained the evolving United States–Australia defence relationship by saying that 'Obviously, as we move to more of a global positioning posture and a more flexible employment of our forces it may be that Australia is even more useful for maintenance and repair functions.'[13]

In addition to these three basic factors which provide the context for regularized trilateral discussions, there are other factors that could sustain the now-established TSD. The first, quite simply, is the level that has been reached in United States–Japan and United States–Australia relations, and to a lesser extent in Australia–Japan relations. As the National Security Strategy of 2006 says about United States–Japan relations:

> With Japan, the United States enjoys *the closest relations in a generation* [emphasis added]. As the world's two largest economies and aid donors, acting in concert multiplies each of our strengths and magnifies our combined contributions to global progress.[14]

And as for Australia, the same document states that 'With Australia, our alliance is global in scope. From Iraq and Afghanistan to our historic FTA, we are working jointly to ensure security, prosperity, and expanded liberty.'[15]

A second factor that underpins the TSD from the US perspective is the increasing emphasis on shared values, and the willingness to build on those values by promoting democracy. The 2006 NSS suggests 'Asian nations that share our values can join us in partnership to strengthen new democracies and promote democratic reforms throughout the region.'[16] Obviously, Japan and Australia among other countries certainly share US values and commitment to democracy and have the means to support its promotion.

Finally, what is striking is how appropriate it is for the United States to work with Japan and Australia in terms of overall US national strategy objectives as laid out in the 2002 and 2006 National Security Strategies (which share eight objectives with only one addition in 2006 – 'Engage the opportunities and confront the challenges of globalization'). The only objective to which Japan and Australia cannot contribute is 'Transform America's national security institutions to meet the challenges and opportunities of the 21st century.' All others, as listed below, are natural areas for the United States, Japan and Australia to work together.

- Champion aspirations for human dignity;
- Strengthen alliances to defeat global terrorism and work to prevent attacks against us and our friends;
- Work with others to defuse regional conflicts;
- Prevent our enemies from threatening us, our allies, and our friends with WMD;

- Ignite a new era of global economic growth through free markets and free trade;
- Expand the circle of development by opening societies and building infrastructure of democracy;
- Develop agendas for cooperative action with other main centers of global power;
- Engage the opportunities and confront the challenges of globalization.[17]

If these factors provide the context within which trilateral dialogue has increased and become formalized, what kinds of challenges might the TSD effort face?

Potential challenges to calibrating the TSD

No security partnership is stress free, and this applies to allies even as close as the United States, Japan and Australia. Throughout postwar history, occasional differences emerged in both United States–Japan and United States–Australia relations. Tensions over the reversion of Okinawa to the Japanese mainland leading to the renegotiation of the United States–Japan Mutual Security Treaty in 1960, over United States–Japan trade relations during the early 1990s and the *Ehime Maru* incident in which an American submarine inadvertently rammed into and sank a Japanese fishing and training vessel off Oahu in 2001 can be cited as intermittent blips in United States–Japan politico-security ties. Australian reluctance to include Taiwan within the ANZUS defence perimeters during the Cold War, American reluctance to offer defence guarantees for Commonwealth defence efforts on the Malayan peninsula during the *Konfrontasi* with Indonesia in the early 1960s and the decidedly independent Australian foreign policy orientation of the Whitlam government in the early 1970s all raised questions about the durability of Australian–American strategic relations. History will record, however, that these intra-alliance strains were overcome and that both bilateral alliances emerged stronger than ever to face ensuing, greater external challenges.

In the context of the TSD, perhaps the most often mentioned difficulty for coordination among the three countries is China. The reason for this is not so much that the United States, Japan and Australia have fundamentally different interests regarding China, but there are clearly different emphases and priorities. In terms of the United States, the Bush administration's emphasis on allies and friends has been partly reflective of its views of China – which seems contradictory. The first was to regard China, in former Secretary of State Colin Powell's words, as a 'competitor, a potential regional rival',[18] and second to treat it as a less central player in US Asia policy. Both approaches deviated sharply from the Clinton administration's formulation of China as a 'strategic partner' and de facto treatment of it as the centrepiece of the United States–Asia relationship. Then Secretary Powell's statement that the United States would 'treat China as she merits'[19] appeared to refer not only to competition and rivalry, but to its proper weight relative to other regional countries. A pattern of statements and contacts were further evidence of an intention to take China off centre-stage of US Asia policy.[20]

But the apparent contradiction of treating China both as a 'potential rival' and as 'peripheral' was really not a contradiction. By treating China as a less integral and determinative country to Asia's international relations, the administration was again reinforcing China's distinctiveness from America's allies and friends while simultaneously highlighting its potential threat. Over the past five years, the war on terrorism, Operation *Enduring Freedom* and Operation *Iraqi Freedom* have certainly reduced the day-to-day centrality of China in US policy.

However, as recent statements and documents from this administration make clear, China remains of prime concern on a range of issues. Indeed, one observer has noted that in the section on shaping the choices of countries at the strategic crossroads (these countries being China, Russia and India), space devoted to China is four times more than that to the other two countries. Much of the concern focuses on China's military potential. For example, the QDR states: 'Of the major and emerging powers, China has the greatest potential to compete militarily with the United States and field disruptive military technologies that could over time offset traditional US military advantages absent US counter strategies.'[21] In a nutshell, current administration policy regarding China, as baldly stated in the 2006 National Security Strategy, is to 'encourage China to make the right strategic choices for its people, while we hedge against other possibilities'.[22]

Meanwhile, it is clear that increasing Sino-Japanese tensions since the late 1990s have had the effect of hardening Tokyo's views of China, while Australia's relations with China have seen something of a boom – primarily fuelled by economic interests, but also by some remarks made by Australia's officials that cast doubt on the country's position in a possible cross-straits crisis. Under such conditions, it is quite natural to wonder whether the three countries can coordinate policies regarding China. Specifically, there is tacit concern occasionally expressed by observers in all three countries that the United States and Japan will tend to be more 'hawkish' towards China while Australia will seek a more accommodative approach. For example, some US observers have worried that former Japanese Prime Minister Koizumi's visits to the Yasukuni shrine seriously worsened Japan's relationships with China and South Korea. Even US policy-makers have expressed concern about the state of Sino-Japanese relations. United States Assistant Secretary of State for East Asia and Pacific Christopher Hill told a US audience during early 2006 when Sino-Japanese animosities appeared to be spiralling towards a new low:

> the US wants to see China and Japan also have an excellent relationship. It does not do us any good whatsoever to see the current difficulties in the relationship. We want them to have a successful relationship. It is not in our interest that they don't have such a relationship.[23]

Conversely, US observers intermittently worry that Australia's booming economic relationship with China could spill over in ways that might undermine that country's extraordinary loyalty to the United States in a future East Asian crisis such as Taiwan where Beijing and Washington confront each other's interests. This concern has been expressed on several occasions by long-time Australia aficionado and former US Deputy Secretary of State, Richard Armitage. It was recently reiterated by American analysts in the aftermath of Australia's April 2006 decision to sell uranium to China who feared that this decision would allow Beijing to 'ramp up' its nuclear weapons capacity.[24]

In fact, a careful reading of the comments of all three countries, and even more important their actions, suggests that the alleged gaps regarding China are narrower than they sometimes appear. All three countries, even the United States and Japan who have forthrightly expressed certain concerns, wish to avoid confrontation. At the same time, notwithstanding booming economic interests for all three countries, and some mixed signals on the political front by Australia, the importance of bilateral alliances with the United States requires caution in dealing with China. It is further worth noting that the joint statement, issued in Sydney in early 2006, addresses China as the first specific matter of the dialogue, but only in the most general of terms – welcoming 'China's constructive engagement in the region'.[25] Even if this comment reflects the minimum consensus regarding China, it difficult to see how the TSD by itself complicates all three countries' stated interest in a positive Chinese role in international and regional affairs. Indeed, the TSD could be one among many important tools or mechanisms for coordinating policy on China. The increasing complexity of 'China policy' in all three countries is evident – and primarily a function of China's rise and, therefore, requirement to address it across a range of constituencies, bureaucracies and interests. Hence, as and if the institutional basis of the TSD develops, the effort could be important in helping to coordinate approaches to China. Nevertheless, it is worth noting that, after China, the next three issues discussed in the joint statement (India and civilian nuclear cooperation with it, North Korea and the Six Party Talks, Burma/ Myanmar and Iran) all elicit far more specific recommendations for coordinated action. A sceptical reading of this would argue that the TSD statement could reach only the most anodyne basis of consensus about China whereas a more positive reading would note the effort to signal China, and others, that the TSD is 'not about China'.

A second potential challenge for the TSD is the degree to which American expectations of 'updated and modernized' alliances can be met. Japanese and Australian support for Operation *Enduring Freedom* and Operation *Iraqi Freedom* has been much appreciated in the United States, but within both countries voices have been raised about future support. In more operational terms, questions have also been raised about how partners in the region can maintain the kind of cooperation the United States seeks given growing technological gaps and resource constraints. This issue came up at this year's Shangri-la Dialogue when Ross Babbage of Australia informed Secretary of Defense Rumsfeld:

> we are seeing these networks of cooperation develop, at the same time the United States is of course pursuing a very strong modernization program ... the challenges of effectively conducting these combined operations and these combined activities when the gulf between the technological and operational level of the United States and most members of this region is widening.[26]

Secretary Rumsfeld's comments essentially counselled a comparative advantage approach to alliances, saying:

> there is no need for every country in the world to have aircraft carriers, for example … There are so many things that need to be done, that in many instances lend themselves to being done by smaller countries. Human intelligence is an example. There are so many things that are needed – niche capabilities – special operations, chemical and biological warfare capabilities. There are many, many things that a nation can do without being a large nation with an enormous defense budget.[27]

Whether this approach of apportioning responsibilities to global, non-traditional security challenges is consistent with respective interests remains to be seen.

A third issue raised in deliberations about the TSD relates to the regional security architecture. The first specific issue here is the impact of the TSD on other regional relationships. To my mind, this is not a particularly daunting problem for the TSD. Indeed, after the comment about welcoming China's constructive engagement with the region, the TSD joint statement concurs in the 'value of enhanced cooperation with other parties such as ASEAN and the Republic of Korea'. It has already been noted that the TSD statement also called for greater cooperation with India. The bottom-line is that the TSD is not a substitute for the three TSD parties' relationships with other regional countries and in fact the TSD can itself facilitate such enhanced cooperation. A second specific issue for the TSD in terms of its relationship to the regional security architecture relates to multilateralism or East Asian community-building. It is difficult to see how a dialogue between half-century-old allies can impede ASEAN or other efforts at regional community-building especially since all members of the TSD are also members of one or more overlapping regional efforts. The TSD actually allows the three parties to influence the development of East Asian multilateralism by coordinating efforts to make it inclusive, as occurred in working with Japan to bring India and Australia into the inaugural East Asia Summit. Notwithstanding the multiple, overlapping efforts at regional institution and norm-building, there appears to be little prospect that such a region-wide or even sub-regional multilateral organization will be the guarantor of conflict prevention, management or resolution.

TSD: the shape of things to come

In light of the context in which trilateral United States–Japan–Australia talks have taken place during the past half decade, and the challenges to cooperation and coordination that exist, what conclusions may be reached about the future of the TSD effort?

First, it is well to remember that the TSD has a critical word – *Dialogue*. This is important because contrary to some perceptions, the TSD is not an organization or a treaty or even an agreement. In the lexicon of foreign and security policy, dialogue is a less concrete and expectant term. Still, dialogue is a mechanism through which perceptions, information and activities can be shared. It remains to be seen when, how and on what such cooperation will take place.

Second, the TSD is not a replacement or substitute for existing bilateral alliances either with Japan or Australia, much less other US regional alliances and partnerships. The TSD is neither a critical piece of the regional security architecture nor mere decoration. Rather, it is a furnishing whose use and relevance will be shaped as interests and requirements evolve.

Third, there is no 'balance' between regional and global efforts of the TSD. Given the challenges that confront the international community, such distinctions are seen by many in the United States as less useful than they were in an earlier age. However, given practical constraints ranging from domestic opinion, constitutions and finances, there may be an allocation of emphasis and duties agreed to by the three countries.

Finally, the United States and Australia share an interest in a more robust Japanese international role, including in Asia, built on the basis of strong United States–Japan and strong Australia–Japan relations. The TSD can assist in facilitating a Japanese role consistent with the United States–Japan alliance and regional expectations. Indeed, the process of the TSD has already had the effect of strengthening the Tokyo–Canberra side of the triangle.

All in all, the Trilateral Security Dialogue between the United States, Japan and Australia represents a worthwhile initiative that could contribute to maintaining a relatively quiescent Asia-Pacific regional order. It will not be, and is not designed to be, the only factor, but is one element of an increasingly active regional political, security and economic environment.

Notes

1 US Department of Defense (2001), *Quadrennial Defense Review Report*, Washington, p. 11.
2 The top Asia hands in the first Bush administration were Japan rather than China 'hands' (e.g. Under Secretary Armitage, Assistant Secretary Kelly, and the National Security Council's Torkel Patterson followed by Dr Michael Green who left the administration in 2005).
3 Assistant Secretary of State for East Asian and Pacific Affairs James A. Kelly noted at his confirmation hearings that 'Singapore, a longtime friend that is not a treaty ally, recently completed new port facilities specifically designed to accommodate visits by US aircraft carriers'.
4 *The National Security Strategy of the United States of America* (2006), Washington, available at: www.whitehouse.gov/nsc/nss/2006/nss2006.pdf (accessed 19 October 2006).
5 US Department of Defense (2006), *Quadrennial Defense Review Report*, Washington, pp. 87–88.
6 Ibid., p. 88.
7 International Information Programs, News from Washington (2006), 'International cooperation vital to fight extremists, Rumsfeld says', International Institute for Strategic Studies Conference at the Shangri-la Hotel, Singapore, 3 June, available at: http://usinfo.state.gov/xarchives/display.html?p=washfile-english&y=2006&m=June&x=20060603140724retnuhb3.754824e-02 (accessed 19 October 2006).
8 Ibid.
9 US Department of Defense (2006), *Quadrennial Defense Review Report*, p. 88.

10 Europe and the Middle East were the other regions identified in the QDR.
11 Admiral Michael McDevitt (2001), 'The Quadrennial Defense Review and East Asia', PACNET no. 43, 26 October.
12 Professor Harry Harding (2001), 'The Bush administration's approach to Asia: before and after September 11', speech to The Asia Society, Hong Kong, 12 November.
13 US Undersecretary for Defense (Industry) Suzanne Patrick cited in John Kerin (2004), 'Diggers get 59 US Abrams tanks', *The Aussie*, 10 March.
14 *The National Security Strategy of the United States of America* (2006), p. 40.
15 Ibid.
16 Ibid.
17 Ibid., p. 1.
18 Colin L. Powell (2001), speech by Secretary of State-Designate to US Department of State Confirmation Hearing, 17 January, available at: www.state.gov/s/index.cfm?docid=443 (accessed 19 October 2006).
19 Ibid.
20 Despite the administration's desire to calibrate China's place in the region, it was difficult to do so. The first country to which then Secretary of State-Designate Powell turns his attention in his confirmation hearings is China. A couple of months later, in a prepared statement at his confirmation hearings, Assistant Secretary of State Kelly makes a brief reference to Japan but immediately turns to China – perhaps understandable in the aftermath of the landing of a US EP-3 electronic surveillance aircraft onto Chinese territory following a collision with a Chinese fighter three weeks earlier.
21 US Department of Defense (2006), *Quadrennial Defense Review Report*, p. 29.
22 *The National Security Strategy of the United States of America* (2006), p. 42.
23 Christopher R. Hill (2006), 'China and the future of the world', Opening Keynote Address to the Chicago Society, University of Chicago, 28 April, available at: http://chicagosociety.uchicago.edu/china/coverage/HillSpeech.pdf (accessed 23 October 2006).
24 Rich Bowdon (2006), 'Concerns expressed over Australia's uranium deal with China', *Worldpress.org*, 26 April, available at: www.worldpress.org/Asia/2327.cfm. On 18 August 2001, the *South China Morning Post* reported that Armitage stated that Australia would be threatened with a backlash from Washington if Canberra failed to support the United States in any future Asian conflict, available at: www.taiwandc.org/scmp-2001-05.htm. Armitage has since modified his position, noting that in regard to Taiwan, 'if we do our jobs correctly, Australia, the US and others who are interested, we won't bring about, we won't have a situation where force has to be brought to bear and we'll never have to face the question of what Australia does with the US, or for that matter, what the US does with Australia'. See an interview on *Lateline*, 19 August 2005, available at: www.abc.net.au/lateline/content/2005/s1442095.htm (all sites accessed 23 October 2006).
25 *Joint Statement Australia–Japan–United States, Trilateral Strategic Dialogue*, Sydney, 18 March 2006, available at: www.foreignminister.gov.au/releases/2006/joint_statement-aus-japan_usa_180306.html (accessed 19 October 2006).
26 International Information Programs, News from Washington (2006), 'International cooperation vital to fight extremists, Rumsfeld says'.
27 Ibid.

Part III
Key issue-areas

12 TSD

The economic dimensions

Charles E. Morrison

This chapter examines several aspects of the economic dimension of the Trilateral Strategic Dialogue (TSD). The author understands the TSD as indeed a 'dialogue', in which three nations with similar political and economic value systems, and with significant common and complementary strategic relationships and interests, share perspectives, consult on policy issues, and enhance the effectiveness of their foreign policies through cooperative behaviour. As such, and also because TSD is 'strategic', it will address 'external' issues, that is, issues associated with the forces in the regional and global environments that have the biggest impact on the common concerns of the three countries. These forces must include economic drivers, such as the 'rise of China' and ongoing processes of technological change and globalization, that are transforming power relationships in Asia and the Pacific and the structure of transnational economic activity, with profound economic, political and security implications. A twenty-first century dialogue that does not include economic drivers cannot be said to be truly strategic.

The way such forces will be reflected in the TSD will typically be over specific and current issues that have broader and longer-term implications. Economics as such were not featured prominently in the joint statement of the first Ministerial Meeting of the TSD in March 2006. However, 'cooperative frameworks' (along with democracy) was a 'particular focus' of the dialogue, and 'pressing non-traditional security issues' were also 'encompassed' in the agenda.[1]

This is consistent with the expertise of the three ministers, none of whom is noted for a deep interest in economics. It also reflects the jurisdiction of their ministries. For Japan and the United States (in contrast to Australia's Department of Foreign Affairs and Trade, which has both foreign affairs and trade ministers), international trade policy is primarily the concern of ministries other than the foreign ministry – Japan's Ministry of the Economy, Trade and Industry (METI) and the Office of the US Trade Representative (USTR) respectively. For all three countries, finance ministries/treasuries are primarily responsible for currencies and macroeconomic imbalances, a huge issue in the Pacific that seems unlikely to be addressed through the TSD.

Economics are deeply intertwined with security issues and thus will undoubtedly be important in future trilateral dialogues, depending in part on the salience of economic issues at the times of the dialogue and the predilections of the particular ministers involved. It can be argued, for example, that the 'rise of China' so far has been much more real in the economic than in the military or diplomatic dimensions, and that it is because of China's growing economic power that it is increasingly able to support these other attributes of power. Similarly frameworks for economic cooperation will continue to be prominent because the architectural issues are perceived to have important political and diplomatic implications. Since all three parties to the dialogue have vital stakes in the health of the regional and global economies and share basic economic values, they have a common interest in sharing perspectives on socio-economic challenges and, to some degree, in coordinating their approaches to these issues in other institutions.

This chapter will examine first the current state of regional economic cooperation frameworks and a related debate over the future of free trade areas in the Asia and Pacific region. It will also briefly review the issues associated with China's economic impact and non-traditional security (or 'human security') issues also of interest to the three countries.

The cooperative architecture

It is not surprising that cooperative frameworks should have been of particular interest to the three ministers at the first TSD meeting. The Asia-Pacific region is still in the formative stages of building economic cooperative frameworks, which were notably lacking only two decades ago.[2] These frameworks suggest putative political and diplomatic alignments and even international identities, and thus they have often been the subject of intense competition and diplomacy out of all proportion with their contemporary economic significance.[3] The most hotly contested issues involve leadership, member composition of a particular framework, how smaller structures relate to larger structures (including global architecture) and the substance and direction of cooperation. Australia, Japan and the United States have certainly not always seen eye-to-eye on these issues, although their current postures on issues of regional frameworks probably converge more than they have in past years.[4]

At the present time there exist three broad regional economic cooperation frameworks: (1) the Asia Pacific Economic Cooperation (APEC) forum, created in 1989, and now encompassing twenty-one 'economies' scattered around the Pacific, including Australia, Japan and the United States;[5] (2) the decade-old ASEAN + 3 (APT) framework of thirteen East and Southeast Asian nations, including Japan, but geographically excluding Australia and the United States; and (3) the brand-new East Asia Summit (EAS) framework of sixteen nations including Australia and Japan, but not the United States. The frameworks are differentiated in large part by geographical definition, APEC covering a broader Asia-Pacific mega-region, the APT defined by the traditional geographical conception of East Asia, and the EAS based on an expanded East Asia that includes neighbouring areas with strong East Asian interests and connections.

Each framework has distinctive assets and liabilities. APEC widened rather than deepened in its early years, resulting in an unwieldy grouping of economies from four continents.[6] The membership of Taiwan and Hong Kong in APEC also inhibits it from developing a more central security agenda. On the other hand, APEC is the only forum in which the top leaders of the most powerful nations of the Pacific rim meet regularly. Its character as a strategic post-Cold War institution linking the United States with Asia is a definite asset. Arguably it is also an asset that APEC has been somewhat selective in bringing in new members; it does not include all ASEAN members, for example, omitting the pariah regime of Myanmar as well as Cambodia and Laos. The APEC economies also interact within the institution on an individual basis rather than as members of blocs or caucuses within the grouping.

The other two frameworks include the entire ASEAN membership and give formal deference to ASEAN as a leadership core group. The APT is a more geographically and culturally compact group of the ten Southeast Asian ASEAN countries plus China, Korea and Japan, all of which traditionally were highly influenced by Chinese power and civilization.[7] However, the prominence of political rivalries in Northeast Asia has forced the leadership to Southeast Asian countries that account for only about a tenth of the APT's combined gross domestic product. Japan has felt increasingly uncomfortable in the APT, and its search for balancers to rising Chinese power has led it to project the larger EAS. The sixteen-nation EAS framework (ASEAN + 3, plus another three of Australia, New Zealand and India) provides a strategic link to India, whose economic and strategic relationship with East and Southeast Asia is growing. It is unclear, however, whether India will be satisfied with a position that gives it a kind of second-class role within a Southeast Asian led institution or if the EAS will comprise much more than an annual meeting alongside the APT meetings.

Historically, Australia, Japan and the United States have all been active in establishing the regional cooperation frameworks in Asia and the Pacific, all of which are of post-Cold War vintage. Prior to 1989, only two Asia-wide governmental regional economic organizations existed, both with limited mandates. The Bangkok-based UN Economic and Social Commission for Asia and the Pacific (ESCAP) has collected statistics and carried out analytical work since 1947, and the Asian Development Bank (ADB) was established in 1966 to supplement World Bank development capital assistance to the region's developing countries. When broad-gauged frameworks for regional cooperation began to emerge, it was first at the sub-regional level. ASEAN was formed among five Southeast Asian countries in 1967, superseding two smaller frameworks established earlier, and the Pacific Island Forum (under a different name) was established in 1971. Although ASEAN was formally limited to economic, social and cultural cooperation, it was first and foremost a political project with a major anti-Vietnam thrust through much of the 1980s.

When a broader Asia-Pacific framework concept was first mooted in the 1960s and 1970s, the intellectual leadership originated in Japan and Australia, while later endorsement by some prominent Americans gave the concept some serious driving force towards the end of the 1970s. A Japanese economist, Kiyoshi Kojima, is usually credited with first proposing a Pacific Free Trade Area in 1965.[8] This idea, modified through the influence of Australian economist Peter Drysdale and others into a proposal for an Organization for Pacific Trade and Development (OPTAD), a kind of mini-Organization for Economic Cooperation and Development for Asia and the Pacific, percolated in a newly formed professional network, the PAFTAD, and lay behind the first Pacific Economic Cooperation conference, held at the Australian National University in 1980. Although the Pacific Economic Cooperation Council (PECC), a non-governmental organization, emerged from Canberra, it was not until the end of the Cold War that the intergovernmental cooperation institution it sought was established as the Asia Pacific Economic Cooperation forum. APEC also emerged with leadership from Australia and Japan.

The post-Cold War changes in the Asia-Pacific region allowed other frameworks to emerge, resulting in some competition among cooperation venues. Most notably, the ASEAN expanded to cover all ten Southeast Asian countries by 1995, and in 1996 it initiated the APT, initially inviting China, Japan and South Korea as ASEAN guests. The East Asia framework was propelled ahead in the late 1990s by two factors. The first was the widely perceived ineffectiveness of APEC in dealing with the 1997–98 economic crisis and a strong feeling in East Asia that the response of the United States and the West generally had been callous.

The failure of the United States to participate directly in the Thai and Indonesian rescue efforts were contrasted throughout the region with an earlier US-led effort to help Mexico overcome a currency crisis. In contrast to the United States, Japan in 1997 proposed an early rescue package, which Washington opposed, and China received much credit in the region for not devaluing its currency.[9] The lesson drawn in East Asia from this episode was that the countries of that region needed their own institutions to overcome emergencies as they could not rely on the broader international community. A second driving force for East Asian cooperation was the leadership of Korean President Kim Dae Jung. President Kim's main interest was Northeast Asian cooperation, but he used the broader APT framework to help overcome the rivalries embedded in the smaller framework.

The high water mark for East Asian cooperation came in the form of a 2001 'Vision Statement' of a regional East Asia Vision Group and the 2002 Report of the East Asia Study Group. These foresaw comprehensive cooperation, including a free trade area and an East Asian summit conference of the thirteen nations acting as equals. However, the East Asian movement lost momentum as Kim's domestic political position weakened in the later years of his 1998 to 2003 term in office. Another factor was the growth of political tensions between Japan and China, which peaked in 2005 and 2006. East Asian cooperation has worked best in the financial arena where the Chiang Mai Initiative has produced the APT Economic Review and Policy Dialogue (ERPD) peer review process and a series of swap arrangements in case of future currency crises. Work continues on an Asian bond market initiative and a regional financial vulnerabilities early-warning system, with support from the ADB.[10]

Australia, Japan and the United States have viewed these developments through somewhat different prisms. The United States has tended to actively oppose or be passively sceptical of groupings in which it has not been a member, regarding them as rivals to APEC, potentially establishing a sphere of influence for a strategic rival and undermining US business interests. Washington strongly opposed the first East Asian proposal, put forward in 1990 by former Malaysian Prime Minister Mohamad bin Mahathir, for an East Asian Economic Group (EAEG). Former Secretary of State James Baker took a deep personal interest in this proposal, which he saw as a threat to the new APEC process. At the time, Washington was also deeply concerned about the differences in American and Japanese business practices and feared that an East Asian grouping might help consolidate a more exclusionary Japanese business culture that would disadvantage Americans. While the Mahathir proposal attracted strong interest in Japan, the American opposition succeeded in preventing the Japanese government from ever endorsing the notion.

Washington has been much less concerned about more recent forms of East Asian cooperation. This may represent more a political judgement that the East Asian cooperation framework will not make much headway than a reassessment of the implications of such proposals for American interests. Washington undoubtedly would be deeply concerned if East Asian cooperation seemed to centre around opposition to US policies, undercut global disciplines and organization that Washington leads or supports, or coalesce around an alternative centre of power.[11] On the other hand, US policy-makers have long supported Asia-based regional cooperation frameworks, such as ASEAN, that contribute to regional stability and order.

Australia and Japan have also been concerned about certain features of the APT framework. Like Washington, Canberra has felt disadvantaged by Asia-only schemes, but it does not have the weight to oppose them. Rather, on the basis of geographical propinquity, Australia has sought membership for itself, presenting itself as part of an extended Asian family.

East Asian-only groupings initially found strong resonance in Japan, which has been a promoter of East Asia community-building processes. Japanese supporters see this concept as a means of re-establishing and reinforcing an Asian identity for Japan that has been put into question by Japan's prominent bilateral alliance with the United States and its membership in such Western-dominated institutions as the Organization for Economic Cooperation and Development (OECD). But while East Asian community-building was initially seen as an arena for Japanese leadership, Japanese enthusiasm for a narrow geography-bound East Asia process has waned with two growing concerns. The first is some fear of isolation within a smaller community, particularly if China plays the leadership role. Although Japan's economy is still much larger than China's in international (exchange rate) terms, Japan has felt more acutely than any other power that the economic rise of China has affected its regional power position. The other concern, based in part on the memory of Secretary Baker's reaction to the EAEG, is that an East Asia-only arrangement will anger Washington, placing Japan in the awkward and unwelcome position of having to choose between the United States and East Asia.

Both these concerns led Japan to seek an expansion of the EAS beyond the APT participants when Malaysia began to push for the Summit. This dovetailed with concern in ASEAN, particularly in Indonesia, that the Summit might undercut ASEAN leadership of the APT process. It also aligned Japan on economic cooperation architecture issues closely with Australia, which sought an invitation to the EAS, and with the United States, whose impulses would be for a larger EAS including close American allies such as Japan and Australia. Japan's desire that the EAS might even include the American president ran up against practical schedule limitations and a lack of significant US interest.

The challenge for Canberra, Tokyo and Washington is to ensure that the frameworks for economic cooperation reinforce rather than compete with each other. At the present time, the indeterminate nature of the economic cooperation structure both encourages some competition as well as subtly dampens it since no one architecture seems to be gaining so much traction as to cause deep concern among outsiders. This could change, particularly if one of the architectures becomes associated with a free trade agreement. This is because free trade agreements are inherently discriminatory; benefit to those within the agreement comes at the expense of those on the outside.[12] It is also because free trade agreements mark a deeper form of cooperation based on negotiation and binding rule-making and thus privilege the framework associated with it.

Free trade agreements (FTAs)

It is odd that free trade agreements have become the preferred symbols of community-building, since the process of negotiating such agreements is so adversarial. However, like 'most favoured nation' treatment in the nineteenth century, 'free trade agreements' have both symbolic political, as well as economic, content and have been repeatedly proposed to cement virtually every form of multilateral economic cooperation architecture. Some members of APEC's Eminent Person's Group (EPG) proposed an APEC FTA within the Group in 1993–94, but this proposal was contradictory with the commitment of many APEC governments to 'open regionalism' that eschews bloc formation. A compromise was worked out in the form of the 1994 'Bogor Goals', in which APEC seeks 'free trade and investment in the region' as a longer-term goal through a process of concerted, voluntary liberalization. Since there is a disconnect between the goal and the voluntary process, there have been new proposals for an APEC FTA, based on binding commitments.[13] However, it is difficult to imagine the US Congress agreeing to a free trade agreement with China any time soon.

The ASEAN + 3 has also been studying free trade. An APT FTA may be slightly more politically feasible than the APEC proposal in that it seems to have attracted governmental support among the members and would exclude the United States, which typically has more demands of free trade agreements in part because of its Congressional approval process. However, there are many political constraints in East Asia itself. To meet World Trade Organization (WTO) standards, the FTA would have to cover substantially all trade, including agriculture, a very sensitive topic for the Northeast Asian economies.

Japan's Minister of Economics, Trade and Industry, Toshihiro Nikai, has proposed an FTA for the EAS group of sixteen, and he foresees a rapid negotiation and the beginning of a process of forming a free trade area by 2010. Moreover, the Japanese government is reportedly prepared to put $100 million for research to support this process.[14] Australia appears to have reacted positively to this proposal, but there is widespread scepticism about the time frame. Washington was obviously disappointed there was no consultation with the United States prior to launching the Nikai initiative in March 2006, but then Nikai's Foreign Ministry counterparts were also surprised.[15] South Korea and China have been reportedly negative, while the ASEAN group's priority is clearly on ASEAN + 1 agreements with outside powers rather than either an APT or EAS-based approach. This is probably more realistic from a negotiating perspective and has the added advantage for ASEAN of keeping it in a hub position.

Australia, Japan and the United States are all pursuing free bilateral or mini-lateral trade arrangements with other nations in Asia.[16] These bilateral agreements, competitive as they may seem to be, apparently do not appear to cause significant problems in trilateral relationships. However, multilateral FTA arrangements, congruent with one of the East Asia cooperation frameworks, excluding one or two of the members of the triangle, could become an important problem. The three countries would have a common interest in ensuring that such FTA arrangements are of 'high quality', as they have all pledged along with their APEC counterparts, and that they are constructed in an 'open' manner that provides building blocks rather than stumbling blocks towards Asia-Pacific and global freer trade. It can be anticipated that the United States would expect Japan and Australia to be pursuing these objectives in any EAS FTA negotiation and that the United States and Australia would be expecting the same of Japan in the smaller APT framework.

The economic rise of China

Much of the tension of alternative economic architectures and associated FTA proposals relates to the underlying issue of the rise of China. The TSD partners have all supported China's emergence into the global economy and membership in open trading institutions such as the WTO and the APEC forum, so they want to ensure that other smaller arrangements have a compatible thrust.

In addition to the regional architecture, the TSD partners have a strong interest in promoting a constructive Chinese role in other wider institutions and in China's economic policies and their impact on trade and investment patterns, commodity prices and the overall stability of the regional and global economies. From their booming trade and investment ties with China, it is clear that all the TSD partners are benefiting from the many opportunities presented by China's growth. But that growth also presents challenges that ought to be discussed among the three countries not out of any effort to 'contain' China's rise, but to try to ensure that it proceeds in a manner that best allows the rest of the region to adjust to it and to place China's own growth on a more secure, less tension-ridden footing. A brief list of important issues would include:

- China's broader engagement in global institutions. The United States is urging China to increase its stake in and responsibility for global systems, and for this purpose supported an increase in China's IMF quota. Another question of particular relevance to Japan and the United States is the question of possible Chinese membership in the now G8 group.
- China's large current account surplus and its implications. In large part, China's growth is export and investment driven. The super-heated Chinese economy, with new capacity being added without clear market-driven reasons, is also of concern to the Chinese. The United States has promoted currency reform as one means of trying to remove distortions and dampen investment, but there is no consensus on this. It bears trilateral consideration.
- China's appetite for raw materials – and particularly energy – is a major factor in commodity prices. This obviously benefits Australia as a commodity producer, but has resulted in competition for energy resources among the Northeast Asian countries. According to some analysts, the rapid increase in China's oil consumption is among the factors that have oil price effects that could 'drive the developing nations into a new debt crisis and represent a serious burden for the global economy'.[17] China's oil security concerns have also driven its state-owned energy companies to invest in such countries as Iran and the Sudan, which are involved in serious confrontations with the OECD countries on nuclear proliferation and/or human rights consideration. It is an obvious interest of all three countries to discuss these issues and to promote greater resource efficiency in China. One positive feature of Sino-Japanese interaction is, in fact, the transfer of fuel efficient technology.
- Changing patterns of competitive advantage on industrial implications. As China moves up the value-added chain in manufacturing and capabilities of Chinese brand-name companies grow, there will be significant implications for Japanese and Korean companies and eventually those of other countries. The TSD countries have an interest in anticipating these trends and facilitating the adjustment of their own companies.

Non-traditional security issues

The joint statement of the first Ministerial Meeting of the TSD leaves the impression that the reference to non-traditional issues (often called 'human security' issues) was more of an afterthought than central to the agenda. However, there is good reason to give these issues more attention. First, some human security issues are critical in the struggle against terrorism. Second, while foreign ministries usually focus on traditional security issues, there is ample evidence that, for the public, non-traditional security issues have the greatest salience. Certainly, the Asian economic crisis of 1997–98 and the SARS epidemic in early 2003 rank as the most significant public concerns of their time.

An explicit discussion of such issues may also help the three TSD partners to develop a greater common understanding of just what comes under the heading of human security. While the shift in the referent from nation to individual is quite commonly understood, the definition of human security remains ambiguous and the priorities differ from society to society. Most developing countries, for example, place a high emphasis on economic development, whereas Western societies frequently give attention to good governance and civil liberties. Japan has given considerable emphasis to human security in its foreign policy and it has generally emphasized economic security ('freedom from want') as opposed to civil liberties and protection of individuals and groups ('freedom from fear').[18]

Both aspects are important in the context of addressing human security challenges that relate to terrorism. While military, police and intelligence resources are needed to control and eliminate existing terrorist groups, political, economic (including aid) and educational policies are the main tools for the task of 'draining the swamp', that is, of depriving terrorists of a supportive environment for recruitment, funds and sympathetic populations.

Australia, Japan and the United States have an enormous impact on the economies of Asia, mostly through market-based trade and investment flows, but also as the largest sources of bilateral and multilateral concessional assistance. Concessional aid remains critically important in areas where isolation and political risks combine to deter most private flows, and these are also the areas most likely to breed terrorism. Japan and the United States have a history of cooperating on assistance programmes, as in the late 1970s, when they agreed that Thailand was a 'front line' state in the Cold War context that was worthy of extra concessional support. However, because of the different ways in which their assistance programmes operate, there has been little actual coordination in the field or joint projects, as had been the aspiration under a Clinton era United States–Japan 'Global Partnership' programme.

As a dialogue process, the TSD is not suited to foreign aid programme coordination, but it can be a venue for strengthening a common sense of priorities, regional and beyond, in light of the struggle against terrorism, and for developing a new listing of 'front line' areas where terrorism is a special problem, so that developmental assistance can be directed with some strategic synergy. The 'freedom from fear' aspect is also important because terrorism is less likely to flourish in environments where human rights and civil liberties are respected and where there are non-violent means of addressing serious public issues, thus depriving terrorists of a key rationale for violence.

Other non-traditional or human security issues – for example, disease, pollution, trafficking – are also matters of deep concern to the people of the region and thus to the trilateral partners. Non-traditional security issues are typically global and broad regional issues that can only be effectively addressed through the institutions with appropriate membership and institutional expertise, such as the World Health Organization (for avian flu) and the International Energy Agency (for energy security issues). However, the TSD can be extremely useful to the three governments in helping them develop a common understanding of issues and shape similar or coordinated approaches or initiatives in the appropriate policy action venues. It is also quite possible that the TSD can be a venue for incubating new programmes or institutions.[19]

Conclusions

As this short overview suggests, there is a rich agenda of issues falling outside the traditional security agenda that are of interest to the three parties' foreign ministries. Other issues, for example, how to revive WTO Doha Development Agenda negotiations, could be of special interest depending on timing. The key question for the future, however, is whether the TSD will become a significant tool for trilateral dialogue or merely a ritualistic series of meetings when senior officials and ministers can fit them in. Two elements might enhance this process.

First, the TSD could be enhanced by a more continuous process, which would include trilateral meetings in a variety of venues, particularly alongside regional meetings, such as APEC or ADB meetings. To make such meetings more productive, commissioned trilateral research work could help provide the three parties with a basis for common understanding of an issue and policy options.

Second, consideration could be given to enhancing the TSD through the inclusion of trade ministers. This could create scheduling complications, but it would also strengthen the coverage and importance of the dialogue process and underscore the obvious point that foreign political and economic policies are closely linked and need to move in parallel and reinforcing directions, both to be strategic and to be effective.

Notes

1 US Department of State, Office of the Spokesman (2006), 'Trilateral Strategic Dialogue Joint Statement', 20 March.
2 R. Foot (1995), 'Pacific Asia: the development of regional dialogue', in L. Fawcett and A. Hurrell (eds), *Regionalism in World Politics: Regional Organization and International Order*, Oxford: Oxford University Press, pp. 228–49.
3 Secretary of State James Baker, for example, made a strong effort to oppose former Malaysian Prime Minister Mahathir's proposed East Asian Economic Group (EAEG), which would not have included the United States. More recently, Japan and China stood on opposite sides in the diplomacy leading to the East Asia Summit (EAS); the former supported an expanded membership while the latter preferred to limit the members to East and Southeast Asian countries.
4 For example, Australia's original APEC proposal did not include the United States as a member.
5 As APEC includes Taiwan as 'Chinese Taipei', APEC members are referred to as economies. This issue does not arise in the EAS or the APT as Taiwan is excluded.
6 For a recent critical analysis, see A. Gyngell and M. Cook (2005), 'How to save APEC', *Policy Brief*, Sydney: Lowy Institute for International Policy.
7 India, of course, was also a source of strong cultural and mercantile influence in much of Southeast Asia.
8 L. T. Woods (1993), *Asia-Pacific Diplomacy: Nongovernmental Organizations and International Relations*, Vancouver: UBC Press, pp. 41–43.
9 Washington opposed the first version of the so-called Miyazawa Plan because it appeared to weaken international disciplines and thus presented a moral hazard problem. For the same moral hazard reason, the United States did not participate in the first rescue package for Thailand, but it became increasingly concerned as time went on, working feverishly at the end of the year to prevent a Korean government default. Even more damaging in the eyes of many Asians were the conditionalities required by the

international financial institutions, now widely regarded as inappropriate to the Asian debt problem.

10 Asian Development Bank (2006), 'Regional cooperation and integration', ADB Strategy Paper, May, p. 16.

11 For elaboration, see Charles E. Morrison (2003), 'Japan, ASEAN, and East Asia from an American perspective', in *ASEAN–Japan Cooperation: A Foundation for East Asian Community*, Tokyo: Japan Center for International Exchange, pp. 199–200.

12 Supporters of FTAs argue, however, that this need not be the case. Some of the arguments are that the boost to the participating economies may increase the benefit for outsiders beyond those that would have taken place had the FTA not existed; outsiders might also benefit from 'locked-in' economic reforms. Another argument is that global liberalization may be facilitated through a 'competitive liberalization' process as outsiders seek to counter FTAs with their own FTA proposals.

13 The foremost advocate has been Fred C. Bergsten, the former chair of the EPG. In 2004, he succeeded in persuading APEC's Business Advisory Committee (ABAC) to urge the governments to 'study' an APEC free trade area proposal, but the governments have so far declined to do so. A joint PECC–ABAC study of the proposal in mid-2006 emphasized the many political obstacles to an APEC-wide free trade arrangement.

14 *The Star* (Malaysia), 20 August 2006.

15 When asked to 'cast light' on how the Nikai proposal would affect Japan's negotiations for an economic partnership with the ASEAN group at a press conference on 11 April 2006, the Ministry of Foreign Affairs press secretary admitted that 'I am personally confused as well', adding that he thought 'we are headed in the same or almost identical direction, but I have to examine what METI is talking about'. Ministry of Foreign Affairs website, available at: www.mofa.go.jp/announce/press/2006/4/0411.html (accessed 19 September 2006).

16 Australia and the United States already have a bilateral FTA; Australia and Japan are studying one; and a United States–Japan FTA is no longer out of the question, particularly if current US–Korean negotiations are successful.

17 F. Müller (2006), 'China's energy prices – geopolitical repercussions', in G. Wacker (ed.), *China's Rise: The Return of Geopolitics?*, Berlin: SWP Research Paper, p. 9.

18 Hiroshi Minami (2006), 'Human security and Japan's foreign policy', *Gaiko Forum*, vol. 4, Winter, pp. 43–51, provides an interesting history of Japan's recent efforts in the United Nations and APEC to promote the freedom from want approach. Canada has been particularly active in pushing the alternative responsibility to protect emphasis.

19 For example, the 2005 Asia-Pacific Partnership on Clean Development and Climate, which was developed by the foreign ministries of the three countries, along with counterparts in China, India and South Korea, is an example of the kind of programme or institution that could be initiated through the TSD.

13 Trilateralism and cooperation on asymmetrical threats

Terrorism, WMD and regional instability

Thomas S. Wilkins

Introduction

Major shifts have occurred in the security architecture of the Asia-Pacific since the end of the Cold War and the 11 September 2001 terrorist attacks. One of the most striking developments has been the deepening and broadening of trilateral security connections between the United States, Japan and Australia: a development which points towards the formation of a nascent triple alliance bloc. The momentum behind this Trilateral Strategic Dialogue (TSD) has been apparent for several years, as the three powers have worked to strengthen and expand their existing bilateral ties. The elevation of its deliberations to ministerial level in 2006 has taken this evolving security forum to the next stage.

The realist perspective of International Relations accounts for the creation of such a bloc by pointing to relative shifts in the regional and global balance of power and highlighting the emergence of a 'superpower', China, as a potential hegemonic actor.[1] While this analysis may appear persuasive at first glance, it is not reflected in the recent security/defence policy 'white papers' published by the trilateral powers, nor in the official content of the TSD agenda.[2] Rather, as this chapter argues, the driver behind this transforming alliance relationship is the common danger of asymmetrical (or 'non-traditional') threats, especially terrorism and weapons of mass destruction (WMD) proliferation. Speaking in Japan, Robert Hill, then Australian Defence Minister, put his finger on this trend when he claimed to be 'struck by the similarities in our perceptions of the threats posed by WMD proliferation and international terrorism'.[3] It is this common sense of danger that has acted to intensify bilateral relations between Australia and Japan, in addition to accelerating their collaboration in these areas with their mutual American ally. With the upgrading of the TSD to the ministerial level (vice-ministerial level trilateral Australian–Japanese–American deliberations were established in 2001) relations between the three states can now be said to be truly 'triangulated'.

It is the fluid and unpredictable global environment that has accorded such asymmetric dangers new prominence in allied security policies and impelled them towards a trilateral partnership. The *National Security Strategy of the United States of America* acknowledges that 'Globalization has exposed us to new challenges and changed the way old challenges touch our security interests and values, while also greatly enhancing our capacity to respond.'[4] Taking this dyad of 'challenge' and 'response' as its organizing mantra this chapter is divided into two parts. The first section briefly looks at how the TSD powers view the nature of the *challenge* posed by terrorism and WMD, and illustrates how wider conditions of instability can exacerbate these dangers. The second section analyses in more detail the ways in which the allies have strengthened their ties and expanded their cooperation to build a more integrated and cohesive trilateral *response* to these multifaceted issues. The primary focus here is on terrorism and WMD proliferation, but these twin threats cannot be separated from the conditions of regional instability from which they are often born – a fact clearly acknowledged in the various defence posture statements of each of the trilateral powers. The chapter is based upon a fusion of policy statements and documents from the three powers and the political and academic discourses that these have generated. Given the usual synchronization of allied policies on these matters a statement on policy from one power can therefore stand as indicative of an evolving, common 'trilateral position'.

Challenge: asymmetric threats

Terrorism

The challenge of terrorism features prominently in both the individual national security strategies and the remit of TSD cooperation, with Washington classifying it foremost among 'irregular challenges' to regional security. The territory, interests and citizens of the United States, Japan and Australia are all targets for radical Islamic terror. Their military forces deployed overseas are also likely to attract terrorist attention in Iraq, Afghanistan, and elsewhere. United States assets have been struck repeatedly by terrorist groups, principally al-Qaeda and its affiliates. The 9/11 attacks on American soil triggered the initiation of a US-led global 'coalition against terror' (in which Japan and Australia play prominent roles). Though the United States has mobilized its forces and allies to fight coalition wars in Afghanistan and Iraq and has had some success in degrading terrorist networks, the threat remains serious and may actually be worsening. 'America is safer, but not yet safe.'[5] Japan has also been victimized by terrorist attacks. Japanese citizens have been killed in New York, Bali and Iraq (in addition to the homegrown Aum Shinryko chemical weapon attack in Tokyo in 1995). Japan's *Action Plan for Prevention of Terrorism* therefore maintains that 'The terrorist threat to Japan should never be underestimated.'[6] Finally, in response to the 9/11 attacks Australia promptly invoked ANZUS to support the United States and joined the coalition in the war against terror.[7] Its citizens and assets have also been attacked, suffering serious casualties in Indonesia in 2002 (Bali), 2004 (Jakarta) and 2005 (Bali again). The *2003 Defence Update* pinpoints 'A critical strategic and security dimension for Australia is that militant extremists in Southeast Asia are prepared to take up the Al Qaida cause and that Australia has been identified as a target.'[8] It lists the Moro Islamic Liberation Front (MILF), the Abu Sayif Group (ASG) and Jemaah Islamiyah (JI) as especially active and dangerous groups in the Asia-Pacific region.

WMD proliferation

The second mutual security challenge faced by the TSD partners is the proliferation of WMD. The United States labels this security issue as a 'catastrophic challenge', reflecting the fact that these are:

> Weapons that are capable of a high order of destruction and/or of being used in such a manner as to destroy large numbers of people. Weapons of mass destruction can be high explosives or nuclear, biological, chemical, and radiological weapons.[9]

Proliferation of the weapons themselves, or the technology and expertise to create them, alongside potential delivery means (such as ballistic missiles), pose a complex and serious threat. A key Australian national security assessment has observed that 'WMD are the ultimate asymmetric threat. WMD allow weak states prepared to defy international norms and non-state actors (like terrorist groups) to strike unilaterally.'[10] The TSD partners are concerned therefore lest rogue regimes or terrorists acquire WMD; either to launch an attack or to act as a deterrent to possible allied interference against their willingness to transfer WMD to other hostile parties.[11] Both of these dimensions warrant further clarification.

First is the extant danger of attacks launched by 'rogue regimes' (those states perceived to violate international norms of behaviour). These include principally the Democratic People's Republic of Korea (DPRK)/North Korea and Iran. The governments of these two states in particular continue to send alarming signals. Pyongyang's withdrawal from the Non-Proliferation Treaty (NPT), admission of possession and subsequent testing of a nuclear weapons capability, recalcitrance in the Six Party Talks and repeated test-firing of long range missiles are indicative (the missiles issue is discussed in further detail in Chapter 14).[12] Likewise Tehran's refusal to allow the International Atomic Energy Agency (IAEA) access to its civilian nuclear programme, its missile testing and the wild threats by President Ahmadinejad to 'Wipe Israel off the map' have similarly created apprehension in allied capitals.[13] Both states persist in seeking to improve their WMD and delivery capabilities.

Second, directly linked to this threat from the rogue states themselves is their ability and intention to disseminate WMD technologies, expertise and delivery vehicles to other actors in the region. The fear in this respect is two-fold. Rogue states could proliferate to other regimes that exercise weak state control or display tenuous friendship towards the TSD partners, such as Pakistan and Indonesia (perhaps also Malaysia or the Philippines). If the government in one of these countries were to turn hostile or implode and be replaced by a more radical (Islamic) regime this would create new security dilemmas. Or rogue regimes may have few qualms about providing terrorists with access to WMD. Washington warns that terrorists 'continue to seek WMD in order to inflict even more catastrophic attacks on us and our friends and allies'.[14] Whether terrorist acquisition of WMD is 'state-sponsored', or acquired from a renegade source such as the black market network created by Abdul Qadeer Khan (a former Pakistani nuclear scientist), or even a transnational criminal organization such as the Russian Mafia (which may possess 'loose nukes' from the former Soviet Union) – whatever the source – the result would be potentially 'catastrophic'.[15] Given the aims of radical terrorist groups and the belief that they desire to inflict maximum and indiscriminate damage, the trilateral alliance shares the conviction that 'There are few greater threats than a terrorist attack with WMD.'[16]

Regional instability

The security strategies of the TSD allies recognize that the challenges of terrorism and WMD proliferation are most likely to intensify under conditions of regional instability. Political, economic or environmental disruptions can create volatile situations in which transnational criminal organizations, terrorism and proliferation can arise and flourish in the absence of competent governance.

Certain areas of the Asia-Pacific region suffer from serious domestic instability. Australia's *2005 Defence Update* describes how 'parts of this region are still characterised by porous borders, weak governance, inequities in the distribution of resources, problems of law enforcement, insurgencies, drug trafficking and transnational crime'.[17] Australia, in particular, is surrounded in its immediate neighbourhood by an 'arc of instability' constituting a belt of delicate states such as Timor, Papua New Guinea, the South Pacific islands (see Chapter 9), and even conceivably Indonesia (for instance, the disturbances in Aceh province). Tokyo also expresses disquiet over its North Korean neighbour, identifying the Pyongyang regime as a 'serious destabilizing factor' and, more generally, 'volatile factors such as threats of the outbreak of complex and diverse regional conflicts'.[18] Washington's wide presence and interests in the region make it sensitive to almost any episode of regional turmoil. The national security strategy of the United States neatly encapsulates the danger that 'Regional conflicts do not stay isolated for long and often spread or devolve into humanitarian tragedy or anarchy.'[19] The overspill from such crises can lead to refugee problems, economic disruptions and calls for intervention. North Korea again features prominently in this respect, as well as Burma and the aforementioned countries.

More specifically, there are strong linkages between regional instability and the appearance of terrorist and WMD threats. Countries with serious governance deficits ('failed' or 'failing' states) or radical regimes can provide fertile ground for the appearance of asymmetric dangers. As noted above, weak states may be susceptible to a seizure of power by anti-Western or 'radical' elements that may result in a creation of new 'rogue regimes' hostile to the West, either possessing or seeking WMD. Furthermore, regimes that are unable to effectively govern their own territory are not able to act efficiently against terrorist threats to themselves or others. United States national security strategy identifies how 'ungoverned areas ... can become safe havens for terrorists'.[20] They may therefore provide recruits for terrorist groups or act as staging grounds for attacks. Given the difficulties in intercepting and destroying terrorist cells in such conditions of anarchy, as demonstrated for example in Afghanistan, Iraq or Pakistan, the challenge of combating terrorism and WMD would be further amplified.

Response: trilateral alliance transformation

These three threats – terrorism, WMD and failed states – intersect to form a dangerous nexus from which asymmetric threats can arise. The Australian government has insisted that 'The risk of *convergence* between failing states, terrorism and the proliferation of WMD remains a major and continuing threat to international security.'[21] Such a multidimensional challenge requires an integrated and coordinated trilateral response from the alliance partners. For the purposes of analytical convenience, cooperative alliance efforts can be loosely broken down into counter-terrorism, counter-proliferation and regional intervention strategies, all directed at the three intertwined issues above.

Counterterrorism

This chapter can only scratch the surface of the momentous developments that have occurred in the wake of a renewed eruption of international terrorism. One thing is clear: each of the allied powers recognizes the need for a 'holistic' approach to tackling terrorist activities using 'diplomatic, economic, information, law enforcement, military, financial, intelligence, and other instruments of power'.[22] The combined counterterrorist strategy of the trilateral powers rests upon several interrelated pillars: national responses, trilateral cooperation, international frameworks and military force.

First, each of the TSD partners has introduced a substantial package of anti-terrorism measures at a national level to upgrade their homeland defences. The domestic anti-terrorism measures – the United States' *National Strategy for Combating Terrorism*, Japan's *Action Plan for Prevention of Terrorism* and *Protecting Australia Against Terrorism: Australia's Counter-Terrorism Arrangements* – all indicate similar vulnerabilities and hence demonstrate a remarkable symmetry in their approaches.[23] Washington, Tokyo and Canberra have each concentrated on a framework for tackling terrorism essentially based upon preparedness, prevention and response. All three have greatly increased the material and financial resources assigned to deter and destroy terrorists, and also to mitigate the effects of a successful attack. They have introduced a profligate amount of new domestic anti-terror legislation and set up specialized committees. They have also undertaken a reorganization of their relevant government agencies (in addition the United States has set up a dedicated Department of Homeland Security). National agencies involved in intelligence gathering, interdicting terrorist financing, hijacking countermeasures, immigration/border control, critical infrastructure protection, NBC (Nuclear, Biological, Chemical) response and 'capacity building' assistance to third party countries have all been strengthened, as has inter-agency coordination.[24]

Second, all the measures outlined above have augmented the capabilities of the trilateral states to cooperate in their *combined* counterterrorism strategy. This can be seen in the 2004 AUSMIN talks, various Memoranda of Understanding (MOU), and, not least, the TSD itself – all of which act to govern trilateral collaboration. These dialogues have resulted in a deepening network of bilateral/trilateral cooperation between national police, intelligence, security, customs, immigration, transportation, military and financial units. Multinational exercises in counter-hijacking, hostage rescue, special forces training and information exchange/assessment are all part of this.[25] Many of these activities were initiated or reinforced at the United States–Australia–Japan Counterterrorism Talks held in September of 2005. One of the crucial elements in cooperation is the expansion of extant intelligence sharing arrangements between the three partners. They all appreciate that 'common situational awareness is a key to well coordinated cooperation, both sides will enhance information sharing and intelligence cooperation in the whole range from unit tactical level through national strategic level'.[26]

Third, the trilateral partners are also fully engaged in the broader international context of counterterrorist regimes. Each of the allied states works to uphold international efforts appropriate to counterterrorism/proliferation such as UN legislation, most recently UN Security Council Resolution 1373, which created the UN Counter-Terrorism Committee (UNCTC) designed to cut off terrorist finances. Each of the powers also participates (where applicable) in other multinational forums, such as the G8 Counter-Terrorism Action Group (CTAG), which concentrates upon transport security and technical assistance to developing countries, and MANPADS, aimed at the counter-proliferation of Man Portable Air Defence Systems (usually surface-to-air missiles), which can be used to down civil airliners. At a regional level, operative actors include: ASEAN + 3, which acts to enhance anti-terrorist cooperation between regional partners, the ASEAN Regional Forum (ARF), which has established an inter-sessional meeting on counterterrorism and issues such as transport security, the APEC (Asia Pacific Economic Cooperation) Counter-Terrorism Task Force (CTTF), the Pacific Islands Forum (for example, Exercise *Ready Pasifika*, 2005), and a plethora of other regional/bilateral talks. Participation in all capacities gives the TSD powers further opportunity to collaborate and refine the nature of their common responses to counterterrorism.

The last platform of allied counterterrorist strategy involves active destruction of terrorist networks through the (joint) application of military force. The United States explicitly upholds its right to take military action against terrorism wherever it may be based. Washington declares that it will 'Deny terrorist groups the support and sanctuary of rogue states' and 'Deny the terrorists control of any nation that they would use as a base and launching pad for terror.'[27] This declaration is endorsed by Tokyo and Canberra, who both support strategies to eradicate terrorists on their native territory (discussed further below). This forms part of the wider 'global war against terror' championed by the United States and now being actively prosecuted by these three powers in Afghanistan (Operation *Enduring Freedom*) and Iraq (Operation *Iraqi Freedom*). Both Japan (within the confines of its 'Peace Constitution') and, to a greater extent, Australia (Operation *Slipper*) have sent troops to assist the United States in these campaigns to destroy the Taliban and al-Qaeda fighters.

Counter-proliferation

As with the case of counterterrorism, each state has undertaken domestic security restructuring to meet the challenge of WMD proliferation. Yet this threat lies largely beyond the domestic realm and requires a comprehensive package of responses, some of them closely intersecting with those mentioned above. Again we see a close correspondence of response measures among the trilateral powers. This section examines cooperation through international regimes, multilateral counter-proliferation initiatives, ballistic missile defence (BMD) and pre-emptive use of force.

First, each of the trilateral partners is committed to upholding and strengthening a network of international/regional proliferation regimes and norms. There is not space here to cite all the international conventions appertaining to WMD proliferation, but the most important of them is the 1968 Non-Proliferation Treaty (NPT).[28] The NPT was revisited at the 2005 Review Conference, which aimed at re-examining existing non-proliferation procedures and reinforcing non-proliferation safeguards in the changed post-Cold War security environment.[29] Before that, in 2002, the G8 Global Partnership Against the Spread of Weapons and Materials of Mass Destruction was inaugurated.[30] Furthermore, in 2004, UN Security Council Resolution 1540 was passed criminalizing WMD proliferation and calling for greater efforts to enforce strict import and export controls on all related materials. Finally, all three allies signed the International Convention for the Suppression of Acts of Nuclear Terrorism, which addresses the issue of WMD acquisition by terrorist non-state actors.[31] International non-proliferation norms have met with some success, notably in the case of Libya's abrogation of WMD capabilities. However, the flagrant disregard of these processes by states such as North Korea and Iran has also brought calls for stronger enforcement apparatus (and a strengthening of the IAEA). With specific regard to North Korea, the United States and Japan are also party to the Trilateral Coordination and Oversight Group (TCOG) alongside South Korea. However, Pyongyang's withdrawal from the Six Party Talks and its subsequent nuclear weapons test in October 2006 exacerbated tensions in this area that were only partially alleviated by the February 2007 breakthrough. Cooperation in these forums and the relevant legislation provides a frame of reference for associated TSD collaboration.

Second, in addition to subscribing to international non-proliferation regimes, the United States, Japan and Australia are all members of the Proliferation Security Initiative (PSI).[32] Founded in 2003, the PSI is a multilateral initiative based upon a Statement of Interdiction Principles (SIP) allowing for stronger combined efforts in intercepting WMD-related cargoes in the Asia-Pacific. According to the SIP it is designed to 'establish a more coordinated and effective basis through which to impede and stop shipments of WMD, delivery systems, and related materials flowing to and from states and non-state actors of proliferation concern'.[33] A number of multinational exercises have been held to reinforce the ability of the signatory powers to carry out its designated tasks, for example Exercise *Pacific Protector* (2003), Exercise *Team Samurai* (2004) and Exercise *Deep Sabre* (2005).[34] These interdiction exercises are also supplemented by adherence to strict import/export controls designed to prevent the flow of WMD-related materials or technologies to unstable regimes or, even worse, non-state actors such as terrorists. This echoes and reinforces the mandate of the Nuclear Suppliers Group (NSG), a voluntary association designed to oversee transfers of civilian nuclear material and nuclear-related equipment and technology to non-nuclear-weapon states. Finally, added to this is the Australia Group, another layer in anti-proliferation regimes, focusing especially on chemical and biological weapons components.[35]

Third, the TSD states are engaged in working together to develop their passive defences and deterrents against ballistic missile attacks from rogue states such as North Korea. Washington and Tokyo are particularly closely involved in dual development and deployment of BMD capabilities (see Chapter 14). The 'US–Japan Alliance: Transformation and Realignment for the Future' document notes that:

> BMD plays a critical role in deterring and defending against ballistic missile attacks, and can dissuade other parties from development and proliferation of ballistic missiles, [so accordingly] both sides stressed the value of closely coordinating improvements in their respective BMD capabilities.[36]

Hence Japan and Australia are working with the United States to develop their combined missile defence technologies. This is driving Japanese and Australian economic/military collaboration with the United States and directly shaping their defence procurement strategies. Added to this is the possibility that Japan, as part of its move towards becoming a 'normal country' (*futsu no kuni e*), may seek to take more immediate responsibility for its own defence. In an extreme scenario Japan may move to deploy nuclear weapons of its own to deter WMD threats (although its new Prime Minister, Shenzo Abe, denied that his country would do this in the aftermath of North Korea's first nuclear test).[37]

A final strand of counter-proliferation strategy is a readiness to employ pre-emptive military force against rogue/proliferator states. The United States and its TSD partners do not rule out the use of force before a WMD attack is launched against them. The American national security strategy states that 'When the consequences of an attack with WMD are potentially so devastating, we cannot afford to stand idly by as grave dangers materialize. This is the principle and logic of preemption.'[38] Former head of the Japanese Defence Agency, Shigeru Ishiba, echoed this doctrine when he made public statements (subsequently softened) upon the possibility of pre-emptive strikes by Japan on North Korea to forestall a missile launch.[39] Prime Minister John Howard has also served notice that Australia would launch pre-emptive strikes against terrorist concentrations in neighbouring states if Australia was imminently threatened.[40]

Indeed, pre-emptive elimination of WMD was in part the raison d'être for the invasion of Iraq in 2003. It was believed that Baghdad had reactivated its WMD programme, and given its previous sponsorship of terrorism, that this could not be countenanced. In the event, reports of Iraqi WMD capability turned out to have been exaggerated. More unexpectedly, the invasion of Afghanistan revealed 'clear evidence that Al Qaida was actively pursuing biological, chemical and nuclear weapons'.[41] Yet, with respect to possible military action against North Korea (or Iran), it is likely that the United States and its allies will exercise much greater caution, since both these states present considerably 'harder targets' than either Afghanistan, Iraq, or most of those states bordering Australia.

Regional intervention

The trilateral powers recognize that general conditions of regional instability provide the milieu in which threats such as terrorism and weapons proliferation can thrive. The TSD states employ an admixture of methods to 'intervene' in areas susceptible to instability. These include conflict management, direct military interventions, dissemination of ideology, and material support (including humanitarian aid) to 'threatened' states. These activities all serve to complement and underwrite the more specific methods to combat terrorism and WMD highlighted above.

First, the trilateral powers are engaged in seeking diplomatic solutions to the prevention and resolution of regional conflicts. This can occur under the umbrella of global organizations such as the United Nations, regional forums such as APEC or the ASEAN + 3, or case-specific apparatus such as the North Korean Six Party Talks. International and regional frameworks are important tools in combating the threat of regional instability. Included in this category is participation in Peacekeeping Operations (PKOs) which often incorporate a wider mandate of post-conflict stabilization and 'nation building'. The United States is a regular and active participant in such contingencies, but Japan and Australia are increasing and maintaining their role in such activities respectively. As a result of its International Peace Cooperation Law (1992) and the National Defence Program Guidelines (2004) Japan is working to 'to tailor [its] policy in the face of the new international situation to participate actively in international peace cooperation'.[42] Since the early 1990s Japan has been involved in a host of PKOs and Peace Support Operations (PSOs), for example in Cambodia, the Golan Heights, and East Timor (in support of Australia). Australia has taken a lead in East Timor/Timor-Leste from INTERFET (International Force East Timor) in 1999 to Operation *Astute* in 2006, where it is supported by its Japanese ally.

Second, the TSD powers are closely coordinating the restructuring of their defence requirements and military force postures to enable more effective (war fighting) coalition intervention (independently of international frameworks, if required). The uncertain global and regional security environments have impelled the TSD states to improve their ability to intervene effectively with military force in a wide spectrum of overseas contingencies (including, but not limited to, PKOs). This focus on 'out of area operations' has necessitated a transformation in the defence doctrine and force structures of the allied powers with a view to increasing trilateral interoperability. Developments are underway to realize a more 'expeditionary strategy' (especially in Japan) and put in place the apparatus for joint operations. The 2005 'American–Japanese Transformation and Realignment for the Future' indicates that a 'Rapid and effective response requires flexible capabilities and can benefit from close US–Japan bilateral cooperation and policy coordination. Regular exercises, including those with third countries, can improve these capabilities.'[43] Periodical multinational exercises such as RIMPAC (Rim of the Pacific) and *Cobra Gold* are designed to build confidence, service-to-service contacts and interoperability.

Thus, each of the three TSD powers is determined to reap the advantages of the Revolution in Military Affairs (RMA) to develop mobile, flexible and potent expeditionary forces and share the TSD military burden more equitably. Japanese Defence Minster Fukushiro Nukaga declared that 'Japan will develop multi-functional, flexible and effective defence forces in order to cope with new threats and diverse contingencies and to participate proactively in international peace cooperation activities.'[44] Australia likewise has largely moved away from its self-reliant 'concentric circles' defence strategy towards an increased emphasis on force projection.

To effect these changes both the Japanese Self-Defence Forces (SDF) and the Australian Defence Force (ADF) are reorganizing their militaries towards a joint force posture (that is, greater combined operations capability). Furthermore, Tokyo and Canberra are working with the United States on joint procurement/ logistical and training activities. The Japanese and Australians also plan to continue, and to expand, their purchases of American military hardware in order to sustain interoperability. A good example of the former is the Acquisition Cross-Servicing Agreements (ACSAs) which allow for provision of goods and service between the SDF or ADF and the US military. In the latter area, each of the allies is also exploring the possibilities of joint basing and training centres (in Australia known as Operation *Talisman Sabre*). While both Japanese and Australian forces are experienced in working alongside American troops, they had little contact with each other. Recent activities in Iraq and East Timor have changed this. Both these deployments have served to heighten 'service-to-service' contact at the armed forces (operational) level.

Third, each of the TSD powers works towards influencing weak or intransigent states through the use of 'soft power'. This involves efforts to win over allies by an appeal to 'values' rather than the use of force or other inducements. It is an attempt to buttress 'moderate' elements within societies susceptible to instability and disorder and win their 'hearts and minds'. In essence, this represents a strategy to influence the future political and economic trajectory of states at a 'crossroads' towards liberal and democratic values (ideology). Washington argues that 'while we do not seek to dictate to other states the choices they make, we do seek to influence the calculations on which these choices are based. We also must hedge appropriately in case states choose unwisely.'[45] Japan and Australia approach the problem in the same way but are perhaps a little less self-righteous in their tone. A strong element of Japanese and Australian efforts in this sphere are attempts to increase the level of 'human security' for people in unstable areas. A key platform for this strategy in Japan is Overseas Development Aid (ODA). Tokyo acts as a pioneer in this field, having established the Trust Fund for Human Security within the United Nations (1999). Likewise, Australia's Regional Assistance Mission to the Solomon Islands in 2003 was designed to stabilize and nurture this weak state as an ally. Taken together, all these measures are designed to help battle against the conditions of poverty, disease and the consequences of natural disasters that allow asymmetric threats to take root.

Lastly, even when potentially unstable states do not adhere to Western preferences in foreign and domestic policy and may even flout international conventions and norms (for example, with regard to human rights), members of the TSD may still provide them with material support. This often includes economic or military sustenance and is justified upon the basis that it is preferable to have an imperfect regime that governs its people reasonably effectively and can cooperate with the TSD partners against terrorism and WMD (for instance, Pakistan), than a situation of weak governance or anarchy which could result in the emergence of a directly hostile regime or haven for terrorist activity (for example, Iraq). The Australian assistance provided to Indonesia in counterterrorism activities, where the establishment of the Indonesian Centre for Law Enforcement was largely funded by Canberra, is a good example of 'such capacity building', as is Australia's counter-terror support to the Pacific Islands Forum. However, in this case as in many others, such as US support for Pakistan, an unwillingness or ineffectiveness on the part of the recipient government in opposing domestic radicalism/terrorism can hamper the efforts of TSD partners.

Conclusions

This chapter has argued that for the trilateral powers 'Defeating the threat of terrorism, countering the proliferation of WMD and supporting regional states in difficulty remain of the highest priority.'[46] In mutual recognition of these interrelated asymmetric challenges, the United States, Japan and Australia have instigated a reinvention and redesign of their alliance relations, since 'the very nature of new threats makes it difficult for a country to deal with them by itself'.[47] Increased cooperation between Tokyo and Canberra has acted to close the triangle of the original (bilateral) 'hub and spokes' model. Now, Dan Blumenthal asserts, 'The building blocks for a trilateral approach are already in place.'[48] The TSD ensures smooth overarching coordination of policies and initiatives that were already in close synchronization between the three partners, such as counterterrorism, counter-proliferation, intelligence sharing, and collaboration on procurement, joint facilities and military interoperability. Hence, the TSD partnership can be said to signify a departure from the traditional 'reactive' alliance models of the Cold War and the emergence of a more 'proactive' and capabilities-based alignment configured to respond to the asymmetric challenges thrown up by globalization.[49]

Yet while the TSD alliance presents an effective instrument for responding to challenges that are asymmetric in nature, it would not be prudent to disregard other partners and organizations in the Asia-Pacific. Indeed, few comprehensive solutions to security in the region can be achieved without the engagement of other major states such as China, Russia and South Korea (and increasingly, India).[50] Thus, the TSD powers all cooperate on certain issue-areas with these states either bilaterally or through international treaties. For instance, China and Russia have been particularly compliant with allied concerns over terrorism and WMD proliferation (by using their influence on North Korea or Iran). Likewise international (for example, the United Nations), regional (for example, ASEAN, APEC) and multilateral (for instance, RIMPAC, *Cobra Gold*) regimes or initiatives all act to complement the close cooperation of the TSD states. However, China and Russia as the key powers in the Shanghai Cooperation Organization (SCO) have not viewed the emergence of the TSD alliance entirely favourably, arguing that it appears like a 'little NATO' designed to (re-)contain them.[51] This caveat notwithstanding, the harmonization of worldviews and national interests among Washington, Tokyo and Canberra means we can expect to see further consolidation of this nascent tripartite alliance in the years to come. As Japan and Australia greatly expand their geopolitical presence and military capabilities alongside the United States, they will be better equipped to meet the challenges of asymmetrical adversaries together in a transformed alliance for the twenty-first century.

Notes

All websites accessed 1 October 2006.

1 IR scholars will need no introduction to realism; the key text is Hans J. Morgenthau (1985), *Politics Among Nations*, 6th edn, New York: Knopf. For alliances consult Glenn Snyder (1997), *Alliance Politics*, Ithaca, NY: Cornell University Press; and Stephen Walt (1987), *The Origins of Alliances*, Ithaca, NY: Cornell University Press. There is abundant literature on 'the China threat' – see for example Zalmay M. Khalilzad *et al.* (1999), *The United States and a Rising China: Strategic and Military Implications*, Santa Monica, CA: Rand Corporation.
2 President George W. Bush (2006), *The National Security Strategy of the United States of America*, Washington, DC: The White House, available at: www.whitehouse.gov/nsc/nss/2006; Japan Defense Agency, *Defense of Japan 2005*, available at: www.jda.go.jp; Department of Defence, Australian Government, *Defence 2000: Our Future Defence Force* (Australian Defence White Paper); *Australia's National Security: A Defence Update 2003*; *Australia's National Security: Defence Update 2005*, all available at: www.defence.gov.au. See also US Department of State, Office of the Spokesman (2006), 'Trilateral Strategic Dialogue Joint Statement', 20 March 2006, available at: www.state.gov/r/pa/prs/ps/2006/63411.htm
3 Robert Hill (2003), 'The war on terrorism and the wider international security situation in East Asia', 719th Wilton Park Conference, Hakone, Japan, 30 September.
4 *The National Security Strategy of the United States of America.*
5 Ibid.
6 Japan Ministry for Foreign Affairs (2004), *Action Plan for Prevention of Terrorism*, 10 December, available at: www.mofa.go.jp/policy/terrorism/action.pdf
7 New Zealand's membership of ANZUS (Australia, New Zealand, United States) has been considered moribund since the mid-1980s. In effect ANZUS has been supplanted by the Australian–US Ministerial consultations (AUSMIN).
8 *Australia's National Security: A Defence Update 2003.*
9 *Department of Defense Dictionary of Military and Associated Terms* (2001/6), available at: www.dtic.mil/doctrine/jel/new_pubs/jp1_02.pdf

10 *Australia's National Security: A Defence Update 2003.*
11 For more relating to this argument, see Derek D. Smith (2006), *Deterring America: Rogue States and the Proliferation of Weapons of Mass Destruction*, Cambridge: Cambridge University Press.
12 The Six Party Talks held from 2003 to 2005 involved the DPRK/North Korea, the United States, Japan, Russia, ROK/South Korea and China.
13 Tim Butcher (2005), 'Wipe Israel off map, says Iran's president', *Telegraph*, 27 October, available at: www.telegraph.co.uk/news/main.jhtml?xml=/news/2005/10/27/wiran 27.xml
14 *The National Security Strategy of the United States of America.*
15 See Gordon Corera (2006), *Shopping for Bombs: Nuclear Proliferation, Global Insecurity, and the Rise and Fall of the A.Q. Khan Network*, Oxford: Oxford University Press; and Graham T. Allison *et al.* (1996), *Avoiding Nuclear Anarchy: Containing the Threat of Loose Russian Nuclear Weapons and Fissile Material*, Boston, MA: The MIT Press.
16 *The National Security Strategy of the United States of America.*
17 *Australia's National Security: A Defence Update 2005.*
18 'Japan's foreign policy in major diplomatic fields', *Diplomatic Bluebook 2004*, Japan Ministry for Foreign Affairs, available at: www.mofa.go.jp/policy/other/bluebook/2004/index.html
19 *The National Security Strategy of the United States of America.*
20 Ibid.
21 *Australia's National Security: A Defence Update 2005* [italics added].
22 *National Strategy for Combating Terrorism*, 2003, available at: www.state.gov/documents/organization/60172.pdf
23 *National Strategy for Combating Terrorism*, Japan's *Action Plan for Prevention of Terrorism*, and *Protecting Australia Against Terrorism: Australia's Counter-Terrorism Arrangements*, available at: www.dpmc.gov.au/publications/protecting_australia/docs/protecting_australia.pdf
24 Plus the United States and Australia are setting up Threat Integration/Assessment Centers.
25 The seizure of the Japanese Ambassador's residence in Peru in 1997 drew attention to the need to prepare for hostage rescue contingencies.
26 'US–Japan Alliance: Transformation and Realignment for the Future', Security Consultative Committee Document, 29 October 2005, available at: www.jda.go.jp
27 *The National Security Strategy of the United States of America.*
28 In addition: the Partial Test Ban Treaty (PTBT), Comprehensive Test Ban Treaty (CTBT), Biological and Toxin Weapons Convention (BWC) and Chemical Weapons Convention (CWC). There are also the proposed Fissile Material Cut-off Treaty (FMCT), the voluntary Missile Technology Control Regime (MTCR) and the Comprehensive Test Ban Treaty (CTBT), currently still awaiting ratification.
29 See *2005 Review Conference of the Parties to the Treaty on the Non-Proliferation of Nuclear Weapons (NPT)*, available at: www.un.org/events/npt2005
30 See the G8 Evian Summit (2003), *Global Partnership Against the Spread of Weapons and Materials of Mass Destruction – A G8 Action Plan*, available at: www.g8.fr/evian/english/navigation/2003_g8_summit/summit_documents/global_partnership_against_the_spread_of_weapons_and_materials_of_mass_destruction-a_g8_action_plan.html
31 See United Nations (2005), *International Convention for the Suppression of Acts of Nuclear Terrorism*, available at: http://untreaty.un.org/English/Terrorism/English_18_15.pdf
32 See Mark J. Valencia (2005), *The Proliferation Security Initiative: Making Waves in Asia*, Adelphi Paper 376, London: IISS.
33 *Statement of Interdiction Principles: The Proliferation Security Initiative*, available at: www.mofa.go.jp/policy/un/disarmament/arms/psi/state.pdf
34 The PSI is not without its pitfalls, however; see Ron Huisken (2006), 'The proliferation security initiative: coming in from the cold', The Nautilus Institute, 20 April, available at: http://nautilus.org; and Michael Richardson (2006), *The Proliferation Security Initiative*

(PSI): An Assessment of its Strengths and Weaknesses, With Some Proposals for Shaping its Future, Singapore: Institute of Southeast Asian Studies.

35 The Australian Group operates along similar lines to the other anti-proliferation regimes focusing on licensing/export controls, yet Washington has been critical of its effectiveness.

36 'US–Japan Alliance: Transformation and Realignment for the Future'.

37 'A nuclear Japan?', *Japan Times*, 16 July 2006, and Chisake Watanabe (2006), 'Japan's prime minister rules out nuclear weapons', *Houston Chronicle,* October 18.

38 *The National Security Strategy of the United States of America.*

39 'Japan threatens force against N Korea', *BBC News*, 14 February 2003, available at: http://news.bbc.co.uk/2/hi/asia-pacific/2757923.stm

40 Laura Tingle (2003), 'The PM and pre-emption politics', *Australian Financial Review*, March 14.

41 *Australia's National Security: A Defence Update 2003.*

42 Mr Yoshinori Ohno, Japanese Defence Minister (2005), 'Responding to WMD challenges in the Asia-Pacific: diplomacy and deterrence', speech, 4 June, Singapore.

43 'US–Japan Alliance: Transformation and Realignment for the Future'.

44 Fukushiro Nukaga, Japanese Defence Minister (2006), 'Japan's defence policy and international peace cooperation activities', speech, 11 January, Royal United Services Institute, UK.

45 *The National Security Strategy of the United States of America.*

46 *Australia's National Security: A Defence Update 2005.*

47 *Defense of Japan 2005.*

48 Dan Blumenthal (2005), 'Strengthening the US–Australian alliance: progress and pitfalls', *Asian Outlook*, April–May, p. 6.

49 Rod Lyon (2005), *Alliance Unleashed: Australia and the US in the New Strategic Age*, Canberra: Australian Strategic Policy Institute, p. 22.

50 For discussion of United States–Japan–Korea trilateralism see Victor D. Cha (1999), *Alignment Despite Antagonism: The United States–Korea–Japan Security Triangle*, Stanford, CA: Stanford University Press. For United States–Japan–China trilateralism see Brad Glosserman (2005), *US–Japan–China Relations: Trilateral Cooperation in the 21st Century – Conference Report*, Honolulu, HI: Pacific Forum Center for Strategic and International Studies (*Issues & Insights*, vol. 5, no. 10), September, available at: www.csis.org/media/csis/pubs/issuesinsights_v05n10.pdf

51 Purnendra Jain (2006), 'A "little NATO" against China', *Asia Times*, 18 March, available at: www.atimes.com/atimes/China/HC18Ad01.html

14 Trilateralism, ballistic missile defence and international arms control

*Richard A. Bitzinger**

Missile defence and international arms control highlight both the promise and pitfalls of Australia–Japan–United States trilateralism in international security. All three countries have mutual and overlapping interests when it comes to both issues, and, in fact, non-proliferation was listed as one of the topics for discussion in the ministerial-level Trilateral Strategic Dialogue held in March 2006. But getting beyond the usual generalities and vague diplomatic statements to craft truly trilateral approaches to arms control and especially missile defence will be much harder. It is particularly difficult for these countries to attempt to inject trilateralism into military issues, given such restrictions as Japan's ban on collective defence and Australia's unique, geographically determined defence requirements. At the same time, whereas Australia, Japan, and the United States may share many common goals when it comes to international arms control, the best forums for dealing with these issues would appear to be even more multilateral. So while trilateralism may succeed in pushing Australia–Japan–United States cooperation on broad security issues further down the road, it does not seem to have much effect on such specific military and defence issues as missile defence and international arms control.

The Asian-Pacific and US missile defence policy

Missile defence remains a top priority for the US government. It is seen as crucial to homeland security, defending the United States from missile attack from rogue states and peer competitors, and even as a hedge against the (however low) likelihood of terrorists or substate actors using weapons of mass destruction (WMD). Missile defences are also intended to protect US armed forces operating overseas in conflicts and hostile areas.[1]

North Korea is the United States' primary motivation in the Asia-Pacific region behind the growing interest in both missile defence in general, and increased US–allied cooperation on missile defences in particular. Together with its ongoing nuclear weapons program, North Korea has constructed, or is developing, an alarming array of medium-range and intermediate-range ballistic missiles. The *Nodong* (a modified Soviet-origin Scud-D) constitutes the most serious immediate missile threat to Northeast Asia. With a range of 1,000 kilometres (approximately 600 miles), it puts most of Japan and US bases in Japan in danger of a conventional or WMD missile attack. North Korea is believed to already possess several hundred *Nodong* missiles. More worrisome to the United States is North Korea's continuing development of longer-range ballistic missiles, particularly the 1,500-kilometre-range (1,000-mile) *Taepodong* I, and the *Taepodong* II, with a range believed to be at least 4,000 kilometres (2,500 miles). The *Taepodong* I was tested in August 1998, and the *Taepodong* II in July 2006.[2]

Although not explicitly mentioned by the US or any other allied government as a raison d'être for missile defences, China's growing arsenal of conventional and WMD-capable ballistic missiles is at least a secondary cause for concern. China has long deployed a number of older medium-range and intermediate-range ballistic missiles capable of targeting both the Asia-Pacific and the United States. More importantly, China has in recent years made some progress towards improving the capabilities of its strategic missile force, and it has added, or is in the process of adding, several ballistic missile systems to its armoury, including two solid-fuel, road-mobile missiles – the 1,800-kilometre-range (1,100-mile) DF-21A and the 8,000-kilometre-range (5,000-mile) DF-31 – and the submarine-launched, 8,000-kilometre-range JL-2.

At the same time, China is believed to possess only a few dozen modern longer-range missiles. Consequently, strategic missile defences could effectively neutralize China's missile-based nuclear option. Not surprisingly, therefore, Beijing has vociferously opposed US missile defences and particularly US efforts to introduce missile defence in Asia in cooperation with its allies. China is concerned that missile defences could contribute to the remilitarization of Japan or provide the technical basis for an offensive Japanese ballistic missile program. More important, in the event of a China–Taiwan conflict, Western missile defences, particularly those based in the Asia-Pacific region, could be used to defend Taiwan from Chinese missile attacks.[3]

In the face of such potential threats, Washington is particularly keen to expand missile defence to include allies and friendly countries, and it is endeavouring to open up missile defence research and development (R&D), production, acquisition and deployment to foreign participation and partnerships. National Security Policy Directive-23 (NSPD-23), one of the Bush administration's leading policy directives on missile defence, states:

> Because the threats of the 21st Century also endanger our friends and allies around the world, it is essential that we work together to defend against them. The Defense Department will develop and deploy missile defenses capable of protecting not only the United States and our deployed forces, but also our friends and allies.

As such, the Defense Department intends to 'structure the missile defense program in a manner that encourages industrial participation by friends and allies … and also promotes international missile defense cooperation'.[4] Consequently, one of the US Missile Defense Agency's key objectives is to 'establish a robust international foundation for missile defense'.[5]

Foreign partnering in missile defence can take place in several ways, including financial investments, technology-sharing, permitting the use of foreign facilities or territory for early warning or the deployment of interceptors, the purchase or co-production of US missile defence systems, or the joint development of missile defence systems and subsystems. In this regard, the United States has in recent years reached out to friends and allies in Europe, the Middle East and the Asia-Pacific to collaborate on building and deploying missile defences. Important non-Asian partners include the United Kingdom, Denmark and Israel. In addition, the United States is working multilaterally with NATO on a variety of missile defence-related initiatives.

Japan and missile defence

United States efforts to promote cooperative missile defence with key Asian-Pacific allies coincides with a period of significant evolution in Japan's postwar security calculus. Tokyo's interest in missile defence was galvanized in August 1998 by North Korea's *Taepodong* I missile test, which alerted Tokyo to the need to reorient its Self-Defence Forces (SDF) to cope with new threats, particularly ballistic missiles and the proliferation of weapons of mass destruction.[6] Japan's 2003 Defence White Paper explicitly noted the danger arising out of the spread of weapons of mass destruction and ballistic missiles. The until recent stalemate in the Six Party Talks to get North Korea to abandon its nuclear weapons program, missile tests by the Kim regime (most recently the test in July 2006 of a *Taepodong* II long-range ballistic missile along with its concurrent launch of several shorter-range missiles), and North Korea's inaugural nuclear weapons test in early October 2006 have only further convinced Japan that it needs missile defences sooner rather than later.

While Japan is most concerned about the missile threat from North Korea, China is also a key factor in Tokyo's interest in acquiring missile defences. China, while officially considered to be only a mid- to long-term security 'concern', is in actuality being regarded more and more as a potential threat to Japan. Japan is increasingly wary of an ever-assertive China, fuelled by its growing economic and military strength. Relations between Beijing and Tokyo have soured considerably in recent years, over such issues as continuing intrusions by Chinese military vessels in Japanese waters – including the November 2004 incident when a Chinese nuclear-powered *Han* submarine was detected off Okinawa – conflicting territorial claims over the Senkaku Islands, and the refusal by Japan's prime minister to stop visiting the Yasukuni shrine. Some in Tokyo increasingly view China's development of more accurate medium-range ballistic missiles as another, and perhaps even more serious, long-term source of concern.[7]

At the same time, Japan's security interests have expanded far beyond Northeast Asia. Now, the SDF has to contend with possible contingency operations much farther afield – for example, in international military stabilization operations (such as in Iraq), or in patrolling sea lanes of communication in the Straits of Malacca (to safeguard access to Middle East/Persian Gulf energy supplies).

All of these developments have caused the United States and Japan to become increasingly more aligned on a number of regional security challenges. Despite Japan's current prohibition on collective defence, the United States and Japan are likely to increase military cooperation when it comes to regional security threats. United States forces based in Japan, for example, would probably be employed in the event of a Taiwan Strait contingency; at the very least, therefore, Japan would have to provide considerable rear-area and logistical support to US forces.

Japan–United States cooperation on missile defence goes back to 1999, with the creation of four joint research programs focusing on upgrades to the *Standard* SM-3 ship-launched air defence missile: a lightweight nose cone, an advanced infrared seeker, a new kinetic energy warhead, and a new booster rocket. These programs were largely low-level technology demonstrator projects, however, never amounting to more than $50 million a year altogether.

In December 2003, however, Tokyo agreed to move from research to development, and to cooperate with the United States in creating a two-tiered missile defence system, comprising the *Aegis*/SM-3 Sea-based Midcourse Defense (SMD) system and the land-based Patriot PAC-3 missile. Plans call for an initial off-the-shelf buy from the United States of missile defence systems, with the concurrent co-development and co-production of next-generation missile defence systems with the United States. These arrangements were formalized in a joint Memorandum of Understanding (MOU) signed in December 2004.

The SMD missile defence system includes improvements to the current *Aegis* air defence system to enhance its range and reaction time in order to handle exo-atmospheric anti-missile engagements. This program entails upgrades to the *Aegis* SPY-1 multifunction phased-array radar and weapons control system for longer-range and higher-altitude search, detection, track, engagement, and control. The SM-3 Block IA missile is an improvement on the SM-2 Block IV missile, with the addition of a third-stage for extended range and a Lightweight Exo-Atmospheric Projectile (LEAP) kinetic warhead for terminal homing and intercept. Japan and the United States successfully tested the SMD missile defence system off the coast of Hawaii in June 2006.[8]

Japan will incorporate the SMD missile defence system into four Kongo-class air defence destroyers, which are already outfitted with the *Aegis* fire-control system and *Standard* SM-2 missile. Japan plans to deploy its first upgraded missile defence destroyer in 2007, with full deployment expected in 2011. Until then, the US Navy will provide limited missile defence coverage of Japan utilizing its own *Aegis*-class SMD destroyers based in the Sea of Japan.

The land-based *Patriot* PAC-3 system will provide endo-atmospheric 'point-defence' protection against missile attacks. Japan's Air Self-Defence Force (ASDF) will deploy PAC-3 units to four locations around Japan between 2006 and 2010.[9] The US Army could also base *Patriot* PAC-3 batteries at US bases in Japan.

Just as critically, in May 2006, Japan and the United States concluded an agreement that, among other things, commits the two countries to fostering closer cooperation in the area of intelligence gathering and sharing when it comes to ballistic missile threats, to increasing interoperability in responding to ballistic missile threats, and working towards greater coordination of missile defence command

and control. As a result, the United States and Japan will establish a bilateral joint operations coordination centre at Yokota Air Base, and the ASDF Air Defence Command will relocate to Yokota in order to support coordinated air and missile defence operations. As a practical matter when it comes to increased cooperation on missile defence, the United States agreed to deploy an X-Band radar for ballistic missile detection at the ASDF base in Shariki.[10] Japan also intends to utilize its new FPS-XX early warning and tracking radar for missile defence, and to share data with US missile defence operators.

Finally, Japan and the United States continue to collaborate on technology upgrades for the SM-3 missile. At least one Japanese-developed component, a clamshell nose cone, has already been incorporated into the SM-3 Block IA missile, and Washington and Tokyo will soon sign an agreement on full-scale cooperative development on the SM-3 Block II/IIA missile configuration. In particular, this co-development program will involve work on a 21-inch diameter (as opposed to the current 13.5-inch diameter) SM-3 missile long favoured by the Japanese, who want a larger and therefore faster and deadlier interceptor. The Japanese – and particularly Japan's defence industry – pin considerable hope on co-producing missile defence systems with the United States, and especially on eventually putting the jointly developed SM-3 Block II/IIA missile into production. If these Block II programs fail to move forward, Japan could reap few industrial or technological benefits from its participation in missile defence.[11]

Altogether, Tokyo will spend at least 1 trillion yen (US$8.6 billion) – including $1 billion for joint research and development – to fully deploy its SMD/*Patriot* missile defence system. Japan's FY2006 defence budget included 141 billion yen (US$1.2 billion) for missile defences in FY2006, and this grew by more than 50 per cent to 219 billion yen (US$1.9 billion) in the FY2007 request.[12] To help fund its missile defence programs, Japan will by 2010 reduce the size of its ground forces by 7,000 troops and cut its number of tanks from 900 to 600, its major surface combatants from 50 to 47, and its fighter aircraft from 300 to 260. In addition, production of the new F-2 fighter jet will be capped at around 100 aircraft, instead of the originally projected 130.[13]

Tokyo's decision to sign on to missile defence, and in particular to engage in cooperative missile defence with the United States, has not been without its compli-cations. With the distinction between theatre and strategic missile defence now abandoned in favour of a seamless, integrated system, Japan has had to quietly reinterpret its ban on collective defence to permit cooperative engagement with the United States against missile threats. In particular, Japan's missile defence system will be highly dependent on US command, control, communications, computing and intelligence (C4I) assets, such as for early warning and tracking. In addition, Japan's missile defences would be likely to share targeting information with US forces, and Japanese interceptors could be used to shoot down missiles intended to attack US territory. Consequently, missile defence ties Japan even closer to the United States in defence and security matters.[14]

Japan has also had to relax its long-standing, near-total ban on arms exports in order to permit cooperation with the United States on missile defence. In December

2004, the Koizumi government agreed to exempt joint missile defence development from the arms export ban. This exception will permit Japan to jointly develop and produce missile defence systems with the United States for use by US forces, and to sell Japanese missile defence-related subsystems and components to the United States. Although Tokyo maintains that this partial lifting applies only to missile defence, some see it as the thin edge of the wedge in eventually repealing the entire ban, and in fact, the Koizumi government also stated that it would examine, on a case-by-case basis, the export ban on other jointly developed weapons.[15]

Australia and missile defence

The current Liberal–National government led by Prime Minister John Howard is a strong supporter of missile defence in general and of US missile defence efforts in particular. In January 2004, Howard stated that it would be 'recklessly negligent' not to explore ways to defend the country against missile attacks.[16] In June 2004, then-Defence Minister Robert Hill refused to rule out the eventual deployment of missile interceptors on Australian soil to protect population centres.[17]

Cooperation with the United States on missile defence is seen as part of a much broader effort on the part of Canberra to expand interoperability and military and defence–industrial partnering with the United States. Overall, the Australian Defence Force (ADF) wants to be capable of making a significant contribution to the United States in coalition and allied operations, while at the same time maintaining an independent deployment capability so as to make an effective contribution to peace and stability within its geographic area of responsibility, operating either on its own or even as a leader in some coalition operations. Consequently, the ADF is currently in a multi-year process of transforming itself into a more expeditionary and firepower-intensive military, capable of being more (and more quickly) deployable and more sustainable over long periods and across long distances, of being able to engage in both low-level and high-intensity high-tech wars, and, finally, of being able to work more closely with US forces in joint missions.[18] Australia already permits the United States to use its Pine Gap communications and relay facility for space-based early warning and detection satellites, such as the Defence Support Program (DSP) and the future Space-Based Infrared System (SBIRS).[19] In December 2003, the Howard government announced its intention to cooperate with the United States on missile defence, and it formally joined the US missile defence program in July 2004, with the signing of an MOU establishing a 25-year framework for joint government-to-government and industry-to-industry cooperation on missile defence R&D and acquisition.[20]

Additionally, Australia is planning to acquire and construct three air warfare destroyers (AWDs), which will be based on the US *Aegis* combat system and the SM-2 *Standard* surface-to-air missile. These AWDs are especially important to the ADF's new expeditionary strategy, as they will provide necessary protection to new amphibious, sealift, and support ships from air-breathing attacks (aircraft and anti-ship cruise missiles).[21] At the same time, since the *Aegis* system is being adapted for the US SMD mid-course missile defence program, the AWD could serve as the central platform for an Australian missile defence system. In fact, these ships would, at a minimum, be capable of providing early warning and tracking of ballistic missiles and passing this information on to US Navy SMD-equipped vessels. In addition, the new AWDs would be likely to be upgradeable to an SMD standard, as their *Aegis* combat systems are likely to incorporate a modular, open architecture, while at the same time space and weight considerations for accepting the SM-3 ballistic missile interceptor are being factored into the ship's design and construction.[22] In March 2004, the US and Royal Australian navies signed a Statement of Principles to expand cooperation on naval surface warfare, one element of which could be improved Australian access to state-of-the-art US technology regarding naval air defence systems for its AWD program.

Other areas of US–Australian cooperation will be joint exploratory R&D on missile defence technologies. A key component of this phase will be studying the prospects for integrating Australia's indigenously developed *Jindalee* over-the-horizon radar network (JORN) into the US missile defence configuration. Australia plans to spend A\$62 million (US\$47.5 million) to upgrade and enhance the JORN system – currently used to detect aircraft at long range – in order to give it greater range and sensitivity to detect incoming missiles during their early boost phase.[23] In addition, Australia and the United States have teamed up to develop high-power active-phased array radar systems that could be applied to missile defences.[24]

Despite statements of support and current exploratory R&D efforts, Canberra has not yet pledged either to acquire missile defences or to host ground-based interceptors on Australian territory. One of the biggest barriers is financial: Australia has not so far committed itself to any long-term capitalization program to underwrite missile defence. In fact, it is interesting to note that missile defences are conspicuously absent from the 2006–16 Defence Capability Plan.[25] At the same time, embracing missile defences could undermine Australia's commitments to transforming the ADF into an expeditionary force and to being able to take part in joint contingency operations with the United States, by diverting funds away from conventional force improvements. In addition, the *Aegis*/SM-3 SMD system would not have the range to protect Australia from missile attacks.[26] Overall, the Howard government faces considerable obstacles to moving forward on missile defence cooperation with the United States, and consequently US–Australian cooperation on missile defence will probably continue to centre around joint R&D.

More importantly, Australia is simply not as immediately concerned as either Japan or the United States with missile threats emanating from either North Korea or China. With regard to North Korea, for once the 'tyranny of distance' works in Australia's favour; the country (and especially its major cities) still lies beyond Pyongyang's missile reach (for now).[27] A Chinese missile threat seems even more remote, although Canberra is very concerned that a United States–China clash (possibly over Taiwan) could drag it into a conflict between its closest ally and a growing economic partner.[28]

Missile defence and trilateralism

In the Asia-Pacific region, partnering the United States in the area of missile defence remains, so far at least, a strictly bilateral affair. Japan and, to a much lesser extent, Australia have made some movement forward in pursuing missile defence, and both countries are cooperating with the United States on various missile defence-related programs. In addition, the fact that all three countries have acquired or are in the process of acquiring the missile defence-capable *Aegis* fire-control/*Standard* missile air defence system points to some potential promise for future three-way cooperation in the area of missile defence. That said, however, the near- and medium-term prospects are dim for any Australia–Japan–United States trilateralism in missile defences. It may be one thing for Tokyo to use cooperative missile defence with the United States as a means of introducing collective defence through the backdoor, watering down the country's so-called 'Peace Constitution', and even loosening its highly inflexible arms export ban – in other words, helping Japan become a more 'normal' country, both in terms of its status in the Asia-Pacific region and its alliance with the United States (also called 'normalization by stealth').[29] It is quite another to push this effort too far by openly engaging in collaboration with third parties on obviously military activities such as missile defence (peacekeeping or stabilization operations do not carry the same stigma, as they are not geared towards dealing with potential conflicts). Japan is simply not prepared yet for anything other than bilateral defence arrangements.

The same may be true for Australia when it comes to missile defence, but for different reasons. Australia currently sees no reason to develop a missile defence capability, either on its own, in bilateral cooperation with the United States, or as part of a broader regional effort. It perceives no pressing missile threat to the continent, and in expeditionary coalition operations where Australian forces might be in danger of short-range missile attacks, it expects that the US military would be likely to provide protection against these threats.[30] Despite its nominal support for US missile defences, therefore, Australia pursues the trilateral security dialogue mainly as a mechanism for bolstering regional security and not for containing China per se.[31]

It is, of course, certainly conceivable that a trilateral Australia–Japan–United States missile shield might be constructed sometime down the road. In particular, these three countries could, with very little in the way of new requirements for technology or system, expand their cooperation when it comes to sharing intelligence, early warning, and tracking of missile threats. And it is also possible that Australia may, sometime in the future, decide to upgrade its air warfare destroyers to the SMD ballistic missile defence standard, thereby permitting a three-way cooperative intercept capability. But in the meantime, missile defence in the Asia-Pacific will mainly be a United States–Japan affair.

Arms control and trilateralism

As opposed to missile defence, Australia–Japan–United States cooperation in international arms control initiatives is much easier to conceptualize. For one thing, all three countries are already members of the leading international arms control regimes, including:

- The Nuclear Suppliers Group: to control the transfer of nuclear-related dual-use items and technologies.
- The Zangger Committee: an informal association of leading nuclear exporting nations that together maintain a list of equipment that may only be exported if safeguards are applied to the recipient facility (the so-called 'Trigger List', because such transfers trigger the requirement for safeguards).
- The Australia Group: to control the transfer of items and technologies that could be used in the development and manufacture of chemical and biological weapons.
- The Missile Technology Control Regime (MTCR): to restrict the export of items and technologies that could be used in the development and manufacture of longer-range ballistic and cruise missiles and other unmanned WMD delivery systems.
- The Proliferation Security Initiative (PSI): an international effort to interdict the transfer of WMD and missile-related weapons and weapons technologies, particularly by permitting interdiction and confiscation of such items at sea.
- Wassenaar Arrangement: an informal association to promote greater transparency and responsibility with regard to the transfer of armaments and sensitive dual-use items and technologies.

Three-way cooperation in the area of arms control was underscored by the fact that, prior to the March 2006 ministerial-level Trilateral Strategic Dialogue, US Secretary of State Rice and Australian Prime Minister Howard both made reference to the usefulness of this dialogue towards 'working together on nonproliferation issues'.[32]

Nevertheless, while these three countries may see expanded trilateral cooperation as useful in pushing international arms control initiatives further down the road, no one as yet sees trilateralism as a substitute for broader multilateral efforts. In fact, given the global nature of WMD and conventional weapons proliferation, trilateralism is probably too narrow an approach to these problems and could perhaps even be a distraction from multilateral arms control regimes. Certainly the United States prefers to see as broadly multinational an effort as possible when it comes to controlling or restricting the transfer of items and technologies relating to weapons of mass destruction and missile delivery systems, or the export of conventional weaponry and dual-use items to countries of concern.

Conclusions

Overall, Australia–Japan–United States trilateralism, and in particular the Trilateral Strategic Dialogue, offers little promise when it comes to missile defence and even international arms control efforts. Missile defence is still too prickly an issue (especially for the Japanese, whose domestic politics make it difficult, if not impossible, to cooperate with the Australians in such an openly military mission) for anything but a bilateral approach, while controlling the proliferation of WMD and missile systems is too important not to be pursued multilaterally. With regard to both undertakings, therefore, a trilateral approach largely falls between two stools.

Regarding the latter, certainly Australia, Japan, and the United States may wish to consult more closely on issues of non-proliferation and to better understand each other's actions, needs and concerns when it comes to such issues as uranium exports, nuclear technology transfers, missile component sales and related matters. Trilateralism, therefore, might help bolster international non-proliferation efforts by providing new (and more confidential) forums for discussion and dialogue. At the same time, however, it is difficult to see how some of these consultations would not also draw the attention of other members of the various international control regimes – other nations besides Australia and Japan would be likely to be very interested in hearing how the United States' proposed nuclear agreement with India does not undermine the Non-Proliferation Treaty, for example.[33] Consequently, in order that Australia–Japan–United States trilateralism does not adversely affect multinational arms control activities, such undertakings should be regarded mainly as adjuncts to, rather than substitutes for, broader control efforts.

So, too, while missile defence may be a perfect candidate for trilateral coordination and cooperation, it is premature to make any predictions as to if or when this might actually come about. To reiterate, given the growing commonality of missile defence-capable platforms and systems on the part of the Australian, Japanese and US forces – such as intelligence-gathering and sharing systems, command, control, and communications infrastructures, and, in particular, the *Aegis–Standard* missile air defence system – the option for some kind of future three-way missile defence engagement strategy is certainly feasible. However, many other matters must be resolved first, on a variety of political and defence-related levels, and additional procurements made of pertinent equipment and technologies, before such a trilateral missile defence system can become a reality. Until that time, such joint missile defence efforts will have to be content with bilateralism – and in this regard, two very different kinds of bilateral efforts, that is, a very robust US–Japanese collaboration in missile defences versus a much more modest US–Australian effort to share intelligence and warning. As of now, therefore, trilateralism is probably still too radical a concept for active defence operations involving Australia, Japan and the United States.

Notes

* The analyses and opinions expressed in this paper are strictly those of the author and do not represent the official position of the Institute of Defence and Security Studies.

1 US Department of Defense, Office of the Secretary of Defense, *Quadrennial Defense Review Report* (QDR) (2006), Washington, DC: Office of the Secretary of Defense, 6 February, pp. 19–20, 24–27; US Department of Defense, Missile Defense Agency (MDA) (2005), *A Day in the Life of the BMDS*, 3rd edn, Washington, DC: Office of the Secretary of Defense, pp. 1, 4–10.

2 Michael D. Swaine, Rachel M. Swanger and Takashi Kawakami (2001), *Japan and Ballistic Missile Defense*, Santa Monica, CA: RAND, pp. 11–14.

3 Center for Nonproliferation Studies, East Asian Nonproliferation Program (CNS-EANP), *EANP Factsheet: China's Opposition to US Missile Defense Programs*, available at: http://cns.miis.edu/research/china/chinamd.htm (accessed 20 September 2006); Alan D. Romberg and Michael McDevitt (eds) (2003), *China and Missile Defense: Managing US–PRC Strategic Relations*, Washington, DC: The Henry L. Stimson Center.

4 *National Security Presidential Directive/NSPD-23* (2002), Washington, DC: The White House, 16 December.

5 MDA (2005), *A Day in the Life of the BMDS*, p. 4.

6 Japan Defense Agency (JDA), Defense Policy Division (2004), *RMA and Japan Defense Agency*, PowerPoint briefing presented to author, 2 March, p. 18.

7 Swaine, Swanger and Kawakami (2001), *Japan and Ballistic Missile Defense*, pp. 11–17.

8 Steven Trimble (2006), 'US and Japan celebrate ballistic missile intercept', *Jane's Defense Weekly*, 28 June.

9 Reiji Yoshida (2006), 'Missile defense plans have their skeptics', *Japan Times*, 28 July.

10 Stephen Trimble (2006), 'Japan and US seal terms of alliance strategy', *Jane's Defense Weekly*, 10 May.

11 Swaine, Swanger and Kawakami (2001), *Japan and Ballistic Missile Defense*, p. 76.

12 Yoshida (2006), 'Missile defense plans have their skeptics'; 'Japan expects to pay part of joint missile system', Agence France-Presse (AFP), 12 December 2005; 'Japan eyes sharp rise in missile defense budget', *SpaceWar*, 29 August 2006.

13 David Fouse (2005), 'Japan's FY2005 National Defense Program outline: new concepts, old compromises', *Asia-Pacific Security Studies Series*, vol. 4, no. 3, p. 3; Shinichi Kiyotani (2004), 'Japan cuts back on F-2 production', *Jane's Defense Weekly*, 18 August.

14 Aurelia George Mulgan (2005), 'Japan's defense dilemma', *Security Challenges*, vol. 1, no. 1, pp. 63–65.

15 Mark Wuebbels (2004/2005), 'Japan revises its three arms export principles', *Asian Export Control Observer*, Issue 5, pp. 10–11.

16 'Son of Star Wars is commonsense: Howard', *Sydney Morning Herald*, 16 January 2004.

17 Tom Allard (2004), 'Home bases for missile defence: Hill', *Sydney Morning Herald*, 23 June.

18 Australian Department of Defence (2005), *Australia's National Security – A Defence Update 2005*, Canberra: Australian Department of Defence; Ian Bostock (2006), 'Country Briefing: Australia – offshore interests', *Jane's Defense Weekly*, 25 January.

19 Richard Brabin-Smith (2004), *Australia and Ballistic Missile Defence: Our Policy Choices*, 'Strategic Insights', Canberra: Australian Strategic Policy Institute, April, pp. 2–3.

20 Ian Bostock (2004), 'Australia fleshes out plans for missile defense', *Jane's Defense Weekly*, 21 January; Ian Bostock (2004), 'Australian destroyers, radars to form part of US missile shield', *Jane's Defense Weekly*, 30 June.

21 Ian Bostock (2004), 'Country Briefing: Australia – reaching out', *Jane's Defense Weekly*, 3 November.

22 Bostock (2004), 'Australian destroyers, radars to form part of US missile shield'.

23 Brendan Nicholson (2004), '$62m update plan for far-view radar', *Age*, 25 February.

24 Richard Scott (2005), 'Australia, US, team on active radar development', *Jane's Defense Industry*, 31 August.
25 Ian Bostock (2006), 'Australia sets out 10-year vision for defense investment', *Jane's Defense Industry*, 1 July.
26 Brabin-Smith (2004), *Australia and Ballistic Missile Defense*, pp. 5–7.
27 Ibid., p. 6.
28 Ian Storey (2002), 'Assertive China gives Australia cause for concern', *Jane's Intelligence Review*, 1 August.
29 Mulgan (2005), 'Japan's defense dilemma', pp. 60–61.
30 Brabin-Smith (2004), *Australia and Ballistic Missile Defense*, p. 6.
31 Storey (2002), 'Assertive China gives Australia cause for concern'; David Gollust (2006), 'Rice participates in security dialogue with Japanese, Australian counterparts', *Voice of America*, 17 March.
32 Gollust (2006), 'Rice participates in security dialogue with Japanese, Australian counterparts'.
33 Ibid.

15 Conclusion

William T. Tow

More than fifty years has passed since Japan, a defeated wartime power, resumed its position as a key player in Asia-Pacific relations under the US security umbrella and as a power ordained to play a major role in shaping regional and global prosperity. Japan is now exploring how it should reconstitute its politico-strategic identity at a time when newly emergent regional and global forces are instigating immense structural and normative change in Asia and around the world and when the future application of American power is increasingly uncertain. Australia likewise has closely linked its own security to affiliation with US regional and global strategy and this pattern has only intensified over the past ten years of conservative government ensconced in Canberra.

As the chapters in this volume have demonstrated, the Trilateral Strategic Dialogue (TSD) is an opportunity for both Japan and Australia to seek reassurance from Washington that their respective bilateral alliances with the United States will be sustainable and credible at a time when international stability is less evident than at any time in postwar history. The TSD's current viability and ultimate fate remain uncertain, however, reflecting the mixed policy motives of its participants, the potentially lethal hostility of its sceptics and the still largely indistinct nature of its purpose and missions.

Yet international relations are nothing if not unpredictable and strategic surprise often serves as an important catalyst for sealing an otherwise amorphous initiative's logic and durability. The explosive nature of ongoing North Korean nuclear and missile politics may well prove to be the glue that ultimately establishes the TSD as an enduring fixture in the Asia-Pacific security environment. Only a few months after the inaugural TSD ministerial session, the North Koreans orchestrated multiple launchings of their missile systems (in July 2006) which, if fitted with commensurate WMD warheads, could easily threaten Japanese cities with widespread destruction and could eventually reach both Australian and US targets. In October 2006, the DPRK shocked the international community by conducting its first nuclear weapons test. Although the UN Security Council unanimously condemned this action, the most important actors required to enforce a subsequent UN resolution (UN Res. 1718) sanctioning Pyongyang from trading or transporting weapons or nuclear technology as punishment for its violation of nuclear non-proliferation norms failed to reach sufficient consensus on how to enforce it. Russia, China and South Korea adopted a 'loose constructionist' interpretation of the UN resolution for fear of alienating Pyongyang to the point of escalating an already severe regional crisis, and refused to view the Proliferation Security Initiative (PSI) as anything other than a provocation against North Korea.

The United States and Japan, in contrast, adopted a hardline posture on sanctions, believing that not doing so could only undermine what little credibility the NPT regime might still retain. Although Japan could not constitutionally participate in sanctions operations, its maritime Self-Defence Force did participate in previously scheduled naval exercises with US 7th Fleet elements off Japan's coast in a show of force bound to be interpreted as a hostile act by the North Korean regime. Australia also sided with Washington and Tokyo on the sanctions issue. Australian policy-planners reportedly weighed (if only briefly) assisting the US Navy in implementing a naval blockade to enforce the sanctions resolution against North Korean shipping.[1] A North Korean diplomat posted in Bangkok responded by warning Australia that it was 'treading a dangerous path' by supporting the US and Japanese position, aggravating tensions not only on the Korean peninsula but also throughout a Southeast Asia which generally favoured diplomacy over coercion as the best means for the resolution of this crisis.[2] By default, then, the TSD powers found themselves united on how to respond to North Korean nuclear policy but isolated from many of their Asia-Pacific counterparts by their determination to pursue tough measures against North Korea.

This episode underscores both the positive and negative aspects of trilateralism that have been addressed throughout this book. Encouragingly, the capacity of the region's three maritime industrialized democracies to coordinate their policy responses to a regionally destabilizing force – a nuclear-threatening North Korea – was validated. Trilateralism appeared to be a more effective pathway than the UN's global multilateralism for invoking clear sanctions in the defence of the existing NPT regime. Moreover, Japan's new conservative Prime Minister, Shinzo Abe, moved quickly to alleviate fears that Japan would 'go nuclear' in response to the North Korean nuclear test and to repair the diplomatic ties with both China and South Korea that had soured under his predecessor, Junichiro Koizumi. All three conditions of 'contingent trilateralism' designated in Chapter 3 of this volume appeared to be at least somewhat in play in the North Korean case. The US response to the North Korean nuclear test was challenged by an increasingly powerful yet trepidatious China and Russia's geopolitical obstinacy in the region. These challenges were exacerbated by the international reverberations of the United States's ill-fated military intervention in Iraq which spilt over to compromise its ability to deal with another member of President George W. Bush's designated 'axis of evil'.

However, Washington was supported strongly by both Japan and Australia as it sought a diplomatic solution to this latest Northeast Asian crisis, with Australian and American (and, constitution permitting, perhaps also Japanese) maritime capabilities being particularly relevant to the prospective enforcement of sanctions against the movement of weapons materials or luxury goods in or out of North Korea, and a potential complement to the Chinese decision to enforce sanctions by land along the China–North Korea border.

Both Japan and Australia moved quickly and decisively to support the new sanctions regime without exacerbating Sino-American differences over the intensity of sanctions enforcement in the process. Balancing and calibration were clear features of the immediate Australian and Japanese responses.

Sceptics of trilateralism, however, could also build a case against the relevance of the TSD to the North Korean crisis and to the overall structural changes unfolding throughout the Asia-Pacific. Most centrally, obvious differences between China and the United States over how to deal with North Korea dominated the international response to the North Korean test. In this context, 'TSD unity' had no real impact on the evolution of the crisis or its outcome because neither Japan nor Australia was able to offer any creative policy alternative for Washington to bridge the gap between Chinese and American strategic interests. South Korean reluctance to adopt a hardline stance on the sanctions issue further underscored the growing impasse between Seoul and Washington–Tokyo over North Korean policy and the glaring irrelevance of the Trilateral Coordination and Oversight Group (TCOG) in addressing the very crisis it was formed to manage. Ultimately, trilateralism or even *ad hoc* multilateralism (represented in this instance by the Six Party Talks) can be successful in Northeast Asia and throughout the Asia-Pacific region only to the extent that China is willing to work within such frameworks.

To employ the predictable aphorism, the 'truth lies somewhere in between' these two positions. Trilateralism is relevant in Asia-Pacific security politics if, and only if, it is applied with sufficient discrimination and subtlety to complement other existing mechanisms for crisis resolution and regional confidence-building. This appears to have been the case in the initial response to the North Korean nuclear test, with the United States underscoring the central relevance of the United States–Japan bilateral alliance – the core of its hub and spokes alliance strategy in the region – to the coordinated effort for sanctions enforcement, along with simultaneous Sino-American collaboration, to force Pyongyang back to the negotiating table. The US alliance system would continue to deter North Korea from militarily escalating the crisis against Japan and South Korea. Meanwhile, US policy leaders hoped, 'the right combination of countries ... can bring the right combination of incentives and disincentives [to achieve] a North Korean reversal – irreversible, verifiable dismantlement of this [nuclear] program'.[3] In this context, the TSD could serve as a potentially critical consultative instrument. It could not, and should not, serve as any type of enforcement spearhead in the event of continued North Korean bellicosity against designated antagonists or the international community-at-large.

The North Korea nuclear test episode is a 'case study' of potential TSD applicability to what Hugh White has designated in his chapter as the 'tectonic changes' now unfolding in the Asian security system. As he correctly notes, such changes raise 'fundamental questions' about future patterns of security alignments and power balancing in the Asia-Pacific and, more specifically, about the future value of Australia and Japan maintaining their strong alliances with the United States and developing stronger bilateral security ties within the TSD framework. It may be, however, that his conclusion that the TSD offers little to addressing wider regional and global imperatives, because the three parties' interests and concerns are shared by many others, underestimates the will, capacity and especially the agility these three countries can bring to the most critical security imperatives of the day.

Australia, Japan and the United States have been involved in the business of alliance management and its fine-tuning for over half a century. Notwithstanding how successful or unsuccessful they have been in pursuing such tasks, these three states are not in the habit of pursuing their mutual security concerns randomly or frivolously. This even applies to such imbroglios as the Vietnam War, where nationalist forces in Southeast Asia were misperceived as part of a Soviet-led global threat to be contained, and to the more recent American-led military intervention in Iraq where concerns about international terrorism and the spread of WMDs led the three allies to participate in what will probably be remembered as a well-intended but ill-fated Western move to neutralize a brutal and unpopular Iraqi government. Against these setbacks, however, one can list the TSD members' cultivation of a relatively stable and increasingly prosperous China into the regional and international security systems, the accommodation of rising Indian power, support for the establishment and steady growth of a Southeast Asian security complex whose member governments threaten no TSD member-state, and the transformation of the Soviet Union/Russia from a Cold War rival to a capitalist, albeit troubled and restless, actor on the international scene. Although their track record is hardly perfect, the United States, Japan and Australia have often addressed the right 'big questions' concerning regional and global change. They have continued to prosper as economic and strategic actors within the world's community of developed states and to play a large role in shaping an increasingly dynamic and prosperous Asia-Pacific region. It is important to recall this important reality at a time when US and allied self-confidence may be reaching a nadir not felt since the fall of Vietnam.

The TSD is at a crossroads and its future will depend on how well it responds to several key factors. First, it will need to succeed in genuinely convincing China that the motives underlying its founding and operations are not to contain that power but to embrace it more effectively as a partner in Asia-Pacific order-building. The TSD states would do well to learn from China's own brief and failed effort to convert the ASEAN + 3 initiative to an 'inclusive' (that is, 'Asians only') body designed to marginalize US power within Asia and to further isolate Japan from the region. The TSD can be employed to identify and sell incentives for China to become the 'responsible stakeholder' that everyone, including Beijing's own leadership, wants that country to become. In this sense, the TSD can be more adroit and reactive to rapidly changing strategic developments than the more cumbersome and consensus-ridden ASEAN Regional Forum (ARF) can ever be. It is well equipped to be a calibrator and interlocutor of the key Asia-Pacific maritime powers' interests with China and other regional actors.

A second and related challenge is for the TSD to become more proficient in responding to and defusing regional flashpoints, particularly on the Korean peninsula and in Taiwan. Harnessing Australia's sensitivities relative to ensuring that it never needs to 'choose' between the United States and China in a future crisis or conflict that may erupt between these two great powers is the critical foundation for meeting this requirement. Canberra must work assiduously to moderate intermittent American, and increasing Japanese, tendencies to regard Taiwan as a definitive bellwether for overall regional security. Ultimately, differences between Taiwan and the Chinese mainland will be resolved by a Chinese formula rather than by international intercession. Korea's tensions are more immediate and potentially more threatening on an international scale, but the TSD might do worse than to emulate the Chinese and South Korean determination to modify North Korea's bellicosity through diplomacy rather than through open confrontation against Pyongyang. The carrot and stick approach embraced by the now defunct Perry Plan (introduced by the former US Secretary of Defense in 1999 and implemented by the Clinton administration as a means to reverse North Korean missile testing) might be revisited in the TSD setting as a long-range approach for moderating North Korean strategic behaviour. A TSD–China coalition could also serve as a possible alternative to the Six Party Talks with Pyongyang if that forum is derailed yet again. As Richard Bitzinger has intimated, however, it might, at best, supplement but cannot actually replace well-established multilateral arms control regimes and instrumentalities already designed to minimize WMD proliferation and to promote other regional and international arms control standards.

A third challenge that, if met successfully, could eventually seal the TSD's relevance as a regional security instrument is to coordinate a specific human security agenda for responding to emerging and future transnational security contingencies. Establishing a formal secretariat at this stage of TSD development to achieve such coordination is unnecessary. Greater organizational infrastructure and resources than those represented by the current annual ministerial meeting, however, would be required to pursue this agenda effectively. The South Pacific region could be a leading candidate for the focusing of such TSD initiatives but other venues in South or Southeast Asia might also be considered. Coordinated disaster relief operations, pandemic control, counterterrorism and drug enforcement initiatives could be earmarked for development and review at a specifically designated TSD office operating out of Tokyo or Canberra. Initial conceptualization and planning for these functions and for overall TSD policy guidance could be undertaken through a comprehensive 'Track II' study sponsored by the three TSD governments. They could subsequently determine and select the most judicious approaches for policy review and implementation.

The real significance of the TSD and similar initiatives is that democratic states are signifying their continued willingness and capacity to engage in order-building and the promotion of more stable security environments, even in the face of substantial challenges on a variety of fronts to their own political values and cultures by hostile elements. The TSD states' determination to unite as a positive force confronting a very complex and often threatening regional and international security environment can be read as an encouraging sign that liberal social values are still able to stand and prevail if their proponents are sufficiently patient and sensitive in promoting their obvious benefits.

Notes

1 Deborah Cameron (2006), 'N Korea faces build-up of naval power', *Sydney Morning Herald*, 20 October.
2 Rowan Callick (2006), 'Rice's call for tough action ignored', *Australian*, 20 October.
3 See 'On-the-record briefing Secretary of State Condoleezza Rice', 17 October 2006 at Elmendorf AFB, Alaska, available at: www.state.gov/secretary/rm/2006/74667.htm (accessed 22 October 2006).

Index

Note: page numbers in **bold** refer to illustrations.

For Product Safety Concerns and Information please contact our EU
representative GPSR@taylorandfrancis.com
Taylor & Francis Verlag GmbH, Kaufingerstraße 24, 80331 München, Germany